The Color Encyclopedia of Daylilies

The Color Encyclopedia

of

DAYLILIES

TED L. PETIT & JOHN P. PEAT

Timber Press
Portland, Oregon

Published in 2000 by
Timber Press, Inc.
The Haseltine Building
133 S.W. Second Avenue, Suite 450
Portland, Oregon 97204, U.S.A.

Designed by Susan Applegate
Half-title page photograph by Ted L. Petit and John P. Peat.
Frontispiece photograph by Pat Sayers.

Printed in Hong Kong

Library of Congress Cataloging-in-Publication Data

Petit, Ted L.
   The color encyclopedia of daylilies/Ted L. Petit and John P. Peat.
     p. cm.
   Includes biographical references (p.).
   ISBN 0-88192-488-1
    1. Daylilies—Encyclopedias. 2. Daylilies—Pictorial works. I. Peat, John P. II. Title.
SB413.D3 P48 2000
635.9'3432—dc21

                                               00-026379

To those who have gone before us
and on whose shoulders we stand,
especially Bill Munson,
who was both friend and mentor

Contents

Foreword

PATRICK MICHAEL STAMILE

> Consider the lilies and how they grow: they toil not, they spin not; and
> yet I say unto you, that Solomon in all his glory was not arrayed like one
> of these.
> LUKE 12:27

No other hardy perennial in history has ever undergone the rapid transmutation that daylilies have. Theirs is a Cinderella story of how a handful of gold, yellow, and fulvous species have been transformed into a fabulous array of dramatic forms, colors, and patterns. Modern hybrid daylily blooms vary in size from 1.5 to 14 inches (3.8–35.6 cm). Modern daylily plants grow anywhere from 9 inches (22.9 cm) to almost 6 feet (1.8 m) tall. At the end of the twentieth century, the expanse of forms—round, triangular, informal, double, spider, unusual, polytepal—and the spectrum of colors—selfs, patterns, eyes, edges—could be taken for a multitude of different kinds of plants rather than hybrids of a few simple flowers. This magic has been accomplished by a devoted core of hybridizers working to develop the potential of the daylily. Their work has been carefully documented in this encyclopedic treatment. The future challenge for hybridizers will be to keep the daylily a relatively insect- and disease-free plant as they continue to expand upon its beauty and garden performance.

Ted Petit and John Peat's simple and concise text on the history, botany, and horticulture of daylilies along with their collection of photographic contributions from colleagues around the world combine to create the most comprehensive and exhaustive work on daylilies to date. No other book so completely catalogs the world of daylilies. The authors' personal acquaintance with major daylily growers and hybridizers make this work a must for all who grow or would like to grow daylilies. Growers and gardeners will find it an invaluable reference. I hope this book will attract and intrigue general readers, pointing them down the path of discovering why daylilies are so special.

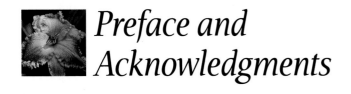 *Preface and Acknowledgments*

Upon completion of this manuscript, more than 40,000 daylilies are registered. Deciding which of these to include was a daunting task. Since each year brings hundreds of new introductions, the look of the daylily is rapidly evolving, which inevitably makes the flowers of older hybrids look dated. However, many older flowers have a beauty that time cannot erase, and we felt that they deserve a place in this book. From this compilation readers will gain a sense of daylily history along with glimpses of the newest cutting-edge daylilies. We even have included some hybrids that are not yet registered and not yet available. We tried to cover as many types of daylilies as possible, in terms of ploidy, form, color, dormancy, and so on. We hope to have reached a balance among these many dimensions.

As we wrap up this project, we are working around the clock during our peak bloom season in Florida, surrounded by stacks of books, slides, catalogs, and correspondence. To compile the information contained in this volume, we relied on slides from many people and referenced many sources of information. We have made every effort to insure that the pictures and information in our final manuscript are accurate, but it is not possible for us to personally know every cultivar in this book. We ask for your understanding if any error has occurred.

Also, understand that daylily cultivars are named by the hybridizers who create them. These names are not necessarily proper English names, and at times they may appear grammatically incorrect. Once registered with the American Hemerocallis Society (A.H.S.), however, these names become the official identification of the plants and cannot be changed. Some names in this book may appear to be misspelled, but we have endeavored to accurately represent the official A.H.S. names for all cultivars. Further, hybridizers do not always provide complete details regarding their cultivars when registering them with the A.H.S. As a result, some cultivars in this book, particularly those registered in the early days of the society, have incomplete information.

We would like to thank those garden and nursery owners who allowed us to photograph daylilies in their gardens over the two-year period we were working on this project. We would also like to thank all the photographers who allowed us to use their slides. Without their help, this undertaking would not have been possible. We owe special thanks to John Eiseman as well as Pat and Grace Stamile, whose contribution of slides and information helped us enormously.

Finally, we thank those closest to us who gave their support during this lengthy effort. After the final details of this book are completed, they are what really matter.

CHAPTER ONE
The Daylily Plant

We who are captivated by the flowers of daylilies may wonder why it is important to know about the daylily plant. A knowledge of the overall plant characteristics will help gardeners in hybridizing, cultivating, and acquiring daylilies and will deepen their appreciation of the flowers. Understanding the total plant, therefore—flowers, foliage, and roots—can greatly increase overall enjoyment of daylilies.

The captions for the daylilies pictured in this book contain descriptions about the plant and flower. These descriptions give information about specific aspects of the plant, including plant parts, flower characteristics, flowering season, ploidy, and dormancy. The following paragraphs explain the terminology used in the figure captions to describe these aspects.

Plant Parts

The primary parts of the daylily, like most other plants, are the root system and foliage. Prior to the bloom season, flower stalks, or scapes, emerge from the base of the plant. Usually flower buds visibly begin forming immediately after the scapes begin to emerge. Plants send up a single scape at a time but can send up two, three, or more scapes during a season. The number of blooms on a scape varies from less than 10 to more than 60. Sometimes small plants known as proliferations form on the side of the flower scape as it matures.

The roots of the daylily are typically fibrous, which allows the plant to store food and water. Thus, bare-rooted daylilies are more easily transported than most other perennials since the plant is capable of sustaining itself with stored nutrients. The point at which the roots meet the foliage is known as the crown and contains the growing point of the plant. The swordlike leaves emerge from the crown in an alternating fashion that creates a fan shape—a single daylily plant is often called a fan.

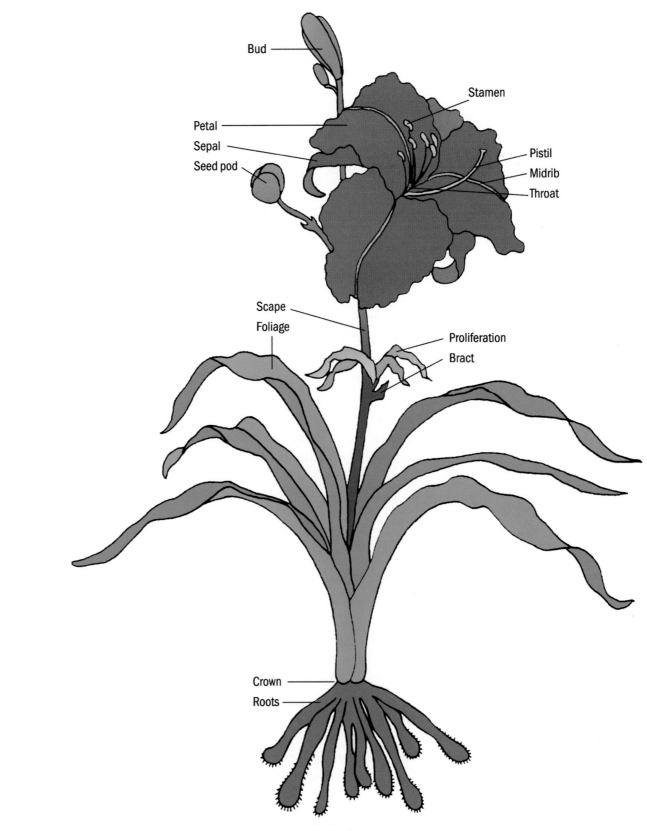

Bud

Stamen

Petal

Sepal

Pistil

Seed pod

Midrib

Throat

Scape

Foliage

Proliferation

Bract

Crown

Roots

Parts of a daylily plant. RICHARD HAYNES

The typical daylily flower is composed of three sepals, three petals, six stamens, and one pistil. The stamens are the male part of the flower and the pistil is the female part. Each stamen contains an anther, or pollen sack, at the tip. The anthers are closed in the early morning when the flowers first open, but as the temperature warms they burst open to reveal the fluffy, yellow-to-orange pollen. At the end of the pistil is the stigma. As the anthers open, the stigma becomes sticky to receive the pollen. The pistil connects to the ovary at the base of the flower and provides the passageway for the pollen to reach the ovary. If successfully pollinated, the ovary will form a seed pod.

Flower Characteristics

In order to describe the different possible flower colors and patterns, the community of daylily growers and hybridizers has divided the flower into several parts, which include the throat, the eye or watermark, the petal self, and the petal edge. The different qualities of these parts are then used to categorize the many daylily hybrids.

The "throat," also sometimes called the "center" or the "heart," is the center of the flower where the petals form a narrow funnel meeting at the base of the pistil. Sometimes "heart" is used to describe a smaller area in the very center of the throat. The throat color is usually green, orange, or yellow. Most newer hybrids have a green throat since gardeners generally find that green gives a cool focal point to the flower.

Daylilies are categorized by two primary characteristics: their self color and the presence of an eye or watermark. The "self" refers to the flattest, widest part of the petal, which carries the primary color of the bloom. The "eye" or "eyezone" is a darker area surrounding the throat of the flower (see those pictured in chapter 5). The eye can be a small dark band or it can take up most of the petal area. If this area surrounding the throat is lighter, rather than darker, than the self color, it is referred to as a "watermark" or a "halo." 'Court Magician' shows an excellent example of a watermark (see page 105). In addition, the petal edges can be darker or lighter than the petal self. Darker petal edges are referred to as a picotee. Picotees and light edges can be very narrow to very wide, taking up to one-third or even half the petal width. Many new tetraploid hybrids have very dramatic gold edges. When a contrasting edge is very narrow it is referred to as a "wire edge," such as a flower with a wire gold edge.

Flower color can be more complex in many cultivars. For example, the petals may contain a blend of more than one color—these are known as polychrome flowers. A bitone flower has petals that are darker or lighter than the sepals. Bicolor flowers are those that have petals and sepals of two entirely different colors. Describing color is very subjective, and the color that results in photographs is dependent upon a wide variety of influences, such as growing conditions, temperature, film type, amount of sunlight, and so on. The color descriptions

'Emperor's Toy' (Elizabeth H. Hudson 1975). Evergreen. Scape 18 in. (45.7 cm); flower 3.75 in. (9.5 cm). Midseason. An example of a lavender and cream bicolor. Diploid. 'Blue Vision' × 'Pixie Prince'. PATRICK STAMILE

'Moonlight Orchid' (Dave Talbott 1986). Semi-evergreen. Scape 28 in. (71.1 cm); flower 6.5 in. (16.5 cm). Early midseason. An example of a lavender and lighter lavender bitone. Diploid. Parents unknown. PATRICK STAMILE

given in this book are from those provided by the hybridizers, who describe a flower color as they see it in their gardens. Therefore, some colors in the photographs may not appear to exactly match those in the descriptions.

Flowering Season

Peak daylily bloom in North America varies from May in the deep South to mid-July in the northern part of the United States and in southern Canada. Of course, in countries south of the equator the bloom season ranges from November to mid-January. Many modern cultivars send up a second or third set of bloom scapes to extend the season. The bloom season of a daylily is categorized according to the start of bloom. Generally, the bloom season is divided into early, midseason, and late. However, in an attempt to be more specific, some hybridizers have divided the season even further, describing the bloom times as extra early, early, early midseason, midseason, midseason late, late, and very late. Since these times can vary markedly between different years and different geographical areas, it is not possible to give exact dates to define them.

Some new hybrids have an extended season and may begin blooming very early and continue through the entire bloom season. Plants that send up more than one scape are referred to as reblooming, or recurrent, cultivars. Many gardeners look for "ever-blooming" hybrids, ones that bloom nearly throughout the whole season. 'Stella de Oro' is a popular reblooming daylily. Though the simple flower form of 'Stella de Oro' has been surpassed by newer cultivars, it remains a long-blooming and widely recognized cultivar.

Diploid vs. Tetraploid

The majority of the older daylily cultivars are diploids, which means they contain the normal number of 22 chromosomes. However, since 1960 a large number of daylilies have been treated with colchicine, a chemical that allows the number of chromosomes in the cell to double as if the cell were about to divide but then prevents normal cell division. This results in tetraploids, plants that contain 44 chromosomes, which is double the normal number. This doubling of the chromosome count in tetraploids leads to larger flowers with heavier substance and more vibrant colors. If a diploid cultivar such as 'Janice Brown' has been successfully treated and converted, then the converted plant will be tetraploid and referred to as 'Tetra Janice Brown' or 'Tet. Janice Brown'. This, then, distinguishes it from the original diploid plant, which, of course, may still be found in many gardens. Each cultivar name is unique to one cultivar; therefore, no two cultivars will have the same name if registered with the American Hemerocallis Society.

Parentage

Understanding the parental background of a cultivar is as important as understanding the parentage of a famous race horse. It is essential for breeding favorable characteristics into future generations. Alternatively, if a cultivar is reported to be susceptible to disease, this undesirable trait can be kept from next generations by not using that cultivar or its prodigy in breeding. Therefore, most serious hybridizers concerned about the overall quality of the plant keep careful records of the genetic background of their daylilies. This means recording both the pod (female) and pollen (male) parents of their seedlings, a simple but time-consuming task. These records can result in long and complex combinations of names, similar to a human family tree. When the parentage is known beyond one generation, the parents of each generation are written within successive sets of parentheses, just like a mathematical formula, in order to clearly track the genetic background of the plant. The simplest parentage formula, going back one generation, is mother × father. A formula showing two generations back would be ((maternal grandmother × maternal grandfather) × (paternal grandmother × paternal grandfather)). Unfortunately, not all hybridizers keep records on parentage, and accidents, such as losing tags, can happen to even the most dedicated hybridizer. Therefore, some cultivars will have a parent listed as unknown or as a generic seedling. The term "F2" is sometimes used as short-hand in parentage formulas to indicate a cross between two plants with the same parents, such as a cross between siblings or between a plant and itself. In these instances the pod parent and pollen parent are identical for the resulting seedling, and the parentage notation can be abbreviated by naming the parents once, followed by F2. For example, the parentage of 'Lunar Sea' is ('Kecia' × 'Chateau Blanc')F2 × seedling. Written out in full, this would be (('Kecia' × 'Chateau Blanc') × ('Kecia' × 'Chateau Blanc')) × seedling. In other words, siblings have been crossed, and their offspring has been crossed with another seedling to produce 'Lunar Sea'.

Dormancy

The winter foliage performance of daylilies is generally categorized as dormant, evergreen, or semi-evergreen. Dormant daylily leaves die back to beneath ground level in the winter. Since these plants lose their leaves in the winter, the term "deciduous" might be more scientifically correct, but since the term "dormant" is so widely used among daylily growers and hybridizers, we use that term in this book. Evergreen daylily foliage remains green throughout the winter. In colder climates the foliage can be killed, or frozen back, but the plant itself is not killed. Semi-evergreens retain varying degrees of foliage on either side of the growing point but become dormant at the center of the plant, showing no new growth until spring.

The topic of dormancy can be relatively complex. Cultivars that go to one extreme end of the dormancy scale are referred to as hard dormants, meaning they go fully dormant, require a long winter chilling period in order to flourish, and will withstand harsh winters—they even may not survive in climates with warm winters. Cultivars at the other end of the extreme are often referred to as

An evergreen daylily. TED L. PETIT & JOHN P. PEAT

A semi-evergreen daylily. TED L. PETIT & JOHN P. PEAT

A dormant daylily emerging in the spring. TED L. PETIT & JOHN P. PEAT

tender evergreens, which implies that the plants grow throughout the winter, require little or no chilling to flourish, and may not survive very cold winters. As a general rule, dormants perform better in cold climates than in warm climates, and evergreens perform better in warm climates. However, hybridizers have been cross-breeding evergreen and dormant daylilies for many generations. The result of their work is that most newer hybrids contain varying degrees of dormancy, allowing them to thrive in a wide climatic range. Also, it is important to realize that there is no direct correlation between dormancy and cold hardiness—remember that some evergreen trees, such as spruce or pine, can survive in more extreme cold climates than can deciduous trees. Most modern evergreen daylilies are extremely cold hardy, growing well into Canada, and some can survive more extreme winters than some dormants. Also, most dormants perform quite well in climates with little winter chilling. Though the three terms dormant, semi-evergreen, and evergreen remain commonplace, be aware that these terms are given as a general description only. More significant is a particular plant's place within the long continuum from fully dormant to fully evergreen, and, more importantly, how cold hardy a plant is, which is often unrelated to dormancy.

Awards

The photo captions also indicate American Hemerocallis Society awards won by the cultivars. Here is a list of these awards.

Stout Silver Medal (or the Stout Medal) is the highest honor bestowed upon a cultivar.

Award of Merit goes to a cultivar that is not only distinctive and beautiful, but also proven to be a good performer over a wide geographical area.

Honorable Mention is the first official stamp of approval from the society.

Donald Fischer Memorial Cup is awarded to the most outstanding miniature cultivar.

Annie T. Giles Award is for the best small-flowered daylily.

Ida Munson Award goes to the best double-flowered daylily.

L. Ernest Plouf Award is for the best consistently fragrant dormant daylily.

Don C. Stevens Award goes to the best bold-eyed or banded daylily.

Eugene S. Foster Award is for the best late- to very-late-blooming cultivar.

Harris Olsen Spider Award is for a cultivar that meets the definition of spider or variant.

Lenington All-American Award is for outstanding performance in different climatic regions.

CHAPTER TWO
History of the Daylily

Daylily history ranges across thousands of years, from their ancient cultivation in Asia, through their discovery and importation by avid collectors in the West, through the early struggles to hybridize and convert the plant to tetraploid, and ultimately into the creation and dramatic craze for the exquisite modern hybrids. The full story is as much about the people who dedicated their lives to acquiring and changing these plants as it is about the plants themselves.

Origin of the Genus

The story begins in Asia, primarily in China, where daylilies have been cultivated for thousands of years. Munson (1989) reports that the earliest known reference to daylilies is from China, dated 2697 BC, when Chi Pai wrote a Materia Medica for Emperor Huang Ti. The people of the region enjoyed the species as much for utilitarian reasons, such as medicine and food, as for the beauty of the flowers. By the 1500s the daylily had made its way into Europe, probably via land and sea trade routes. The herbalists Dodonaeus, Clusius, and Lobelius described and illustrated the daylily in the late 1500s. When Linneaus introduced the now standard binomial system of nomenclature in 1753, he placed daylilies in the genus *Hemerocallis* within the family Liliaceae. The term *Hemerocallis* is from the Greek *hemera*, meaning "a day," and *kallos*, meaning "beauty," literally "beauty for a day." The nomenclature was altered by Dahlgren, Clifford, and Yeo, who in 1985 proposed a new system of classification, now widely accepted, that placed daylilies in their own family, Hemerocallidaceae. Several books describe much of the early history of daylilies in greater detail. Excellent reviews are available from Walter Erhardt, *Hemerocallis: Daylilies* (1992), R. W. Munson Jr., *Hemerocallis: The Daylily* (1989), and A. B. Stout, *Daylilies* (1934).

The period from 1700 to 1900 was the era of plant hunting, a time marked by the search for new daylily species. A theory popular among Westerners at this time was that the Garden of Eden could be re-created by gathering together all the beautiful plants that had been scattered around the globe at the fall of

Adam and Eve. Perhaps this romantic pursuit has been the quiet, subconscious dream of all gardeners through the ages. In the eighteenth and nineteenth centuries botanists and plant collectors set out around the world to discover new plants and bring them to the West. The excitement of discovery and adventure in new lands filled this period. Individuals such as Ernest Wilson, George Forrest, Francis Kingdon Ward, and Joseph Rock brought many new species of daylilies to Europe and America. Despite their efforts, by 1900 only half the known species of *Hemerocallis* had been introduced to the West.

Ultimately, it was the collaboration of Albert Steward and Arlow B. Stout that had the greatest impact on collecting new *Hemerocallis* species and advancing our knowledge about them. Steward lived in China and taught botany at the University of Nanking, regularly gathering daylilies from their native habitat. He sent these specimens to Stout, then the director of the New York Botanical Garden. As Sydney Eddison describes him in *A Passion for Daylilies*, "By all accounts, Dr. Stout was a dedicated scientist but not a gregarious man." After the death of his only son, Stout sought solace and refuge in his garden where "this starchy old gentleman" fell in love with daylilies. Stout received more than 50 shipments of seed and plants from China during his time at the New York Botanical Garden. He became the foremost authority on daylilies, undertaking the first comprehensive description and classification of the species. He also began a rigorous breeding program which opened the doors to future hybridizing efforts by others. As a tribute to his contributions, the Stout Medal is the highest award bestowed on a daylily by the American Hemerocallis Society.

The daylilies now found in gardens and in commerce around the world are hybrids many, many generations from the species. Indeed, the species have become primarily of historical interest. It takes some effort now to locate *Hemerocallis* species, for they have been surpassed by modern hybrids and are rarely seen for sale in commercial gardens. The most likely place to find them is in older home sites in North America and Europe, still forming lovely color accents where they have been growing wild for generations.

Species of *Hemerocallis*

Stout's 1934 book *Daylilies* remains the definitive work on the species, but other botanists have published reports describing additional species. The end result is that authorities do not completely agree upon the number of species in existence. However, most classification schemes suggest approximately 20 *Hemerocallis* species. Writers also divide the species into groups differently. For example, Erhardt (1992) suggests that the species be broken into five main groups, while Munson (1989) suggests the classification described below.

A detailed description of the species is of more than purely academic interest, for within these plants lies the key to all the many facets of modern daylilies. The variety of colors, scape heights, branching, forms, doubling, and so on, are all held within this small gene pool. Perhaps even more interesting are the phenomenal changes that have occurred in daylilies in the mere 50 to 60 years since hybridizing seriously began in the 1940s. A quick glance at the species shows the petals narrow and without ruffling, and the colors restricted to yellow, orange, and rust. This limited gene pool has given forth immense diversity. Hybridizers have created flowers varying in size from 2 in. (5.0 cm) to more than 1 ft. (30.5 cm) in diameter, from round and ruffled to the narrow spiders, and in virtually every color of the rainbow—all in little over half a century. Given the phenomenal diversity in flower form, color, and other aspects of modern daylilies now at our disposal, what will the next half-century bring?

Another important factor about the species is that we may not have taken complete advantage of all the characteristics offered from the very beginning. The race to improve the daylily may have left behind some very important species traits. For example, *Hemerocallis fulva* var. *kwanso* has rust-colored double flowers. Though few people are likely to suggest that it is as beautiful as the latest cultivars, it has many extra layers of true petals; this many layers has not yet been achieved in modern hybrids. Or, consider *H. multiflora*, which can carry 75 to 100 blooms—what happened to this heavy-blooming characteristic? Perhaps most interesting is *H. graminea*, whose flowers stay open for two to three days: imagine how this would change the way we think about our "beauty for a day." The species offer dwarf plants as well as plants with 6-ft. (1.8-m) scapes. Some plants bloom very early, some in midseason, and some very late in the season. Some are fully dormant and some are fully evergreen. And finally, some flowers are pure selfs of one color and some have a distinctly darker eye. Though interest in the species may be primarily historical, the species have supplied all the building blocks on which to create entire hybridizing programs. Hybrids have not fully highlighted the features of the species, a fact that should prompt daylily hybridizers to reconsider the possibilities these remarkable plants offer.

A detailed description of *Hemerocallis* species is beyond the scope of this book, but the following is a brief overview derived from the published sources by Stout, Erhardt, and Munson, mentioned above.

George Forrest documented a group of compact dwarf plants with very short scapes in southwest China—*Hemerocallis nana, H. plicata,* and *H. forrestii. Hemerocallis nana* has slender scapes generally bearing only one flower, *H. plicata* bears eight flowers with a faint rust halo, and *H. forrestii* produces five to ten orange blooms.

Several species of daylilies have yellow flowers. *Hemerocallis flava*, mentioned in botanical literature as early as 1570, has been popular in European gardens for centuries. It has bright lemon-yellow flowers that begin blooming early and re-bloom into the season. *Hemerocallis minor* has low-growing, lemon-yellow flowers with brownish-red-tinged sepals. It has fully dormant foliage and also begins blooming early in the season. *Hemerocallis thunbergii* bears yellow flowers on well-branched scapes that can reach 3–4 ft. (0.9–1.2 m) in midsummer. *Hemerocallis citrina* is also dormant and bears yellow flowers in midsummer on very tall, well-branched scapes that hold more than 60 buds, and the blooms are nocturnal.

Hemerocallis fulva is distinct for its brownish to rusty red color. The plants are semi-evergreen, with scapes reaching 50 in. (1.3 m) carrying day-blooming flowers that peak during midseason. The species has a number of single-flowered variants, including the rosy-red-flowered *H. fulva* var. *rosea* and *H. fulva* 'Europa', a rusty red flower with a brownish eye and apricot midrib. *Hemerocallis fulva* var. *kwanso* and *H. fulva* 'Flore Pleno' are double flowered and have white-striped foliage. Unfortunately, these two doubles are virtually, if not completely, sterile.

Several species have orange flowers. *Hemerocallis aurantiaca*, an evergreen believed to have come from Japan, has 3-ft. (0.9-m), top-branched scapes. *Hemerocallis exaltata* carries light orange flowers on 4- to 5-ft. (1.2- to 1.5-m) scapes that bloom in midseason. *Hemerocallis multiflora* is a dormant plant with 3-ft. (0.9-m), highly branched scapes carrying numerous flowers that bloom from mid- to late season until frost. *Hemerocallis dumortierii* blooms very early in the spring on scapes that can be shorter than the foliage. *Hemerocallis middendorffii* has 3-in. (7.6-cm) flowers of a uniform orange on unbranched scapes.

Shiu-Ying Hu described the following species in 1968. *Hemerocallis altissima* has 4- to 6.5-ft. (1.2- to 2.0-m) scapes with pale yellow, nocturnal, 3-in. (7.6-cm) flowers. *Hemerocallis coreana* has yellow flowers on 20- to 32-in. (50- to 81-cm) scapes, and *H. esculenta* has 25- to 35-in. (64- to 89-cm) scapes carrying five to six orange flowers. *Hemerocallis graminea* is a dwarf plant with 30-in. (76-cm) scapes bearing unique orange flowers that remain open for two to three days. *Hemerocallis hakuunensis* has 34- to 40-in. (86- to 102-cm) scapes carrying six to eleven orange flowers. *Hemerocallis littorea* bears orange flowers with a dark brown eyezone.

Hemerocallis thunbergii. CARL SIGEL

Hemerocallis fulva var. *rosea.* CARL SIGEL

Hemerocallis citrina. CARL SIGEL

Hemerocallis fulva var. *kwanso.* CARL SIGEL

Hemerocallis minor. CARL SIGEL

Hemerocallis fulva. CARL SIGEL

Hemerocallis dumortieri. CURTIS & LINDA SUE BARNES

Hemerocallis aurantiaca. CARL SIGEL

Hemerocallis fulva 'Flore Pleno'. CARL SIGEL

Hemerocallis altissima. CARL SIGEL

Hemerocallis multiflora. CARL SIGEL

Hemerocallis hakuunensis. CARL SIGEL

Hemerocallis middendorffii. CURTIS & LINDA SUE BARNES

CHAPTER THREE
History of Daylily Hybridizing

The flowers of the hybrid daylilies are different from those of the species shown in chapter 2. The progressive change from the species flowers to the daylilies of today is a tribute to the hard work of amateur and professional hybridizers around the world. Hybridizing can take the daylily flower in literally any direction, depending on the vision of the breeder—each bloom pictured in this book started as an inspiration in the mind of a hybridizer. Since the hybrid story is as much about people, their personalities and their dreams, as it is about flowers, the road from the species plants to today's hybrids has been fraught with clashes of ego and personality. Sydney Eddison in *A Passion for Daylilies* tells the full tale of the people behind the plants.

Daylily hybridizing began with the early collectors who had access to the original species plants. Little plant material was available and progress was slow. Gradually, new hybrids were introduced, more material became available, and the daylily flower became more diverse in form, color, and other characteristics. Gradually the rate of advancement increased. Many breeders have contributed to these advancements, some through their backyard gardens, others through major hybridizing programs. It is impossible to discuss everyone who has played a role in the progress of the daylily, but below are those whose energy and vision have left an indelible stamp on the plant.

Early Efforts

Arlow B. Stout was the unquestionable father of daylily hybridizing in North America. While director at the New York Botanical Garden he received plants of *Hemerocallis* species from Asia, which he classified and with which he began to hybridize. In his classic book *Daylilies* (1934), he describes in detail his efforts to cross the different species plants to produce new daylily varieties with novel features. For example, his book contains a full-color plate tracing "'Theron', the first truly red daylily" back to *H. flava*, *H. fulva* 'Europa', *H. aurantiaca*, and *H. thunbergii*. He produced his first cultivar, 'Mikado', in 1929 and continued to work with daylilies until his retirement from the botanical garden in 1948. During the 1930s and 1940s, Stout was a dominant figure in the daylily world in the United States.

These early years did not belong to Stout alone, however. Even before the turn of the century, George Yeld and Amos Perry had begun their hybridizing programs in England. Their breeding was also necessarily based on work with species plants. Some of their hybrids became very important in more extensive breeding programs in the United States, but the impact of their efforts was greatly reduced because of difficulties in transporting plants across the ocean. Despite Yeld and Perry's very important contributions, the vast majority of daylily hybridizing was, and continues to be, conducted in the United States. A number of serious hybridizers, though, now operate in other parts of the world, especially Europe and Australia.

As more hybridizers began to work with daylilies in the 1940s and 1950s, the look of the flower began to change. The progressive winners of the American Hemerocallis Society's Stout Silver Medal illustrate the history of these changes. The photographs in this chapter show representative flowers from the Stout Medal collection, pictured in chronological order.

Early hybridizing efforts had a number of hurdles to overcome. The most important first goals included clarifying the color of the flower, particularly the rusty color of *Hemerocallis fulva*. The colors found in the species were limited to yellow, orange, and rusty red; therefore, the early hybridizers worked toward increasing the color range. Some of the initial efforts, even by Stout, produced true reds and clear pinks. The first hybrids also had narrow petals with no ruffling, prompting efforts to widen and ruffle the petals.

Some major hybridizers involved in these efforts during the 1940s and 1950s included Elizabeth Nesmith, Ophelia Taylor, and Ralph Wheeler. All accounts of Nesmith, proprietor of Fairmount Gardens in Lowell, Massachusetts, indicate that she was a strong, determined, extraordinarily focused person—she turned this energy toward producing flowers of clear color, particularly pinks, purples, and reds. Taylor, of Ocala, Florida, concentrated her efforts on flower form and style. Her 'Prima Donna' was one of the first clear pastel daylilies, large and wide petaled. It was used heavily in hybridizing and went on to win the Stout Medal in 1955. Wheeler, born in New York, fell in love with *Amaryllis* and then, after a move to Florida, *Hemerocallis*. He concentrated on flowers that he considered unique and special. Nesmith's 'Potentate' and Wheeler's 'Amherst' became two foundation plants for breeding purples. The work of these three hybridizers carried the daylily forward from the early "post-species" plants of the Stout era toward larger, clearer flowers in a variety of colors.

The period from 1950 to 1975 saw dramatic changes in the look of the daylily, in no small part due to the increasing number of people interested in the flower. During this time, enthusiasm for the daylily grew dramatically. As the flower became more attractive, more people were drawn to it, which in turn increased the interest in breeding. The registration of new hybrids increased to over 15,000, and a new group of breeders surfaced. A group of hybridizers emerged in the Chicago area led by Ezra Kraus, David Hall, and Elmer Claar, turning their region into the center of daylily hybridizing. Kraus, then chair of the Department of Botany at the University of Chicago had assembled the most extensive daylily collection in the Midwest. A bachelor and serious scientist, Kraus dedicated himself to a carefully planned, structured breeding program, focusing primarily on reds, pinks, and melons. Hall, an attorney and friend of Kraus, bred daylilies as a hobby and created reds, very clear pinks, and roses. Claar, who constructed and managed real estate and hotel projects, was an avid collector of many things, including daylilies. His hybridizing hobby led to broad-petaled, ruffled yellows and a line of reds that had a major impact on red breeding.

Outside the Chicago area, several other breeders were working diligently. W. B. MacMillan of Abbeville, Louisiana, managed to produce seedlings that bloomed in one year instead of the usual two to three, thus racing ahead in the hybridizing field. His greatest successes in color were cream-pinks, pastels, and yellows, but he is best known for the flower form he developed. His daylilies were very round and ruffled for their time, so much so that "the MacMillan form" came to define round and ruffled flowers. Edna Spalding was another Louisiana breeder of that era. Although she bred daylilies merely for pleasure and forced them to compete with her vegetable garden, she had a keen eye and a strong sense for quality and made great advances with pinks and purples. Two other southerners, Frank and Peggy Childs of Georgia, worked for 30 years with daylilies of every conceivable color in both single and double forms. Their 'Catherine Woodbery', a clear lavender-pink, was eventually converted to a tetraploid and formed the basis of much work at the tetraploid level.

Since 1975, the tetraploid revolution has dominated daylily hybridizing, but a number of breeders have continued to work with diploid daylilies. Ra Hansen carried out an extensive program producing bold and dramatic flowers that reflect the dynamic persona of this former Miss Texas finalist. Pauline Henry is another prominent diploid hybridizer who continues to work on her famous Siloam Series. She produces a large number of prize-winning cultivars in a range of colors that vary in form from miniatures, to large flowers, to doubles.

Emergence of the Tetraploids

While breeders were hard at work hybridizing new diploid daylilies, a behind-the-scenes revolution quietly and forever changed *Hemerocallis*. The 1940s saw the first attempts to treat daylilies with colchicine and convert them from diploid to tetraploid, but the efforts were difficult to confirm and caused little notice in daylily circles. Hamilton Traub, Quinn Buck, and Robert Schreiner each reported successfully converting a daylily in 1947, 1948, and 1949, respectively. They introduced tetraploid plants in the following years, but the plants were primitive compared to the diploids of the day and garnered little attention. It was not until the now famous 1961 American Hemerocallis Society convention in Chicago that the tetraploid daylily made known its true impact.

Two years prior to the convention, Orville Fay and Bob Griesbach self-pollinated their induced tetraploid 'Crestwood Ann', producing a pod with four viable seeds. These seedlings established a line of seed-grown tetraploids that bloomed in 1961. To say the least, this created a stir among the attendees. Adding to the excitement, Fay proclaimed that within 10 years diploid daylilies would be obsolete, a statement that raised a furor among diploid breeders and growers who were being told the efforts of their hard work were soon to be made obsolete. Only a handful of the more visionary hybridizers clearly saw the importance of this break. Most diploid hybridizers were offended and saw the breakthrough as a challenge to be defeated at every possible turn.

R. W. Munson Jr., a quiet, reserved architect who began hybridizing daylilies when he was still a teenager, was a major player in this new tetraploid revolution. He was a bachelor living with his mother and sister, dedicated to working with diploids to create a line of clear pastels. After 27 years of hybridizing diploids, Munson attended the 1961 Chicago convention. There he realized the potential importance of tetraploid daylilies and decided to change his program to a tetraploid line. He made a pact with Steve Moldovan and Virginia Peck to pursue tetraploids, despite the obstacles. The early converted daylilies were almost sterile, so that a season of hard work that would have produced tens of thousands of new diploid daylilies produced only a handful of tetraploid seedlings. The undertaking was arduous, and the work was frustrating. Munson, Peck, and Moldovan, along with Charles Reckamp, against a background of great pessimism, and what initially seemed insurmountable odds, pioneered the tetraploid daylily and brought it to its present position at the forefront of daylily growing.

But the people of the American Hemerocallis Society remained divided into two hostile camps, diploid supporters and tetraploid supporters. While the diploid hybridizing programs raced ahead, creating round, ruffled flowers, the tetraploid breeding was painfully slow, and hybridizing efforts lagged behind. The vast majority of society members refused to accept the new tetraploids, seeing them as coarse and unrefined. As a result, those that pioneered the tetraploid daylily paid dearly for their vision. Munson, Reckamp, and Peck died without receiving the Stout Medal, and at the time of this writing, Moldovan has not yet received it either. Though tetraploid breeding seriously began in the 1960s, only two tetraploid cultivars won the Stout Medal prior to 1996: 'Mary Todd' (Fay) and 'Ruffled Apricot' (S. Baker). This is further testament that the 1980s, halcyon days for diploid hybridizers, were dark days for tetraploid breeders, when only a select few believed that tetraploids could succeed. In the later years of the 1990s the hostility began to subside—tetraploids are now mainstream in most large, prominent hybridizing efforts.

Peck made remarkable advances in breeding full and ruffled forms into a variety of colors. Her cultivar 'Dance Ballerina Dance' was widely used in hybridizing because of its excellent ruffling. Another tetraploid breeder, Charles Reckamp at Mission Gardens in Techny, Illinois, created a line of dormant tetraploid pastel flowers with ruffled petals and gold edges. Both he and Steve Moldovan began working with diploids before becoming interested in tetraploids. Moldovan bred dormant northern cultivars with evergreen southern cultivars in an effort to produce hybrids that were more widely adaptable.

Munson worked with his mother, Ida, and together they produced daylilies in every available color. Their plants 'Betty Warren Woods' and 'Ida's Magic' became the standards for refinement and have been among the most important and widely used hybrids in the late 1990s. Despite Munson's many extraordinary accomplishments, his passion was always for purples and pastels. While many hybridizers focused merely on improving the flower, Munson's primary focus was always on improving the overall plant habit. He was ever mindful of the pitfalls of short-sighted hybridizing and painfully aware of the problems that hybridizers had ignored in their breeding of other flowers. He was determined to keep the daylily safe from such shortcomings as susceptibility to black spot fungus that had come to plague the modern hybrid tea rose, or sensitivity to the rot that had been bred into the newer irises. His primary goal was to make the daylily a carefree, ever-blooming perennial that would grow across a broad climatic range with no dependence on chemicals or special treatment. The flowers pictured throughout this book include the contributions of many other prominent hybridizers of tetraploids.

Hybridizers of Today

At the end of the twentieth century, the tides have turned, and most top hybridizers are either breeding with tetraploid daylilies or are in the process of converting their programs from diploid to tetraploid. Few top hybridizers are continuing exclusively with diploid lines.

Currently prominent hybridizers include Patrick and Grace Stamile, former school teachers who have applied their methodical nature to daylilies. Patrick has worked on medium- to large-flowered tetraploids, including his famous Candy Series, and more recently his very refined pinks. Grace has focused on small and miniature flowers, including miniature tetraploid doubles. The Stamiles began their hybridizing career on Long Island, but moved their nursery to central Florida, which has become the center of daylily hybridizing efforts. Also in central Florida are Jeff and Elizabeth Salter, another team of prominent hybridizers. Jeff, a quiet, reserved man by nature and an attorney by training, took the daylily to new levels in terms of full-formed, wide-petaled, ruffled, heavily substanced flowers. Elizabeth, the granddaughter of Ida Munson and niece of R. W. Munson, grew up among daylilies. She has concentrated on small and miniature flowers and has created a line with unique, complex, blue eyes. David Kirchhoff and Mort Morss are another well-known and respected team in central Florida. Kirchhoff is an outspoken character with a keen eye, razor sharp wit, and little patience for mediocrity. A survivor in the often cutthroat world of daylilies, he has dedicated himself to advancing and improving double forms as well as large-flowered tetraploids, especially the reds. The quiet and calming Morss became enamored with the eyed and edged tetraploids and has created a number of large dramatic flowers with complex eyes and ornate edges. Ted Petit, a professor of neuroscience and co-author of this book, has concentrated on creating large, ornate single and double flowers, many of which are heavily ruffled with gold edges. His neighbor Bob Carr has focused on large-flowered tetraploids, especially the reds. E. R. Joiner has made a great impact on double daylilies. Curt Hanson and John Benz are two tetraploid hybridizers who have struggled to produce beautiful flowers hardy in cold northern climates.

In addition, a group of newer hybridizers have begun making major changes to the face of the daylily. Dan Trimmer, another Long Island hybridizer to move to central Florida, continues to focus on bringing modern converted diploids into the tetraploid lines. Matthew Kaskel, a man with enormous energy and humor, has concentrated on well-branched, large, single and double flowers, as well as smaller flowers for the commercial trade. John Peat, a computer systems analyst and co-author of this book, has begun to impact large-flowered, patterned tetraploid daylilies as well as tetraploid spiders. Larry Grace, another tetraploid breeder, has made improvements in the round, ruffled, gold-edged flowers.

These and other hybridizers are working to increase the range of climate conditions in which daylilies thrive and are putting their own vision of a new look on the daylily. The photographs throughout this book illustrate the work of more hybridizers who have made an impact on the daylily. Chapter 12 features some of their latest achievements.

'Hesperus' (Hans P. Sass 1940). Dormant. Scape 48 in. (122 cm); flower size unknown. Midseason. Yellow to light orange. Diploid. Parents unknown. Stout Silver Medal 1950. FRANCIS GATLIN

'Fairy Wings' (Mary Lester 1953). Dormant. Scape 36 in. (91.4 cm); flower size unknown. Early midseason. Light yellow. Diploid. Parents unknown. Award of Merit 1957. Stout Silver Medal 1960. FRANCIS GATLIN

'Satin Glass' (Orville Fay and W. Hardy 1960). Dormant. Scape 34 in. (86.4 cm); flower size unknown. Midseason. Pale melon-yellow with a green throat. Diploid. Parents unknown. Award of Merit 1965. Stout Silver Medal 1968. Lenington All-American Award 1971. FRANCIS GATLIN

'Prima Donna' (B. Taylor 1946). Evergreen. Scape 36 in. (91.4 cm); flower size unknown. Midseason. Pastel red-orange-lavender. Diploid. Parents unknown. Award of Merit 1952. Stout Silver Medal 1955. FRANCIS GATLIN

'Dauntless' (Arlow B. Stout 1935). Semi-evergreen. Scape 36 in. (91.4 cm); flower size unknown. Early midseason. Yellow to light orange. Diploid. Parents unknown. Award of Merit 1951. Stout Silver Medal 1954. CURTIS & LINDA SUE BARNES

'Ava Michelle' (Wilmer Flory 1960). Semi-evergreen. Scape 18 in. (45.7 cm); flower size unknown. Late midseason. Light yellow self with a green throat. Diploid. Seedling × 'High Noon'. Award of Merit 1965. Stout Silver Medal 1970. FRANCIS GATLIN

'Ruffled Pinafore' (G. Milliken 1948). Evergreen. Scape 30 in. (76.2 cm); flower size unknown. Midseason. Orange to yellow. Diploid. Parents unknown. Award of Merit 1954. Stout Silver Medal 1957. FRANCIS GATLIN

'Bess Ross' (Elmer Claar 1951). Dormancy unknown. Scape 36 in. (91.4 cm); flower size unknown. Midseason. Orange-red. Diploid. Parents unknown. Award of Merit 1957. Stout Silver Medal 1962. FRANCIS GATLIN

'May Hall' (David F. Hall 1957). Dormant. Scape 35 in. (88.9 cm); flower size unknown. Early midseason. Pink blend. Diploid. Parents unknown. Award of Merit 1965. Stout Silver Medal 1969. CURTIS & LINDA SUE BARNES

'Green Glitter' (Mattie Harrison 1964). Evergreen. Scape 32 in. (81.3 cm); flower 7 in. (17.8 cm). Early midseason. Pale yellow with a chartreuse throat. Diploid. 'Nobility' × seedling. Award of Merit 1973. Stout Silver Medal 1977. CURTIS & LINDA SUE BARNES

'Mary Todd' (Orville Fay 1967). Semi-evergreen. Scape 26 in. (66.0 cm); flower 6 in. (15.2 cm). Early. Buff self. Tetraploid. Seedling × 'Crestwood Ann'. Award of Merit 1973. Stout Silver Medal 1978. JOHN EISEMAN

'Bertie Ferris' (Ury G. Winniford 1969). Dormant. Scape 20 in. (50.8 cm); flower 2.5 in. (6.4 cm). Early. Persimmon-orange self. Diploid. 'Corkey' × seedling. Award of Merit 1975. Stout Silver Medal 1980. Donald Fischer Memorial Cup 1973. FRANCIS GATLIN

'Lavender Flight' (Edna Spalding 1963). Semi-evergreen. Scape 34 in. (86.4 cm); flower 6.25 in. (15.9 cm). Early midseason. Deep lavender self with green-yellow throat. Diploid. Parents unknown. Award of Merit 1968. Stout Silver Medal 1973. FRANCIS GATLIN

'Green Flutter' (W. Williamson 1964). Semi-evergreen. Scape 20 in. (50.8 cm); flower 3 in. (7.6 cm). Late. Canary yellow with a green throat. Diploid. Parents unknown. Award of Merit 1973. Stout Silver Medal 1976. Annie T. Giles Award 1970. Lenington All-American Award 1980. MARY ANNE LEISEN

'Ed Murray' (Edward Grovatt 1971). Dormant. Scape 30 in. (76.2 cm); flower 4 in. (10.2 cm). Midseason. Black-red self with a green throat. Diploid. 'Tis Midnight' × seedling. Award of Merit 1978. Stout Silver Medal 1981. Annie T. Giles Award 1976. Lenington All-American Award 1983. FRANCIS GATLIN

'Moment of Truth' (W. B. MacMillan 1969). Scape 23 in. (58.4 cm); flower 6 in. (15.2 cm). Midseason. Near white self. Diploid. Seedling × 'Julia Tanner'. Award of Merit 1976. Stout Silver Medal 1979. PATRICK STAMILE

'Stella de Oro' (Walter Jablonski 1975). Dormant. Scape 11 in. (27.9 cm); flower 2.75 in. (7.0 cm). Early midseason. Gold self with tiny green throat. Diploid. Parents unknown. Award of Merit 1982. Stout Silver Medal 1985. Donald Fischer Memorial Cup 1979. PATRICK STAMILE

'My Belle' (Kenneth Durio 1973). Evergreen. Scape 26 in. (66.0 cm); flower 6.5 in. (16.5 cm). Early. Flesh-pink self with green throat. Diploid. 'Sug' × seedling. Award of Merit 1980. Stout Silver Medal 1984. PATRICK STAMILE

'Janet Gayle' (Lucille Guidry 1976). Evergreen. Scape 26 in. (66.0 cm); flower 6.5 in. (16.5 cm). Early. Pink-cream blend with green throat. Diploid. Parents unknown. Award of Merit 1982. Stout Silver Medal 1986. JOHN EISEMAN

'Ruffled Apricot' (S. Houston Baker 1972). Dormant. Scape 28 in. (71.1 cm); flower 7 in. (17.8 cm). Early midseason. Apricot with lavender-pink midribs and gold-apricot throat. Tetraploid. Seedling × 'Northbrook Star'. Award of Merit 1979. Stout Silver Medal 1982. TED L. PETIT & JOHN P. PEAT

'Becky Lynn' (Lucille Guidry 1977). Semi-evergreen. Scape 20 in. (50.8 cm); flower 6.75 in. (17.2 cm). Extra early. Rose blend with green throat. Diploid. Parents unknown. Award of Merit 1983. Stout Silver Medal 1987.
TED L. PETIT & JOHN P. PEAT

'Martha Adams' (Elsie Spalding 1979). Evergreen. Scape 19 in. (48.3 cm); flower 6.75 in. (17.2 cm). Early midseason. Pink self with green throat. Diploid. Parents unknown. Award of Merit 1985. Stout Silver Medal 1988.
JOHN EISEMAN

'Brocaded Gown' (Bryant Millikan 1979). Semi-evergreen. Scape 26 in. (66.0 cm); flower 6 in. (15.2 cm). Early midseason. Lemon-cream self with chartreuse throat. Diploid. 'Buttermilk Sky' × 'Sabie'. Award of Merit 1986. Stout Silver Medal 1989. FRANCIS GATLIN

'Sabie' (W. B. MacMillan 1974). Evergreen. Scape 24 in. (61.0 cm); flower 6 in. (15.2 cm). Early. Golden yellow self with green throat. Diploid. Parents unknown. Award of Merit 1979. Stout Silver Medal 1983. TED L. PETIT & JOHN P. PEAT

'Betty Woods' (David Kirchhoff 1980). Dormant. Scape 26 in. (66.0 cm); flower 5.5 in. (14.0 cm). Early. Bright yellow self with green throat. Diploid. (('Winning Ways' × seedling) × 'Keith Kennon') × 'Cosmic Treasure'. Award of Merit 1987. Stout Silver Medal 1991. Ida Munson Award 1983. PATRICK STAMILE

'Fairy Tale Pink' (Charlie Pierce 1980). Semi-evergreen. Scape 24 in. (61.0 cm); flower 5.5 in. (14.0 cm). Midseason. Pink self with green throat. Diploid. 'Quiet Melody' × 'Janet Gayle'. Award of Merit 1987. Stout Silver Medal 1990.
OSCIE WHATLEY

'Janice Brown' (Edwin C. Brown 1986). Semi-evergreen. Scape 21 in. (53.3 cm); flower 4.3 in. (10.8 cm). Early midseason. Bright pink with rose-pink eyezone and green throat. Diploid. Parents unknown. Award of Merit 1992. Stout Silver Medal 1994. Annie T. Giles Award 1990. Don C. Stevens Award 1990. TED L. PETIT & JOHN P. PEAT

'Siloam Double Classic' (Pauline Henry 1985).
Dormant. Scape 16 in. (40.6 cm); flower 5 in.
(12.7 cm). Early midseason. Bright pink self
with green throat. Diploid. Parents unknown.
Award of Merit 1991. Stout Silver Medal 1993.
Ida Munson Award 1988. L. Ernest Plouf
Award 1985. PATRICK STAMILE

'Neal Berrey' (Sarah Sikes 1985). Semi-evergreen. Scape 18 in. (45.7 cm); flower 5 in. (12.7
cm). Midseason. Rose-pink blend with green-
yellow throat. Diploid. 'Ronda' × (('Sophisticated Miss' × 'My Belle') × 'Blue Happiness').
Award of Merit 1992. Stout Silver Medal 1995.
TED L. PETIT & JOHN P. PEAT

'Barbara Mitchell' (Charlie Pierce 1985). Semi-
evergreen. Scape 20 in. (50.8 cm); flower 6 in.
(15.2 cm). Midseason. Pink self with green
throat. Diploid. 'Fairy Tale Pink' × 'Beverly Ann'.
Award of Merit 1990. Stout Silver Medal 1992.
TED L. PETIT & JOHN P. PEAT

'Always Afternoon' (Mort Morss 1989). Semi-
evergreen. Scape 22 in. (55.9 cm); flower 5.5 in.
(14.0 cm). Early. Buff-edged medium mauve
with purple eye and green throat. Tetraploid.
('Ring of Change' × 'Tiffany Palace') × 'Opus
One'. Award of Merit 1995. Stout Silver Medal
1997. Ida Munson Award 1995. TED L. PETIT &
JOHN P. PEAT

'Wedding Band' (Patrick Stamile 1987). Semi-
evergreen. Scape 26 in. (66.0 cm); flower 5.5 in.
(14.0 cm). Midseason. Yellow edges on cream-
white with green throat. Tetraploid. 'French
Frosting' × 'Porcelain Pleasure'. Award of Merit
1993. Stout Silver Medal 1996. PATRICK STAMILE

CHAPTER FOUR
Singles

Single daylilies in their myriad colors are by far the most popular form. The flower has a pleasing simplicity that so many gardeners and enthusiasts find serene and peaceful. While many people love the doubles, minis, spiders, or complex patterns, the self-colored singles have retained their devoted following. As R. W. Munson once said, "There is a beauty in the simplicity of the flower, like a serene Japanese garden where less is often more."

However, hybridizers have not been happy to simply leave these flowers alone. The years have seen many hybridizing achievements, and new features have enhanced the beauty of these flowers. From what began as narrow-petaled, triangular flowers, hybridizers have gradually widened the petals to form increasingly more round flowers. As the petals increased in width, ruffling began to emerge, so that many daylilies have both a round and ruffled form. From this initial ruffling has emerged ever increasing types of ruffles, from soft looping ruffles to tightly crimped edges on some of the newer hybrids. Indeed, some of the newest hybrids are so ruffled that much of the petal is consumed in ruffling that extends well into the throat area. Ruffling has also led to several types of ornate edging, such as hooks and horns, shark's teeth, and heavy gold edging.

From the original color palette of yellow, orange, and rusty red, hybridizers have developed flowers of virtually every color. Through the hybridizing of the 1980s and 1990s, reds have been clarified and intensified, and pinks have been purified into an ever increasing range from baby-ribbon-pink to deep rose. Purples and lavenders have been created in a broad color range, from a deep royal purple to light bluish lavender. A true blue daylily has not yet been developed, but hybrids do have eyezones of violet through powder blue to dark navy blue. White daylilies have emerged from light pink and yellow to hybrids of pure ivory white. The black daylily has slowly emerged from the dark red and purple lines. Along with color range, flower substance has increased, allowing greater weather resistance and sun tolerance.

The daylilies pictured in this chapter have been grouped into general color categories: white (cream to white), yellow (yellow to gold), orange (apricot, melon to orange), pink (peach to rose-pink), lavender (lavender to purple), and red (red to black-red).

WHITE (cream to white)

'Admiral's Braid' (Patrick Stamile 1993). Semi-evergreen. Scape 21 in. (53.3 cm); flower 5.5 in. (14.0 cm). Midseason. An ivory-white and pink flower heavily edged in gold with green throat. Tetraploid. 'Wedding Band' × ('Pink Scintillation' × seedling). PATRICK STAMILE

'Alpine Snow' (Patrick Stamile 1994). Dormant. Scape 20 in. (50.8 cm); flower 5.5 in. (14.0 cm). Midseason. A highly ruffled near-white self with heavy substance and green throat. Tetraploid. 'Ptarmigan' × 'Tet. Monica Marie'. PATRICK STAMILE

'Anniversary Gold' (Ted L. Petit 1994). Evergreen. Scape 20 in. (50.8 cm); flower 5.75 in. (14.6 cm). Midseason. A very refined ivory-cream-pink with gold edge and green throat. Tetraploid. 'Wedding Band' × 'Ida's Magic'. TED L. PETIT

'Beautiful Edgings' (Nita Copenhaver and Donald Copenhaver 1989). Semi-evergreen. Scape 30 in. (76.2 cm); flower 7 in. (17.8 cm). Midseason. A triangular cream flower with petals edged in rose and a green throat. Diploid. 'Best of Friends' × seedling. JOHN EISEMAN

'Ben Adams' (Jeff Salter 1994). Dormant. Scape 25 in. (63.5 cm); flower 5.5 in. (14.0 cm). Early midseason. A heavily ruffled cream self with green throat. Tetraploid. 'Walking on Sunshine' × 'Alexandra'. TED L. PETIT & JOHN P. PEAT

Bernie Bryslan' (Henry Lorrain and Douglas Lycett 1994). Dormant. Scape 20 in. (50.8 cm); flower 5.5 in. (14.0 cm). Late. A ruffled pale cream-ivory self with green throat. Tetraploid. 'President Hadley' × 'Michelle Reid'. HENRY LORRAIN & DOUGLAS LYCETT

'Cameron Quantz' (Charlotte Holman 1979). Dormant. Scape 28 in. (71.1 cm); flower 7 in. (17.8 cm). Early midseason. A triangular lightly ruffled near-white with a pink blush and green throat. Diploid. 'Moment of Truth' × seedling. TED L. PETIT & JOHN P. PEAT

'Capture the Magic' (Jeff Salter 1996). Semi-evergreen. Scape 28 in. (71.1 cm); flower 6 in. (15.2 cm). Early midseason. A pale cream self with a pink blush, a heavily ruffled gold edge, and a green throat. Tetraploid. Parents unknown. TED L. PETIT & JOHN P. PEAT

'Dan Tau' (W. H. Smith 1981). Semi-evergreen. Scape 24 in. (61.0 cm); flower 6 in. (15.2 cm). Early. A smooth-textured, recurved cream self with a pink blush and lime-green throat. Diploid. Parents unknown. Award of Merit 1987. TED L. PETIT & JOHN P. PEAT

'Diamonds and Pearls' (Jeff Salter 1994). Semi-evergreen. Scape 24 in. (61.0 cm); flower 5.5 in. (14.0 cm). Early midseason. An opulently formed cream self with a heavily ruffled gold edge and a green heart. Tetraploid. Parents unknown. TED L. PETIT & JOHN P. PEAT

'Dripping with Gold' (Ted L. Petit 1998). Evergreen. Scape 25 in. (63.5 cm); flower 5.5 in. (14.0 cm). Midseason. An ivory flower with a cream pink blush, green throat, and heavy gold ruffling. Tetraploid. ('Wedding Band' × 'Wrapped in Gold') × 'Deanna's Gift'. TED L. PETIT

'Elegance Supreme' (Edwin C. Brown 1987). Semi-evergreen. Scape 19 in. (48.3 cm); flower 5 in. (12.7 cm). Early midseason. A nicely ruffled cream-near-white self with green throat. Diploid. Seedling × 'Wendy Glawson'. TED L. PETIT & JOHN P. PEAT

'Eloquent Silence' (Jeff Salter 1993). Evergreen. Scape 28 in. (71.1 cm); flower 6 in. (15.2 cm). Midseason. A large cream-white ruffled flower with a crimped wire gold edge and a green throat. Tetraploid. Seedling × 'Tet. Inspired Word'. TED L. PETIT & JOHN P. PEAT

'English Trifle' (Betty Harwood 1995). Dormant. Scape 27 in. (68.6 cm); flower 5 in. (12.7 cm). Midseason. A lightly ruffled pale cream self with a green throat. Diploid. Seedling × 'Fairy Tale Pink'. BETTY HARWOOD

'Gentle Shepherd' (Clarke Yancey 1980). Semi-evergreen. Scape 29 in. (73.6 cm); flower 5 in. (12.7 cm). Early midseason. One of the most popular near-white flowers. Classic shape and lightly ruffled with a green heart. Diploid. (('Call to Remembrance' × 'Robert Way Schlumpf') × seedling) × ('Light the Way' × (seedling × 'Tender Love'). Award of Merit 1987. TED L. PETIT & JOHN P. PEAT

'Glacier Bay' (Patrick Stamile 1995). Evergreen. Scape 28 in. (71.1 cm); flower 5.5 in. (14.0 cm). Midseason. Crimped gold ruffles edge this cream-white self with green throat. Tetraploid. 'Arctic Ruffles' × 'Admiral's Braid'. PATRICK STAMILE

'Honey Jubilee' (Charlie Pierce 1980). Semi-evergreen. Scape 24 in. (61.0 cm); flower 6 in. (15.2 cm). Midseason. A loosely ruffled cream self with a green throat. Diploid. 'My Belle' × 'Holiday in Dixie'. PATRICK STAMILE

'Ice Carnival' (Frank Childs 1967). Dormant. Scape 28 in. (71.1 cm); flower 6 in. (15.2 cm). Midseason. A time-honored near-white, triangular, tailored self with a green throat. Diploid. Parents unknown. Award of Merit 1974. TOM ROOD

'Inspired Word' (Bob Dove 1979). Semi-evergreen. Scape 24 in. (61.0 cm); flower 6 in. (15.2 cm). Midseason. A pale off-white with green highlights and a green throat. Diploid. 'White Angel' × seedling. R. W. MUNSON JR

'Joan Senior' (Kenneth Durio 1977). Evergreen. Scape 25 in. (63.5 cm); flower 6 in. (15.2 cm). Early midseason. Among the all-time most popular near whites. Recurved, creped flower with a lime-green throat. Diploid. 'Loving Memories' × 'Little Infant'. Award of Merit 1984. Lenington All-American Award 1990. PATRICK STAMILE

'Karl Petersen' (Ted L. Petit 1995). Semi-evergreen. Scape 24 in. (61.0 cm); flower 6.5 in. (16.5 cm). Midseason. A luxuriously formed, wide-petaled, large, ivory-cream, creped self with a green throat. Tetraploid. 'Ida's Magic' × 'Wedding Band'. TED L. PETIT

'Lenox' (R. W. Munson Jr. 1984). Evergreen. Scape 24 in. (61.0 cm); flower 6 in. (15.2 cm). Early midseason. A classically formed, pale cream self with a cream-green throat. Tetraploid. Parents unknown. TED L. PETIT & JOHN P. PEAT

'Lime Frost' (Patrick Stamile 1990). Dormant. Scape 27 in. (68.6 cm); flower 5.75 in. (14.6 cm). Very late. A lightly ruffled green and white blend with a green throat. Tetraploid. ('Arctic Snow' × 'White Tie Affair') × Tet. Gentle Shepherd'. Eugene S. Foster Award 1997. PATRICK STAMILE

'Luverne' (Sarah Sikes 1991). Dormant. Scape 28 in. (71.1 cm); flower 5.75 in. (14.6 cm). Mid-season. A wide-petaled, circular, ivory flower with tints of pink and a green heart. Diploid. 'Someone Special' × 'Lauren Leah'. JOHN EISEMAN

'Marble Faun' (Bryant Millikan 1983). Evergreen. Scape 20 in. (50.8 cm); flower 5 in. (12.7 cm). Early. A very recurved, round, cream to lemon-yellow flower with a light green heart. Diploid. 'Wynnson' × 'Brocaded Gown'. Award of Merit 1994. PATRICK STAMILE

'Marquee Moon' (Dan Trimmer 1998). Dormant. Scape 24 in. (61.0 cm); flower 5.25 in. (13.3 cm). Midseason late. A heavily ruffled, gold-edged near white with a green throat. Tetraploid. 'Admiral's Braid' × 'Enchanted April'. DAN TRIMMER

'Monica Marie' (Lee Gates 1982). Evergreen. Scape 24 in. (61.0 cm); flower 5 in. (12.7 cm). Early midseason. A heavily creped, wide-petaled, near-white self with a green throat. Tetraploid. Parents unknown. Award of Merit 1991. JOHN EISEMAN

'Moonlit Caress' (Jeff Salter 1996). Semi-evergreen. Scape 26 in. (66.0 cm); flower 5.5 in. (14.0 cm). Midseason late. A near-white self with a green throat. Tetraploid. Parents unknown. TED L. PETIT & JOHN P. PEAT

'Nell Keown' (Charlie Pierce 1979). Evergreen. Scape 18 in. (45.7 cm); flower 6.5 in. (16.5 cm). Early. A loosely ruffled cream-yellow self with a green throat. Diploid. 'Hazel Monette' × 'Janet Gayle'. PATRICK STAMILE

'Pearl Harbor' (Robert Carr 1997). Evergreen. Scape 27 in. (68.6 cm); flower 5.75 in. (14.6 cm). Midseason. A cream-yellow blend with a gold edge and a green throat. Tetraploid. 'Wedding Band' × 'Ida's Magic'. ROBERT CARR

'Presumed Innocent' (Robert Carr 1998). Evergreen. Scape 28 in. (71.1 cm); flower 5.5 in. (14.0 cm). Early midseason. An ivory-cream with heavy ruffling over a green throat. Tetraploid. 'America's Most Wanted' × 'Quality of Mercy'. ROBERT CARR

'Ptarmigan' (Patrick Stamile 1989). Dormant. Scape 20 in. (50.8 cm); flower 5.75 in. (14.6 cm). Midseason late. A lightly ruffled, slightly recurved, smooth, substantial, near-white flower with a green heart. Tetraploid. 'Arctic Snow' × 'White Tie Affair'. PATRICK STAMILE

'Quality of Mercy' (Robert Carr 1994). Semi-evergreen. Scape 27 in. (68.6 cm); flower 6 in. (15.2 cm). Early midseason. A very special near-white self with a green throat. Tetraploid. 'Wedding Band' × 'Tet. Inspired Word'.
TED L. PETIT & JOHN P. PEAT

'Queens Gift' (Edwin C. Brown 1984). Semi-evergreen. Scape 23 in. (58.4 cm); flower 5 in. (12.7 cm). Early midseason. A nicely ruffled cream self with a deep olive-green center. Diploid. Parents unknown.
JOHN EISEMAN

'Raining Violets' (Allen Wild 1983). Dormant. Scape 20 in. (50.8 cm); flower 4.75 in. (12.1 cm). Midseason late. A diamond-dusted cream to ivory-white edged in lavender-violet with raised cream midribs and a yellow-green throat. Diploid. Parents unknown. PATRICK STAMILE

'Rose Goodman' (Betty Harwood 1995). Semi-evergreen. Scape 28 in. (71.1 cm); flower 6.5 in. (16.5 cm). Early. A large near-white self with a pink blush and a large green throat. Diploid. 'New Series' × 'Janet Gayle'. BETTY HARWOOD

'Ruffled Dude' (R. W. Munson Jr. 1986). Evergreen. Scape 20 in. (50.8 cm); flower 5 in. (12.7 cm). Early midseason. A heavily ruffled cream self with a chartreuse throat. A tetraploid critical for breeding ruffling. Tetraploid. Seedling × 'Fred Ham'. JOHN EISEMAN

'Ruffled Ivory' (Edwin C. Brown 1982). Semi-evergreen. Scape 27 in. (68.6 cm); flower 5.25 in. (13.3 cm). Midseason. A smooth-textured, recurved, lightly ruffled near-white with a pink blush and a chartreuse throat. Diploid. Seedling × 'Dream Awhile'. WILLIAM JARVIS

'Sea Swept Dreams' (Jeff Salter 1996). Semi-evergreen. Scape 28 in. (71.1 cm); flower 6 in. (15.2 cm). Midseason. A large, nicely formed, ruffled ivory-cream self with a green throat. Tetraploid. Parents unknown. TED L. PETIT & JOHN P. PEAT

'Siloam Ralph Henry' (Pauline Henry 1988). Dormant. Scape 18 in. (45.7 cm); flower 5.5 in. (14.0 cm). Midseason. A very popular ruffled pale-ivory-blushed-pink self with a green throat. Diploid. Parents unknown. Award of Merit 1997. PATRICK STAMILE

'Slade Brown' (Edgar W. Brown 1981). Evergreen. Scape 23 in. (58.4 cm); flower 9 in. (22.8 cm). Early. A narrow-petaled, triangular cream-chartreuse self with a green throat. Diploid. Seedling × 'Estelle Whitmire'. TED L. PETIT & JOHN P. PEAT

'Snow Ballerina' (R. W. Munson Jr. 1978). Semi-evergreen. Scape 26 in. (66.0 cm); flower 5 in. (12.7 cm). Early midseason. A lightly ruffled cream-white self with a green throat. Tetraploid. Parents unknown. R. W. MUNSON JR

'So Lovely' (George Lenington 1969). Semi-evergreen. Scape 30 in. (76.2 cm); flower 5.5 in. (14.0 cm). Midseason. A narrow-petaled near-white self with a green throat. Diploid. Seedling × 'White Formal'. CURTIS & LINDA SUE BARNES

'True Gertrude Demarest' (Gertrude Demarest and Elsie Spalding 1986). Semi-evergreen. Scape 20 in. (50.8 cm); flower 7.5 in. (19.1 cm). Early midseason. A wide-petaled, tailored to lightly ruffled ivory with a pink overcast and a green throat. Diploid. Parents unknown. Award of Merit 1994. JOHN EISEMAN

'Tuscawilla Tranquillity' (Ra Hansen 1988). Semi-evergreen. Scape 21 in. (53.3 cm); flower 5.5 in. (14.0 cm). Extra early. A very popular near-white self with a lemon-lime throat. Diploid. ('Monica Marie' × 'Ruffled Ivory') × ('Monica Marie' × 'Gentle Shepherd'). RA HANSEN

'Wendy Glawson' (Edwin C. Brown 1986). Semi-evergreen. Scape 19 in. (48.3 cm); flower 5 in. (12.7 cm). Early midseason. A wide-petaled, ruffled cream-white self with a green throat. Diploid. Seedling × 'Morning Madonna'. JOHN EISEMAN

'White Crinoline' (Patrick Stamile 1992). Dormant. Scape 21 in. (53.3 cm); flower 6 in. (15.2 cm). Early midseason. An exceptional near-white self with green throat. Tetraploid. 'Ptarmigan' × 'Tet. Gentle Shepherd'. PATRICK STAMILE

'White Hot' (Patrick Stamile 1992). Dormant. Scape 25 in. (63.5 cm); flower 6.25 in. (15.9 cm). Early midseason. An exceptionally formed nearly pure white self with a green throat. Tetraploid. ('Arctic Snow' × 'White Tie Affair') × 'Tet. Gentle Shepherd'. PATRICK STAMILE

'White Temptation' (Van Sellers 1978). Semi-evergreen. Scape 32 in. (81.3 cm); flower 5 in. (12.7 cm). Midseason. A very nearly white self with a green throat. Diploid. Parents unknown. Award of Merit 1985. TED L. PETIT & JOHN P. PEAT

'White Tie Affair' (Virginia Peck 1982). Dormant. Scape 24 in. (61.0 cm); flower 6 in. (15.2 cm). Midseason. A time-honored near-white self with a green throat. Tetraploid. Seedling × 'Tet. Iron Gate Glacier'. TED WHITE

'Whiter Shade' (Patrick Stamile 1992). Semi-evergreen. Scape 21 in. (53.3 cm); flower 6 in. (15.2 cm). Early midseason. A broad-petaled lightly ruffled near-white self with a green throat. Tetraploid. 'Ptarmigan' × 'Tet. Homer Howard Gilden'. PATRICK STAMILE

'Winter Palace' (Ted L. Petit 1998). Semi-evergreen. Scape 23 in. (58.4 cm); flower 5.5 in. (14.0 cm). Midseason. An ivory to cream flower with a heavy gold edge and a green throat. Tetraploid. 'Untamed Glory' × 'Admiral's Braid'. TED L. PETIT

YELLOW (yellow to gold)

'Alec Allen' (Kate Carpenter 1982). Evergreen. Scape 26 in. (66.0 cm); flower 5.5 in. (14.0 cm). Early midseason. A wide-petaled, ruffled creamy yellow self with a lime-green center. Diploid. Parents unknown. Award of Merit 1988. JOHN EISEMAN

'All the Magic' (Jeff Salter 1996). Semi-evergreen. Scape 26 in. (66.0 cm); flower 5.5 in. (14.0 cm). Early midseason. A heavy-substanced cream-yellow-peach blend with a green heart. Tetraploid. Parents unknown. TED L. PETIT & JOHN P. PEAT

'America's Most Wanted' (Robert Carr 1997). Evergreen. Scape 27 in. (68.6 cm); flower 6 in. (15.2 cm). Early. A highly ruffled, well-branched golden cream-melon-yellow self with a green throat. Tetraploid. 'Sherry Lane Carr' × seedling. ROBERT CARR

'Anastasia' (Jeff Salter 1985). Evergreen. Scape 20 in. (50.8 cm); flower 6.5 in. (16.5 cm). Midseason. A cream-yellow self with petals pleated deep into a lime-green throat. Tetraploid. Seedling × 'Jade Lady'. TED L. PETIT & JOHN P. PEAT

'Atlanta Full House' (Trudy Petree 1984). Dormant. Scape 27 in. (68.6 cm); flower 6.5 in. (16.5 cm). Midseason. A large, triangular yellow self with a green heart. Tetraploid. (('Mary Todd' × 'Jared') × 'Proselyte') × 'Tet. Carondelet'. Award of Merit 1991. TED L. PETIT & JOHN P. PEAT

'Atlanta Moonlight' (Trudy Petree 1982). Dormant. Scape 27 in. (68.6 cm); flower 6 in. (15.2 cm). Midseason. A light cream-yellow lightly ruffled self with a green throat. Tetraploid. (('Mary Todd' × 'Jared') × 'Baruch') × 'Tet. Driven Snow'. TED L. PETIT & JOHN P. PEAT

'Beauty to Behold' (Van Sellers 1978). Semi-evergreen. Scape 24 in. (61.0 cm); flower 5.5 in. (14.0 cm). Midseason. A wide-petaled lemon self with a green center. Diploid. 'Wynn' × 'Springtime Sonata'. Award of Merit 1985. TED L. PETIT & JOHN P. PEAT

'Betty Warren Woods' (R. W. Munson Jr. 1987). Evergreen. Scape 24 in. (61.0 cm); flower 4.75 in. (12.1 cm). Midseason late. A highly ruffled cream-yellow self with a green center. Very important for breeding vigor and fertility. Tetraploid. ('Capella Light' × 'India House') × 'Ruffled Dude'. PATRICK STAMILE

'Bill Norris' (David Kirchhoff 1993). Semi-evergreen. Scape 29 in. (73.7 cm); flower 5 in. (12.7 cm). Midseason. A brilliant sunny gold self with very wide, heavily ruffled petals. An extremely popular flower. Tetraploid. Seedling × 'Bit More Class'. DAVID KIRCHHOFF

'Blake Allen' (Kate Carpenter 1981). Evergreen. Scape 28 in. (71.1 cm); flower 7 in. (17.8 cm). Early midseason. A deep yellow, wide-petaled, lightly ruffled self with a green throat. Diploid. Seedling × 'Sabie'. Award of Merit 1989. PATRICK STAMILE

'Blonde is Beautiful' (Harrold Harris and John Benz 1985). Semi-evergreen. Scape 28 in. (71.1 cm); flower 6 in. (15.2 cm). Midseason. A creamy lemon-yellow, triangular, lightly ruffled self with a green heart. Tetraploid. Seedling × 'Demetrius'. TED L. PETIT & JOHN P. PEAT

'Chasing Windmills' (Ted L. Petit 1996). Semi-evergreen. Scape 19 in. (48.3 cm); flower 6 in. (15.2 cm). Midseason. A cream-tangerine-gold very ruffled round flower with a green throat. Tetraploid. 'Betty Warren Woods' × 'Pharaoh's Gold'. TED L. PETIT

'Cherished Treasure' (R. W. Munson Jr. 1991). Evergreen. Scape 30 in. (76.2 cm); flower 6 in. (15.2 cm). Early midseason. A lightly ruffled yellow-washed-peach self with a yellow-green throat. Tetraploid. 'Betty Warren Woods' × ('Ethiopia' × ('Tet. Betty Barns' × 'Royal Heiress')). R. W. MUNSON JR

'Childhood Treasure' (Jeff Salter 1992). Semi-evergreen. Scape 24 in. (61.0 cm); flower 5 in. (12.7 cm). Midseason. A wide-petaled very ruffled yellow-gold self with a green throat. Tetraploid. 'Walking on Sunshine' × 'Alexandra'. TED L. PETIT & JOHN P. PEAT

'Christina Maartense' (Henry Lorrain and Douglas Lycett 1998). Semi-evergreen. Scape 33 in. (83.8 cm); flower 5.5 in. (14.0 cm). Early. A pastel yellow with a creped texture, green highlights, and a lime-green throat. Tetraploid. 'Edessa' × 'Edna'. HENRY LORRAIN & DOUGLAS LYCETT

'Circle of Life' (Ted L. Petit 1996). Semi-ever-green. Scape 23 in. (58.4 cm); flower 5 in. (12.7 cm). Midseason. A very round, heavy sub-stanced gold self with a green throat. Tetra-ploid. 'Betty Warren Woods' × 'Pharaoh's Gold'. TED L. PETIT

'Collier' (Edwin C. Brown 1993). Semi-evergreen. Scape 28 in. (71.1 cm); flower 6 in. (15.2 cm). Early midseason. A wide-petaled polychrome combining pink, gold, cream, and yellow with a green throat. Tetraploid. 'Most Noble' × 'Kathleen Salter'. TED L. PETIT & JOHN P. PEAT

'Crystal Singer' (Elizabeth H. Salter 1996). Ever-green. Scape 28 in. (71.0 cm); flower 4 in. (10.2 cm). Midseason. A small, ruffled yellow-cream with a heavy gold edge and a lime-green throat. Tetraploid. 'Sweet Southern Sunshine' × 'Tropical Freeze'. TED L. PETIT & JOHN P. PEAT

'Darrell' (Kenneth Durio 1981). Evergreen. Scape 26 in. (66.0 cm); flower 7 in. (17.8 cm). Early midseason. A very large light butter-yellow with pink highlights and a green-yellow throat. Tetraploid. 'Decoy' × 'Tet. Bril-liant Luster'. PATRICK STAMILE

'Creative Art' (Charlie Pierce 1981). Semi-evergreen. Scape 16 in. (40.6 cm); flower 6 in. (15.2 cm). Midseason. A triangular light yellow self with a green throat. Diploid. 'Jade Chalice' × 'Richly Blessed'. Award of Merit 1988. JOHN EISEMAN

'Deanna's Gift' (Ted L. Petit 1994). Evergreen. Scape 20 in. (50.8 cm); flower 6 in. (15.2 cm). Early midseason. A peach-yellow ruffled self with a pink blush and wire gold edge above a green throat. Tetraploid. 'Betty Warren Woods' × 'Ida's Magic'. TED L. PETIT

'Deloris Gould' (Wallice Gould 1992). Semi-evergreen. Scape 25 in. (63.5 cm); flower 5 in. (12.7 cm). Early midseason. A very round deep yellow self with a small green throat. Tetraploid. ('Pittsburgh Golden Triangle' × 'Shock-wave') × ('Indonesia' × 'Dance Ballerina Dance'). TED L. PETIT & JOHN P. PEAT

'Demetrius' (Harrold Harris 1977). Dormant. Scape 24 in. (61.0 cm); flower 5.5 in. (14.0 cm). Early midseason. A chrome-yellow self with green throat. Tetraploid. (('Mary Todd' × 'Jared') × 'Proselyte') × seedling. TED WHITE

'Ed Kirchhoff' (David Kirchhoff 1981). Semi-evergreen. Scape 23 in. (58.4 cm); flower 5 in. (12.7 cm). Early. A saffron-yellow self with a darker yellow ruffled edge and an olive-green throat. Tetraploid. (('Double Jackpot' × 'Amber Sunset') × ('Evening Gown' × 'Yasmin')) × seedling. Eugene S. Foster Award 1995.
PATRICK STAMILE

'Devonshire' (R. W. Munson Jr. 1987). Evergreen. Scape 30 in. (76.2 cm); flower 7 in. (17.8 cm). Early midseason. A very large ivory-yellow self with a yellow-chartreuse throat. Tetraploid. ('Pagoda Goddess' × ('Kecia' × 'Wilbur Harling')) × ('Tet. Shibui Splendor' × 'Chateau Blanc'). JOHN EISEMAN

'Emerald Brooch' (Jean Duncan 1995). Evergreen. Scape 22 in. (55.9 cm); flower 5 in. (12.7 cm). Early midseason. A bright lemon-yellow with a deep green throat and wide, overlapping, heavily ruffled petals. Tetraploid. 'My Darling Clementine' × seedling. JEAN DUNCAN

'Emperor's Choice' (John Benz 1991). Dormant. Scape 24 in. (61.0 cm); flower 5 in. (12.7 cm). Midseason late. A very wide-petaled, ruffled lemon-yellow self with a deep green throat. Tetraploid. ('Seth' × 'Atlanta Antique Satin') × 'Matt'. JOHN BENZ

'Ever So Ruffled' (Patrick Stamile 1983). Semi-evergreen. Scape 22 in. (55.9 cm); flower 5 in. (12.7 cm). Midseason. A very popular classic deep yellow self with a dark green throat. Wide-petaled and ruffled. Tetraploid. 'Lahaina' × 'Supersonic Prize'. Award of Merit 1994. PATRICK STAMILE

'Ferengi Gold' (Ted L. Petit 1994). Dormant. Scape 19 in. (48.3 cm); flower 5.5 in. (14.0 cm). Early midseason. Cream yellow with a pink blush, green throat, and tightly crimped ruffled edges. Very vigorous grower. Tetraploid. 'Betty Warren Woods' × ('Emerald Dawn' × 'Betty Warren Woods'). TED L. PETIT

'Floyd Cove' (Patrick Stamile 1987). Dormant. Scape 21 in. (53.3 cm); flower 5 in. (12.7 cm). Midseason. An extremely wide-petaled, ruffled, circular yellow self with a green-yellow throat. Diploid. 'Ever So Ruffled' × 'Daydream Believer'. PATRICK STAMILE

'Fred Ham' (R. W. Munson Jr. 1982). Evergreen. Scape 24 in. (61.0 cm); flower 7 in. (17.8 cm). Midseason. A cream-yellow self with a green heart. Tetraploid. 'Chateau Blanc' × ('Tet. Ruth Bastian' × ('Astarte × Embassy')). Award of Merit 1991. TED L. PETIT & JOHN P. PEAT

'Glory Days' (Patrick Stamile 1987). Dormant. Scape 24 in. (61.0 cm); flower 5.5 in. (14.0 cm). Midseason late. An extraordinarily heavily ruffled, very wide-petaled gold self. Tetraploid. (seedling × 'Shockwave') × (('Lahaina' × 'Shockwave') × 'Ever So Ruffled'). PATRICK STAMILE

'Golden Dimples' (Jean Duncan 1995). Evergreen. Scape 24 in. (61.0 cm); flower 5.25 in. (13.3 cm). Early midseason. A wide, flat, sculpted, heavily ruffled gold self. Tetraploid. 'Ever So Ruffled' × 'Booger'. JEAN DUNCAN

'Golden Prize' (Virginia Peck 1968). Dormant. Scape 26 in. (66.0 cm); flower 7 in. (17.8 cm). Late. A triangular bright yellow-gold flower of classic form and long-standing popularity. Tetraploid. Parents unknown. Lenington All-American Award 1987. PATRICK STAMILE

'Good Morning America' (Jeff Salter 1992). Semi-evergreen. Scape 26 in. (66.0 cm); flower 6 in. (15.2 cm). Midseason. A wide-petaled, heavily ruffled cream-gold blend with a green throat. Tetraploid. 'Lady Arabella' × seedling. TED L. PETIT & JOHN P. PEAT

'Grace and Grandeur' (Jeff Salter 1992). Semi-evergreen. Scape 22 in. (55.9 cm); flower 6 in. (15.2 cm). Early midseason. A cream-yellow blend with a green throat. Wide-petaled with heavy ruffles. Tetraploid. 'Walking on Sunshine' × 'Kathleen Salter'. TED L. PETIT & JOHN P. PEAT

'Grand Marshal' (Edwin C. Brown 1993). Semi-evergreen. Scape 28 in. (71.1 cm); flower 6.5 in. (16.5 cm). Early midseason. A large, full-formed, ruffled ivory-yellow self with a green throat. Tetraploid. 'Kathleen Salter' × 'Tet. Ruffled Ivory'. JOHN EISEMAN

'Grander Dreams' (Ted L. Petit 1995). Semi-evergreen. Scape 19 in. (48.3 cm); flower 6 in. (15.2 cm). Midseason. A cream-yellow flower with a pink blush, crunchy ruffled edges, and a green throat. Tetraploid. 'Betty Warren Woods' × 'Ida's Magic'. TED L. PETIT

'Helaman' (R. Roberson 1981). Evergreen. Scape 29 in. (73.7 cm); flower 9 in. (22.9 cm). Early midseason. An extremely large, triangular yellow blossom edged in bronze with a chartreuse throat. Diploid. 'Mormon' × 'Cashmere'. JOHN EISEMAN

'Hudson Valley' (Virginia Peck 1971). Dormant. Scape 32 in. (81.3 cm); flower 8.5 in. (21.6 cm). Midseason. A greenish yellow self with a green throat. Classic triangular form. Tetraploid. 'Bonnie John Seton' × seedling. Award of Merit 1977. JOHN EISEMAN

'Iowa Greenery' (Elsie Spalding 1988). Evergreen. Scape 20 in. (50.8 cm); flower 5.5 in. (14.0 cm). Early midseason. A bright yellow self with an extremely large green center bleeding out into the petals. Diploid. Parents unknown. JOHN EISEMAN

'Jerusalem' (Donald Stevens and Robert Seawright 1985). Dormant. Scape 28 in. (71.1 cm); flower 5 in. (12.7 cm). Midseason. A famous bright gold self with yellow-green heart. Wide petaled nicely formed. Tetraploid. 'Truffles' × 'Dance Ballerina Dance'. JOHN EISEMAN

'Joel' (Harrold Harris 1978). Dormant. Scape 24 in. (61.0 cm); flower 5.5 in. (14.0 cm). Early midseason. A triangular, lightly ruffled yellow self with a green throat. Tetraploid. (('Mary Todd' × 'Jared') × 'Proselyte') × 'Tet. Carondelet'. JOHN EISEMAN

'John Allen' (Kate Carpenter 1987). Dormant. Scape 23 in. (58.4 cm); flower 6 in. (15.2 cm). Midseason. A pale yellow-gold self with a green throat. Diploid. 'Lake Norman Sunrise' × 'Alec Allen'. TED L. PETIT & JOHN P. PEAT

'Joint Venture' (Ted L. Petit 1998). Evergreen. Scape 22 in. (55.9 cm); flower 6 in. (15.2 cm). Midseason. A heavily ruffled, large gold with a green throat and strong substance. Tetraploid. 'Betty Warren Woods' × 'Glory Days'. TED L. PETIT

'Joy and Laughter' (David Kirchhoff 1995). Evergreen. Scape 28 in. (71.1 cm); flower 6 in. (15.2 cm). Early. A golden yellow self with a golden green throat. Tetraploid. 'Kathleen Salter' × 'Bill Norris'. DAVID KIRCHHOFF

'Julian Carter' (Mac Carter 1998). Dormant. Scape 24 in. (61.0 cm); flower 6 in. (15.2 cm). Early midseason. A wide-petaled, very ruffled golden yellow self with a green throat. Tetraploid. 'Golden Glow' × 'Betty Warren Woods'. MAC CARTER

'Kathleen Salter' (Jeff Salter 1989). Semi-evergreen. Scape 28 in. (71.1 cm); flower 6 in. (15.2 cm). Early midseason. A very ruffled yellow self with a green throat. Tetraploid. 'Anastasia' × 'Betty Warren Woods'. MELANIE MASON

'Kecia' (R. W. Munson Jr. 1977). Evergreen. Scape 28 in. (71.1 cm); flower 6 in. (15.2 cm). Early midseason. A pale yellow self with a green throat. Tetraploid. Parents unknown. Honorable Mention 1981. R. W. MUNSON JR

'Lady Arabella' (Jeff Salter 1992). Semi-evergreen. Scape 28 in. (71.1 cm); flower 5 in. (12.7 cm). Early midseason. A ruffled cream-ivory-gold blend with heavy substance and a green throat. Tetraploid. Parents unknown.
JOHN EISEMAN

'Larry Grace' (Jeff Salter 1994). Semi-evergreen. Scape 24 in. (61.0 cm); flower 6 in. (15.2 cm). Early midseason. A large, wide-petaled yellow self with a gold edge and a green throat. Tetraploid. 'Untamed Glory' × 'Kathleen Salter'.
TED L. PETIT & JOHN P. PEAT

'Las Vegas Gold' (Ted L. Petit 1998). Semi-evergreen. Scape 20 in. (50.8 cm); flower 6 in. (15.2 cm). Early. A heavily ruffled bright gold to tangerine-orange flower with a green throat. Tetraploid. 'Betty Warren Woods' × ('Glory Days' × 'Betty Warren Woods'). TED L. PETIT

'Lunar Sea' (R. W. Munson Jr. 1982). Evergreen. Scape 22 in. (55.9 cm); flower 6 in. (15.2 cm). Early midseason. A lemon self with a chartreuse heart and ruffling. Tetraploid. ('Kecia' × 'Chateau Blanc')F2 × seedling.
PATRICK STAMILE

'Mary's Gold' (Harold McDonell 1984). Dormant. Scape 34 in. (86.4 cm); flower 6.5 in. (16.5 cm). Midseason. A large, very popular, brilliant golden orange self with a green throat. Tetraploid. 'Creepy Crawler' × 'Spellbinder'. Award of Merit 1991. TED L. PETIT & JOHN P. PEAT

'Matt' (Harrold Harris 1982). Dormant. Scape 20 in. (50.8 cm); flower 5.5 in. (14.0 cm). Midseason. A popular yellow flower with bronze overlay and a green throat. Tetraploid. 'Demetrius' × ('Matthias' × 'Tet. Frank Hunter'). Award of Merit 1988. JOHN EISEMAN

'Moon' (Mac Carter 1996). Semi-evergreen. Scape 32 in. (81.3 cm); flower 6 in. (15.2 cm). Midseason. A very ruffled yellow self with a dark green center. Tetraploid. 'Omomuki' × 'Moon Dust'. MAC CARTER

'Moon Dazzle' (Patrick Stamile 1989). Semi-evergreen. Scape 27 in. (68.6 cm); flower 6.5 in. (16.5 cm). Midseason late. A large, lightly ruffled, triangular yellow self with a green throat. Tetraploid. ('Super Nova' × 'Ever So Ruffled') × (('Lahaina' × 'Shockwave') × 'Ever So Ruffled'). PATRICK STAMILE

'Most Noble' (R. W. Munson Jr. 1980). Evergreen. Scape 28 in. (71.1 cm); flower 6 in. (15.2 cm). Midseason. A deep yellow self, slightly ruffled with a green throat. Tetraploid. Parents unknown. Award of Merit 1987. PATRICK STAMILE

'My Darling Clementine' (Jeff Salter 1988). Evergreen. Scape 21 in. (53.3 cm); flower 4.5 in. (11.4 cm). Early. A very early-blooming, wide-petaled yellow self with a green throat. Tetraploid. Parents unknown. Award of Merit 1997. PATRICK STAMILE

'Natchez Moon' (Jeff Salter 1994). Dormant. Scape 20 in. (50.8 cm); flower 5 in. (12.7 cm). Early midseason. One of the finest round, ruffled cream-yellow flowers currently available. Tetraploid. 'Alexandra' × seedling. TED L. PETIT & JOHN P. PEAT

'Newberry Frilly Lady' (Velerie Rushing 1987). Dormant. Scape 20 in. (50.8 cm); flower 6 in. (15.2 cm). Early midseason. A narrow-petaled, classically formed, frilly medium yellow self with a green throat. Tetraploid. 'Lahaina' × 'Newberry Real Frills'. TED L. PETIT & JOHN P. PEAT

'Olympic Showcase' (Patrick Stamile 1990). Semi-evergreen. Scape 24 in. (61.0 cm); flower 6.2 in. (15.9 cm). Early midseason. A popular triangular, large, brilliant gold self with a green throat. Tetraploid. 'Norma Jean' × ('Lahaina' × 'Shockwave'). PATRICK STAMILE

'Omomuki' (Patrick Stamile 1991). Dormant. Scape 26 in. (66.0 cm); flower 5 in. (12.7 cm). Early midseason. A heavily ruffled chartreuse-yellow self with a large green center. Tetraploid. ('Ever So Ruffled' × ('Lahaina' × 'Shockwave')) × 'Floyd Cove'. PATRICK STAMILE

'Oriental Opulence' (Jeff Salter 1992). Semi-evergreen. Scape 28 in. (71.1 cm); flower 6.5 in. (16.5 cm). Early midseason. A very large yellow-gold and amber-peach blend with a green throat. Very round and ruffled. Tetraploid. 'Walking on Sunshine' × 'Alexandra'. TED L. PETIT & JOHN P. PEAT

'Pearl Lewis' (Virginia Peck 1984). Dormant. Scape 24 in. (61.0 cm); flower 6 in. (15.2 cm). Midseason late. A deep cream-gold self with an olive-green throat and light ruffling. Tetraploid. 'Eighteen Karat' × 'Sheer Class'. Award of Merit 1994. JOHN EISEMAN

'Ruffled Magic' (Edwin C. Brown 1981). Semi-evergreen. Scape 25 in. (63.5 cm); flower 5.25 in. (13.3 cm). Early midseason. A clear pastel yellow with pink blush, looping ruffles on the petal edges, and a green throat. Diploid. 'Martha Adams' × 'Jade Chalice'. PATRICK STAMILE

'Ruffled Masterpiece' (Edwin C. Brown 1987). Semi-evergreen. Scape 24 in. (61.0 cm); flower 5.25 in. (13.3 cm). Early midseason. Among the most popular flowers, a virtually circular, heavily ruffled cream-yellow with a green throat. Diploid. 'Queens Gift' × seedling. JOHN EISEMAN

'Ruffled Perfection' (Jack Carpenter 1989). Semi-evergreen. Scape 24 in. (61.0 cm); flower 7 in. (17.8 cm). Early. A very large cream-lemon-yellow self with heavy substance and ruffling. Diploid. Parents unknown. JOHN EISEMAN

'Shaman' (Lee Gates 1985). Evergreen. Scape 20 in. (50.8 cm); flower 5.5 in. (14.0 cm). Early. A canary-yellow self with soft looping ruffles and a green throat. Tetraploid. Parents unknown. TED L. PETIT & JOHN P. PEAT

'Sherry Lane Carr' (Robert Carr 1993). Evergreen. Scape 23 in. (58.4 cm); flower 6.5 in. (16.5 cm). Early midseason. This well-branched cream-butter-yellow self with a heavily ruffled gold edge has a very high bud count. Tetraploid. Parents unknown. TED L. PETIT & JOHN P. PEAT

'Siloam Amazing Grace' (Pauline Henry 1989). Dormant. Scape 24 in. (61.0 cm); flower 5.5 in. (14.0 cm). Early midseason. A ruffled yellow self with a strong green throat. Diploid. Parents unknown. Award of Merit 1996. TED L. PETIT & JOHN P. PEAT

'Siloam Mama' (Pauline Henry 1982). Dormant. Scape 24 in. (61.0 cm); flower 5.75 in. (14.6 cm). Early midseason. A wide-petaled, textured yellow flower with a green throat. Diploid. Parents unknown. L. Ernest Plouf Award 1984. TED L. PETIT & JOHN P. PEAT

'Siloam Medallion' (Pauline Henry 1982). Dormant. Scape 26 in. (66.0 cm); flower 6.5 in. (16.5 cm). Early midseason. A very round, large yellow self with a green throat. Diploid. Parents unknown. JOHN EISEMAN

'Sorrento Song' (Patrick Stamile 1990). Dormant. Scape 24 in. (61.0 cm); flower 5 in. (12.7 cm). Midseason. A wide-petaled, very bright yellow to gold ruffled flower with a green throat. Tetraploid. ('Ever So Ruffled' × ('Lahaina' × 'Shockwave')) × 'Ever So Ruffled'. PATRICK STAMILE

'Southern Romance' (Ted L. Petit 1994). Semi-evergreen. Scape 21 in. (53.3 cm); flower 5.5 in. (14.0 cm). Midseason. An ivory-cream to pink flower with golden watermark, green throat, and crimped gold edge. Tetraploid. 'Ruffian's Apprentice' × ('Wedding Band' × 'Desert Jewel'). TED L. PETIT

'Stone Ponies' (Ted L. Petit 1995). Semi-evergreen. Scape 29 in. (73.7 cm); flower 5 in. (12.7 cm). Midseason. A heavily sculpted tangerine to gold flower with a green throat and very heavy substance. Tetraploid. 'Ever So Ruffled' × 'Ida's Magic'. TED L. PETIT

'Spring Willow Song' (R. W. Munson Jr. 1983). Semi-evergreen. Scape 25 in. (63.5 cm); flower 6 in. (15.2 cm). Early midseason. A lightly ruffled yellow-cream self with a green throat. Tetraploid. Parents unknown. PATRICK STAMILE

'Sun King' (R. W. Munson Jr. 1980). Evergreen. Scape 30 in. (76.2 cm); flower 6 in. (15.2 cm). Early midseason. A ruffled gold-yellow self with a green throat. Tetraploid. Parents unknown. R. W. MUNSON JR

'Sun' (Mac Carter 1995). Evergreen. Scape 22 in. (55.9 cm); flower 7 in. (17.8 cm). Early midseason. A very ruffled, large, clear light yellow self with a green throat. Tetraploid. 'Mary Timmons' × 'Olympic Showcase'. MAC CARTER

'Sunlit Splendor' (Jeff Salter 1988). Semi-evergreen. Scape 24 in. (61.0 cm); flower 6 in. (15.2 cm). Early midseason. A pale ivory-yellow ruffled self with a green throat. Tetraploid. Parents unknown. TED L. PETIT & JOHN P. PEAT

'Supreme Empire' (Curt Hanson 1996). Dormant. Scape 33 in. (83.8 cm); flower 6 in. (15.2 cm). Midseason late. A carved, or grooved, yellow-gold self with a green throat. Unusual and distinctive. Tetraploid. 'Alpha Centauri' × 'Tet. Siloam Medallion'. CURT HANSON

'Tiffany Gold' (R. W. Munson Jr. 1982). Evergreen. Scape 24 in. (61.0 cm); flower 7 in. (17.8 cm). Early midseason. A very creped, triangular pink-gold flower with a gold throat. Diploid. 'Shibui Splendor' × 'Sabie'. TED L. PETIT & JOHN P. PEAT

'Top Honors' (Frank Childs 1976). Semi-evergreen. Scape 24 in. (61.0 cm); flower 7.5 in. (19.1 cm). Midseason. A tailored pale yellow self with a green throat. Diploid. Parents unknown. Award of Merit 1984. TED WHITE

'Top Show Off' (Edwin C. Brown 1991). Semi-evergreen. Scape 23 in. (58.4 cm); flower 4.75 in. (12.1 cm). Early midseason. A bright yellow ruffled self with a green heart. Diploid. Parents unknown. JOHN EISEMAN

'Untamed Glory' (Jeff Salter 1991). Semi-evergreen. Scape 26 in. (66.0 cm); flower 5.5 in. (14.0 cm). Early midseason. A yellow-bronze polychrome with a green throat and tightly crimped edges. A critical breeder. Tetraploid. Parents unknown. JOHN EISEMAN

'Velma Gibson' (R. W. Munson Jr. 1989). Evergreen. Scape 18 in. (45.7 cm); flower 5 in. (12.7 cm). Early midseason. A wide-petaled, ruffled lemon-cream self with a chartreuse throat. Tetraploid. ('Fred Ham' × 'Lunar Sea') × 'Ruffled Dude'. R. W. MUNSON JR

'Victorian Collar' (Patrick Stamile 1988). Semi-evergreen. Scape 24 in. (61.0 cm); flower 6.25 in. (15.9 cm). Early midseason. A large, round gold self with a green throat. Very popular. Tetraploid. 'Ever So Ruffled' × 'Tet. Homeward Bound'. Award of Merit 1996. PATRICK STAMILE

'Whiskey on Ice' (Lucille Guidry 1983). Evergreen. Scape 28 in. (71.1 cm); flower 7 in. (17.8 cm). Early midseason. An amber-lemon blend with a lemon throat. Triangular and tailored. Diploid. Parents unknown. JOHN EISEMAN

'Wild One' (Allen Wild 1978). Dormant. Scape 34 in. (86.4 cm); flower 7.25 in. (18.4 cm). Midseason. A diamond-dusted deep golden-yellow with a rose-red edge and a yellow-green throat. Diploid. Parents unknown. JOHN EISEMAN

'Yazoo Elsie Hintson' (W. H. Smith 1986). Semi-evergreen. Scape 32 in. (81.3 cm); flower 8 in. (20.3 cm). Early midseason. An extremely large, ruffled butter-cream self with a pale lime throat. Diploid. Parents unknown. TED L. PETIT & JOHN P. PEAT

'Yuma' (Oscie Whatley 1979). Dormant. Scape 25 in. (63.5 cm); flower 6 in. (15.2 cm). Midseason late. A very popular yellow-rose blend with knobby edge and a yellow-green throat. Tetraploid. 'Maja' × 'Kanani'. TED L. PETIT & JOHN P. PEAT

ORANGE (apricot, melon to orange)

'Bursting Loose' (Enman R. Joiner 1988). Ever-green. Scape 26 in. (66.0 cm); flower 8 in. (20.3 cm). Early midseason. A light apricot poly-chrome with pink highlights and a light green throat. Diploid. Seedling × 'Homeward Bound'. TED L. PETIT & JOHN P. PEAT

'Cause for Pause' (David Kirchhoff 1998). Ever-green. Scape 32 in. (81.3 cm); flower 7 in. (17.8 cm). A very large burnt-orange-rose flower, wide-petaled and ruffled. Striking. Tetraploid. Parents unknown. TED L. PETIT & JOHN P. PEAT

'Chestnut Mountain' (Jeff Salter 1989). Ever-green. Scape 24 in. (61.0 cm); flower 5.5 in. (14.0 cm). Midseason. A nicely ruffled, wide-petaled chestnut-copper and orange-yellow blend with a green throat. Tetraploid. 'Royal Autumn' × 'Betty Warren Woods'. MELANIE MASON

'Cotopaxi' (R. W. Munson Jr. 1989). Semi-ever-green. Scape 28 in. (71.1 cm); flower 5 in. (12.7 cm). Midseason. An orange-amber and cream-amber bicolor with a gold-orange throat and a lighter wire edge. Tetraploid. Parents unknown. R. W. MUNSON JR

'Crested Gold Surf' (Jean Duncan 1995). Ever-green. Scape 26 in. (66.0 cm); flower 5 in. (12.7 cm). Early midseason. A very wide-petaled ruf-fled pink-apricot-gold with a green throat. Tetraploid. 'Ever So Ruffled' × seedling. JEAN DUNCAN

'Edna Mabel Jean' (Henry Lorrain and Douglas Lycett 1995). Dormant. Scape 23 in. (58.4 cm); flower 5 in. (12.7 cm). Midseason. A ruffled melon-pink blend with a green throat. Tetra-ploid. 'Kate Carpenter' × 'Femme Osage'. HENRY LORRAIN & DOUGLAS LYCETT

'Forty Carats' (John Benz 1988). Dormant. Scape 30 in. (76.2 cm); flower 5.5 in. (14.0 cm). Midseason. A yellow to soft pumpkin-orange flower with a large, deep green center. Tetraploid. 'Judah' × 'Tet. Mavis Smith'. TED WHITE

'Gail Fox' (Ted L. Petit 1996). Semi-evergreen. Scape 21 in. (53.3 cm); flower 6.5 in. (16.5 cm). Midseason. A large, heavily ruffled, deep tangerine-orange with a green throat. Tetraploid. ('Calais' × ('Jade Lady' × 'Suva')) × (('Ida's Magic' × 'Desert Jewel') × 'Betty Warren Woods'). TED L. PETIT

'Golden Scroll' (Lucille Guidry 1983). Dormant. Scape 19 in. (48.3 cm); flower 5.5 in. (14.0 cm). Early. A lightly ruffled cream-tangerine self with a green throat. Diploid. Parents unknown. Award of Merit 1988. L. Ernest Plouf Award 1989. TED L. PETIT & JOHN P. PEAT

'Heavenly Crown' (Charles Reckamp and Charles Klehm 1979). Dormant. Scape 26 in. (66.0 cm); flower 5.5 in. (14.0 cm). Midseason late. An orange-melon blend with ornately hooked edges above a green heart. Tetraploid. Seedling × 'Devine Gift'. TED L. PETIT & JOHN P. PEAT

'Hot Wire' (Patrick Stamile 1986). Evergreen. Scape 30 in. (76.2 cm); flower 6 in. (15.2 cm). Early midseason. A bright, burnt orange self. Tetraploid. 'Sound and Fury' × 'Frank Gladney'. PATRICK STAMILE

'Leprechaun's Luck' (David Kirchhoff 1994). Evergreen. Scape 30 in. (76.2 cm); flower 5.5 in. (14.0 cm). Early midseason. A whisky-orange with patterned throat. Tetraploid. ('Bitter Sweet Holiday' × 'Ming Porcelain') × 'Gilded Mosaic'. DAVID KIRCHHOFF

'Inca Prince' (R. W. Munson Jr. 1989). Evergreen. Scape 24 in. (61.0 cm); flower 5 in. (12.7 cm). Midseason. A bright copper-orange self with a large orange watermark above a green throat. Tetraploid. Parents unknown. R. W. MUNSON JR

'Marie Hooper Memorial' (Jack Carpenter 1988). Dormant. Scape 26 in. (66.0 cm); flower 8.25 in. (21.0 cm). Midseason. A ruffled, triangular melon-cream-pink blend with a yellow-green throat. Diploid. Parents unknown. JOHN EISEMAN

'Light of Heaven' (Jeff Salter 1988). Dormant. Scape 24 in. (61.0 cm); flower 6 in. (15.2 cm). Early midseason. An extremely ruffled, very wide-petaled pale cream self with a green throat. Extraordinary. Tetraploid. Parents unknown. TED L. PETIT & JOHN P. PEAT

'Living on the Edge' (Ted L. Petit 1998). Semi-evergreen. Scape 26 in. (66.0 cm); flower 5 in. (12.7 cm). Early midseason. A pastel cream-melon to peach-pink blend with a green heart and heavy gold crimped edges. Tetraploid. 'Ferengi Gold' × 'Admiral's Braid'. TED L. PETIT

'My Pirate Days' (Ted L. Petit 1996). Evergreen. Scape 30 in. (76.2 cm); flower 6.5 in. (16.5 cm). Midseason. A strong tangerine and pink-blush flower with heavy substance and a green throat. Tetraploid. ('Ruffled Dude' × seedling) × 'Betty Warren Woods'. TED L. PETIT

'Orange Velvet' (Enman R. Joiner 1988). Semi-evergreen. Scape 30 in. (76.2 cm); flower 6.5 in. (16.5 cm). Midseason. A lightly ruffled medium orange self with a green heart. Diploid. 'Copper Lantern' × 'Golden Scroll'. Award of Merit 1995. TED L. PETIT & JOHN P. PEAT

'Pat Mercer' (Enman R. Joiner 1982). Semi-evergreen. Scape 28 in. (71.1 cm); flower 7 in. (17.8 cm). Midseason. A large amber-orange with a large lighter halo above a green throat. Diploid. 'Emerald Crown' × 'Shibui Splendor'. TED L. PETIT & JOHN P. PEAT

'Pharaoh's Gold' (John Benz 1991). Dormant. Scape 24 in. (61.0 cm); flower 5 in. (12.7 cm). Midseason late. A very wide-petaled, circular flower of rich orange-gold with a deep green throat. Tetraploid. 'Gentleman Lou' × 'Matt'. PATRICK STAMILE

'Primal Scream' (Curt Hanson 1994). Dormant. Scape 34 in. (86.4 cm); flower 7.5 in. (19.1 cm). Midseason late. An orange-tangerine self with a green throat. Tetraploid. 'Tangerine Parfait' × 'Mauna Loa'. CURT HANSON

'Pure and Simple' (Jeff Salter 1993). Semi-evergreen. Scape 28 in. (71.1 cm); flower 5.5 in. (14.0 cm). Early midseason. A ruffled, deep, clear orange sherbert with an olive-green throat. Nice substance and form. Tetraploid. 'Alexandra' × seedling. JOHN EISEMAN

'Rags to Riches' (Robert Carr 1997). Evergreen. Scape 28 in. (71.1 cm); flower 5.5 in. (14.0 cm). Midseason. A very ruffled, heavy-substanced orange blend with an olive-green throat. Tetraploid. 'Victorian Collar' × ('Sherry Lane Carr' × seedling). TED L. PETIT & JOHN P. PEAT

'Santiago Heat' (Jeff Salter 1993). Evergreen. Scape 28 in. (71.1 cm); flower 6 in. (15.2 cm). Midseason. An intense orange-red-coral blend with a yellow-green throat. Nicely formed flower. Tetraploid. Parents unknown. TED L. PETIT & JOHN P. PEAT

'Senegal' (Matthew Kaskel 1994). Evergreen. Scape 24 in. (61.0 cm); flower 5.5 in. (14.0 cm). Early midseason. A highly ruffled pastel bronze blend with heavy substance and a yellow-green throat. Tetraploid. (('Island Empress' × 'Lemonade Supreme') × 'Ming Porcelain') × ('Most Noble' × seedling). TED L. PETIT & JOHN P. PEAT

'Slow Burn' (Jeff Salter 1996). Semi-evergreen. Scape 27 in. (68.6 cm); flower 5 in. (12.7 cm). Midseason. A nicely ruffled orange-red blend with a green throat. Tetraploid. Parents unknown. TED L. PETIT & JOHN P. PEAT

'Song of Spring' (Jack Carpenter 1991). Dormant. Scape 22 in. (55.9 cm); flower 6 in. (15.2 cm). Early midseason. A tailored lightly ruffled light cream-apricot self with green heart. Diploid. Parents unknown. TED L. PETIT & JOHN P. PEAT

'Sparkling Orange' (Joseph Barth 1983). Dormant. Scape 34 in. (86.4 cm); flower 6 in. (15.2 cm). Early midseason. A large, brilliant orange self. Tetraploid. Parents unknown. JOHN EISEMAN

'Storyville Child' (Ted L. Petit 1997). Dormant. Scape 22 in. (55.9 cm); flower 5.5 in. (14.0 cm). Early. An extremely ruffled flower of melon to peach-pink with heavy substance. Tetraploid. 'Betty Warren Woods' × 'Angelus Angel'. TED L. PETIT

'Sweet Shalimar' (Ra Hansen 1986). Evergreen. Scape 24 in. (61.0 cm); flower 5.5 in. (14.0 cm). Midseason. A smoothly textured, deep persimmon-orange with an olive throat. Diploid. ('Dynasty Gold' × 'Martha Adams') × ('Orange Joy' × 'Janet Gayle'). Eugene S. Foster Award 1994. RA HANSEN

'Tycoon's Treasure' (Robert Carr 1995). Evergreen. Scape 29 in. (73.7 cm); flower 6.5 in. (16.5 cm). Early midseason. A large, very ruffled, deep gold-orange blend with a green throat. Tetraploid. 'Cherished Treasure' × 'Moon Dazzle'. TED L. PETIT & JOHN P. PEAT

'Wildfire Tango' (David Kirchhoff 1992). Evergreen. Scape 26 in. (66.0 cm); flower 6 in. (15.2 cm). Extra early. A lightly ruffled, strong gold-orange self with an olive throat. Tetraploid. ('Bittersweet Holiday' × 'Palace Lantern') × ('Milanese Mango' × 'Tet. Nepenthe'). CURTIS & LINDA SUE BARNES

PINK (peach to rose-pink)

'Alexandra' (Jeff Salter 1991). Semi-evergreen. Scape 24 in. (61.0 cm); flower 5.5 in. (14.0 cm). Early midseason. A heavily ruffled, wide-petaled peach-pink self. Tetraploid. Parents unknown. PATRICIA LOVELAND

'Allegheny Sunset' (Patrick Stamile 1996). Dormant. Scape 20 in. (50.8 cm); flower 5.5 in. (14.0 cm). Midseason. A wide-petaled, ruffled pink-rose blend with a green throat. Tetraploid. ('Ming Porcelain' × ('Pink Scintillation' × seedling)) × 'Seminole Wind'. BETH CREVELING

'Alvatine Taylor' (R. W. Munson Jr. 1982). Evergreen. Scape 30 in. (76.2 cm); flower 6 in. (15.2 cm). Early midseason. A pale ivory-pink-beige with a cream-yellow throat. Tetraploid. 'Silver Potentate' × seedling. TED L. PETIT & JOHN P. PEAT

'American Original' (Patrick Stamile 1994). Semi-evergreen. Scape 24 in. (61.0 cm); flower 6 in. (15.2 cm). Early. A large, wide-petaled, ruffled pink self with a dark green throat. Tetraploid. (seedling × 'Silken Touch') × 'Seminole Wind'. PATRICK STAMILE

'Angel Sigh' (Jean Duncan 1998). Evergreen. Scape 32 in. (81.3 cm); flower 5.25 in. (13.3 cm). Early midseason. A very full-formed ivory-cream with pink infusion and a darker edge but no eye. Tetraploid. ('Spode' × 'Celestial Virtue') × seedling. JEAN DUNCAN

'Angelus Angel' (Howard Hite 1985). Dormant. Scape 24 in. (61.0 cm); flower 5 in. (12.7 cm). Early midseason. A wide-petaled, ruffled cream-peach-pink blend with a green throat. Tetraploid. 'Tonga Dancer' × (('Aquarius' × 'Jade Bowl') × 'Virginia Miller'). PATRICK STAMILE

'Autumn Wood' (Hazel Dougherty 1991). Dormant. Scape 24 in. (61.0 cm); flower 5.5 in. (14.0 cm). Midseason. A ruffled, wide-petaled peach and green polychrome with peach-green throat. Diploid. Parents unknown. TOM ROOD

'Antique Rose' (Sarah Sikes 1987). Semi-evergreen. Scape 25 in. (63.5 cm); flower 5.5 in. (14.0 cm). Midseason. A loosely ruffled rose-pink with a green-yellow throat. Diploid. 'Ronda' × (('Sophisticated Miss' × 'My Belle') × 'Blue Happiness'). Award of Merit 1994. TED L. PETIT & JOHN P. PEAT

'Awash with Color' (Patrick Stamile 1994). Evergreen. Scape 32 in. (81.3 cm); flower 5.75 in. (14.6 cm). Early midseason. A deep rose-pink blend heavily ruffled with a green throat. Tetraploid. 'Trudy Harris' × 'Silken Touch'. PATRICK STAMILE

'Bathsheba' (Harrold Harris 1983). Evergreen. Scape 25 in. (63.5 cm); flower 6 in. (15.2 cm). Early midseason. A triangular, deep cream-pink self with a green throat. Tetraploid. (('Hadassah' × 'Tet. Chosen Love') × 'Tet. Sudie') × 'Tet. Sophisticated Miss'. JAY TOMPKINS

'Beijing' (R. W. Munson Jr. 1986). Evergreen. Scape 24 in. (61.0 cm); flower 5 in. (12.7 cm). Midseason. A ruffled, pale flesh-colored self with a cream-yellow throat. Tetraploid. 'Kecia' × 'Dance Ballerina Dance'. JOHN EISEMAN

'Beloved Ballerina' (R. W. Munson Jr. 1983). Semi-evergreen. Scape 28 in. (71. cm); flower 6 in. (15.2 cm). Early midseason. A ruffled ivory-pink blend with a lemon-cream throat. Tetraploid. Parents unknown. R. W. MUNSON JR

'Best Kept Secret' (David Kirchhoff 1992). Semi-evergreen. Scape 28 in. (71.1 cm); flower 5.5 in. (14.0 cm). Midseason. A rose-pink flower with a coral-rose watermark. Tetraploid. ('Ming Porcelain' × 'Inner View') × 'Tet. Blue Happiness'. DAVID KIRCHHOFF

'Betty Benz' (Harrold Harris and John Benz 1987). Dormant. Scape 32 in. (81.3 cm); flower 6 in. (15.2 cm). Midseason. A ruffled cream-pink self with a green throat. Diploid. 'Janet Gayle' × 'Sent from Heaven'. JOHN EISEMAN

'Beverly Ann' (Charlie Pierce 1979). Semi-ever-green. Scape 24 in. (61.0 cm); flower 6.5 in. (16.5 cm). Early. A very large, wide-petaled rose-pink self with a green throat. Diploid. ('My Belle' × seedling) × 'Janet Gayle'. PATRICK STAMILE

'Booger' (Kenneth Durio 1985). Evergreen. Scape 26 in. (66.0 cm); flower 6.5 in. (16.5 cm). Early midseason. A very large, beautiful baby-ribbon-pink with a faint rouging above a green throat. Very popular. Tetraploid. ('Decoy' × 'Tet. Sophisticated Miss') × 'Tet. Carmen Marie'. TED L. PETIT & JOHN P. PEAT

'Bookmark' (R. W. Munson Jr. 1982). Evergreen. Scape 24 in. (61.0 cm); flower 5 in. (12.7 cm). Early midseason. A wide-petaled pink-beige self with a yellow-green throat. Tetraploid. Parents unknown. PATRICK STAMILE

'Borders on Pink' (Judith Weston 1990). Semi-evergreen. Scape 17 in. (43.2 cm); flower 5 in. (12.7 cm). Midseason late. A fuchsia-pink with wide powder-pink edges and a bright green throat. Diploid. Parents unknown. TED L. PETIT & JOHN P. PEAT

'Canton Harbor' (R. W. Munson Jr. 1984). Dormancy unknown. Scape 32 in. (81.3 cm); flower 5 in. (12.7 cm). Early midseason. A ruffled, wide-petaled copper-coral self with a gold-green throat. Tetraploid. 'Mayan Poppy' × (('Tet. Sari' × 'Magnifique') × 'Chinese Poet'). JOHN EISEMAN

'Carefree Beauty' (Charlie Pierce 1982). Semi-evergreen. Scape 24 in. (61.0 cm); flower 6.5 in. (16.5 cm). Midseason. A lightly ruffled pale-cream-pink self with a green throat. Diploid. Parents unknown. JOHN EISEMAN

'Castle Camelot' (Steve Moldovan 1983). Semi-evergreen. Scape 24 in. (61.0 cm); flower 5.5 in. (14.0 cm). Early. An orchid-pink to rose-pink with a green center. Tetraploid. (seedling × 'Royal Watermark') × ('Astart' × ('Kwan Yin' × 'Catherine Woodbery')). STEVE MOLDOVAN

'Catherine Woodbery' (Frank Childs 1967). Dormant. Scape 30 in. (76.2 cm); flower 6 in. (15.2 cm). Midseason late. A classic triangular orchid self with a green throat. Diploid. Parents unknown. Award of Merit 1973.
TED L. PETIT & JOHN P. PEAT

'Cezanne' (R. W. Munson Jr. 1990). Evergreen. Scape 24 in. (61.0 cm); flower 7 in. (17.8 cm). Early midseason. A peach and rose blend with a large watermark and a green throat. Tetraploid. ('Kecia' × 'Judy Koltz') × 'Bookmark'.
R. W. MUNSON JR

'Chance Encounter' (Patrick Stamile 1994). Evergreen. Scape 25 in. (63.5 cm); flower 6 in. (15.2 cm). Early midseason. A lightly ruffled, deep raspberry-rose blend with a wire gold edge and a deep green throat. Tetraploid. ((seedling × 'Love Goddess') × 'Crush on You') × 'Tet. Barbara Mitchell'. PATRICK STAMILE

'China Bride' (Lucille Guidry 1989). Evergreen. Scape 24 in. (61.0 cm); flower 6 in. (15.2 cm). Early. Rose-pink and cream-pink bicolor with a rose halo and a green throat. Diploid. Parents unknown. JAY TOMPKINS

'Codie Wedgeworth' (Thomas Wilson 1986). Evergreen. Scape 26 in. (66.0 cm); flower 6 in. (15.2 cm). Early. A lightly ruffled, deep pastel pink self with a green throat. Diploid. 'Pink Pioneer' × 'Beverly Ann'. Award of Merit 1992. JAY TOMPKINS

'Contessa D'Iberville' (Ted L. Petit 1995). Semi-evergreen. Scape 18 in. (45.7 cm); flower 6 in. (15.2 cm). Midseason. Very ruffled, wide-petaled light pink with a gold edge and a green throat. Tetraploid. ('Ida's Magic' × 'Moon Twilight') × 'Ida's Magic'. TED L. PETIT

'Coral Stone' (Patrick Stamile 1996). Dormant. Scape 22 in. (55.9 cm); flower 6 in. (15.2 cm). Early midseason. A wide-petaled, large, lightly ruffled coral-pink blend with a green throat. Tetraploid. 'Silken Touch' × 'Only You'. PATRICK STAMILE

'Corona Del Mar' (Ted L. Petit 1998). Semi-evergreen. Scape 30 in. (76.2 cm); flower 6 in. (15.2 cm). Midseason. A ruffled coral-rose with a lighter watermark and a green throat. Tetraploid. 'Deanna's Gift' × 'Richard Taylor'. TED L. PETIT

'Crush on You' (Patrick Stamile 1992). Ever-green. Scape 22 in. (55.9 cm); flower 6 in. (15.2 cm). Early midseason. A ruffled pink self with a green throat and white midribs. Heavy sub-stance. Tetraploid. 'Enchanted Empress' × seedling. PATRICK STAMILE

'Dance Ballerina Dance' (Virginia Peck 1976). Dormant. Scape 24 in. (61.0 cm); flower 6 in. (15.2 cm). Midseason. A ruffled apricot-pink self. One of the most used plants in breeding. Tetraploid. Seedling × 'Round Table'. Award of Merit 1983. TED L. PETIT & JOHN P. PEAT

'Darling' (Patrick Stamile 1992). Evergreen. Scape 23 in. (58.4 cm); flower 5 in. (12.7 cm). Early midseason. A wide-petaled, ruffled, deep rose-pink self with a green throat. Tetraploid. ('Ming Porcelain' × 'Love Goddess') × 'Tet. Martha Adams'. PATRICK STAMILE

'Days of Wine' (Henry Lorrain and Douglas Lycett 1994). Dormant. Scape 42 in. (106.7 cm); flower 5 in. (12.7 cm). Midseason late. A wine-rose-pink blend with a gold edge and lighter watermark above a green throat. Tetraploid. 'Exaltation' × ('Temple Goddess' × seedling). HENRY LORRAIN & DOUGLAS LYCETT

'Decatur Piecrust' (Clyde Davidson 1982). Dormant. Scape 22 in. (55.9 cm); flower 5 in. (12.7 cm). Midseason. A salmon-pink self with crunchy ruffled edges. Tetraploid. 'Waving Winds' × 'Round Table'. PATRICK STAMILE

'Desert Jewel' (R. W. Munson Jr. 1990). Evergreen. Scape 30 in. (76.2 cm); flower 6 in. (15.2 cm). Early midseason. A classically triangular, lightly ruffled peach-sand with gold edges and a green throat. Tetraploid. 'Ruffles Elegante' × ('Winter Reverie' × 'Chinese Temple Flower'). R. W. MUNSON JR

'Doma Knaresborough' (Ted L. Petit 1994). Semi-evergreen. Scape 19 in. (48.3 cm); flower 6 in. (15.2 cm). Early midseason. A large, ruffled peach-pink with yellow-cream watermark and a green throat. Tetraploid. 'Betty Warren Woods' × 'Shishedo'. TED L. PETIT

'Dorothy O'Keefe' (Ted L. Petit 1998). Evergreen. Scape 22 in. (55.9 cm); flower 5.5 in. (14.0 cm). Midseason. A pale ice-pink self with a green throat and a gold edge. Tetraploid. 'Ida's Magic' × 'Ever So Ruffled'. TED L. PETIT

'Ed Brown' (Jeff Salter 1994). Semi-evergreen. Scape 28 in. (71.1 cm); flower 5.5 in. (14.0 cm). Early midseason. A clear pale-pink self with a gold edge and a green throat. Tetraploid. 'Something Wonderful' × 'Elizabeth's Dream'. TED L. PETIT & JOHN P. PEAT

'Effay Veronica' (Ted L. Petit 1995). Dormant. Scape 21 in. (53.3 cm); flower 5.5 in. (14.0 cm). Early midseason. Extremely ruffled, wide-petaled pink self with a green throat. Tetraploid. 'Betty Warren Woods' × 'Shishedo'. TED L. PETIT

'Elizabeth Yancey' (Clarke Yancey and D. Harrison 1973). Semi-evergreen. Scape 28 in. (71.1 cm); flower 5.5 in. (14.0 cm). Early. A light pink self with a deep green throat. Diploid. 'Tender Love' × seedling. Award of Merit 1981. TED L. PETIT & JOHN P. PEAT

'Elizabeth Salter' (Jeff Salter 1990). Semi-evergreen. Scape 22 in. (55.9 cm); flower 5.5 in. (14.0 cm). Midseason. A wide-petaled, ruffled, salmon-pink self with a green throat. Very popular. Tetraploid. Parents unknown. TED L. PETIT & JOHN P. PEAT

'Elusive Dream' (Ted L. Petit 1998). Semi-ever-green. Scape 21 in. (53.3 cm); flower 5 in. (12.7 cm). Early midseason. A pale cream-pink with heavy substance, a green throat, and ruffled gold edges. Tetraploid. 'Ferengi Gold' × 'Admiral's Braid'. TED L. PETIT

'Enchanted April' (Dan Trimmer 1993). Dormant. Scape 24 in. (61.0 cm); flower 5.5 in. (14.0 cm). Midseason late. A lavender-pink self with a heavy gold edge outside a darker picotee and a yellow-green throat. Tetraploid. 'Techny Peach Lace' × 'Wedding Band'. DAN TRIMMER

'Enchanting Blessing' (W. M. Spalding 1983). Evergreen. Scape 19 in. (48.3 cm); flower 5.25 in. (13.3 cm). Midseason. A very ruffled, pale peach-pink blend with a green throat. Diploid. Parents unknown. JOHN EISEMAN

'English Cameo' (Patrick Stamile 1996). Dormant. Scape 26 in. (66.0 cm); flower 5.5 in. (14.0 cm). Early midseason. A wide-petaled, ruffled, circular flower of a light cream-peach blend with a green heart. Tetraploid. ('Ming Porcelain' × ('Pink Scintillation' × seedling)) × 'Seminole Wind'. PATRICK STAMILE

'Esoteric Affair' (Ted L. Petit 1995). Semi-ever-green. Scape 20 in. (50.8 cm); flower 6 in. (15.2 cm). Midseason. A pale peach-pink with a cream watermark, green throat, and loosely ruffled gold edge. Tetraploid. 'Dessert Jewel' × ('Ida's Magic' × 'Velma Gibson'). TED L. PETIT

'Evelyn Stout' (David Kirchhoff 1973). Ever-green. Scape 20 in. (50.8 cm); flower 7 in. (17.8 cm). Early midseason. A very large, lightly ruf-fled dusty pink self with a gold throat. Diploid. Seedling × 'Passion Pink'. TOM ROOD

'Farmer's Daughter' (David Kirchhoff 1991). Evergreen. Scape 28 in. (71.1 cm); flower 5.5 in. (14.0 cm). A warm, clear pink self with a gold to green throat. 'Grand Merci' × ('Dance Ballerina Dance × ('Ring of Change' × 'Sherry Fair')). JOHN EISEMAN

'Forestlake Ragamuffin' (Fran Harding 1993). Dormant. Scape 28 in. (71.1 cm); 5.5 in. flower (14.0 cm). Early midseason. A shell-pink self with gold shark's tooth, crimped, and ruffled edges and a green throat. Very popular. Tetraploid. 'Decatur Piecrust' × (seedling × ('Lahaina' × 'Yuma')). FRAN HARDING

'Gentle Rose' (Patrick Stamile 1989). Dormant. Scape 22 in. (55.9 cm); flower 6 in. (15.2 cm). Early midseason. A wide-petaled rose blend with a deep green throat. Tetraploid. ('Houdini' × 'Yesterday Memories') × 'Pink Monday'. PATRICK STAMILE

'Gilded Mosaic' (Mort Morss 1988). Evergreen. Scape 27 in. (68.6 cm); flower 5 in. (12.7 cm). Early. A rose-lavender flower edged in yellow with an iridescent lime-green throat. Tetraploid. Seedling × ('Ming Porcelain' × ('Silver Veil' × 'Zinfandel')). DAVID KIRCHHOFF

'Gingham Maid' (Lucille Guidry 1986). Dormant. Scape 23 in. (58.4 cm); flower 7.25 in. (18.4 cm). Early. A very large, triangular, pink-cream, slight bitone with a lime-green throat. Diploid. Parents unknown. L. Ernest Plouf Award 1995. JOHN EISEMAN

'Glory in Ruffles' (Lucille Guidry 1982). Evergreen. Scape 21 in. (53.3 cm); flower 7 in. (17.8 cm). Early. A triangular, classically formed, slightly ruffled cream-pink blend with a green throat. Diploid. Parents unknown. TOM ROOD

'Glittering Elegance' (John Benz 1996). Dormant. Scape 28 in. (71.1 cm); flower 5 in. (12.7 cm). Midseason late. A wide-petaled, heavily ruffled rose-pink self with a green throat. Tetraploid. 'Trudy Harris' × 'Tet. Barbara Mitchell'. JOHN BENZ

'Graceful Exit' (Ted L. Petit 1998). Semi-evergreen. Scape 28 in. (71.1 cm); flower 6 in. (15.2 cm). Midseason. A coral blend with pink highlights and a green heart. Tetraploid. ('Fred Ham' × 'Sun King') × 'Elizabeth Salter'. TED L. PETIT

'Gypsy Quilt' (Ted L. Petit 1997). Semi-ever-green. Scape 23 in. (58.4 cm); flower 5.5 in. (14.0 cm). Midseason. A peach to salmon-rose-pink with tangerine watermark above a green throat. Very creped. Tetraploid. 'Majestic Morning' × (('Ida's Magic' × 'Desert Jewel') × 'Betty Warren Woods'). TED L. PETIT

'Grand Merci' (David Kirchhoff 1985). Semi-evergreen. Scape 22 in. (55.9 cm); flower 5.25 in. (13.3 cm). Early midseason. A rose with a deeper edge and a green throat. Tetraploid. 'Chicago Candy Cane' × ('Inner View' × 'Ming Porcelain'). DAVID KIRCHHOFF

'Heavenly Dragon' (Mort Morss 1989). Dormant. Scape 22 in. (55.9 cm); flower 5 in. (12.7 cm). Midseason. A rose self with gold edges and a yellow throat. Tetraploid. ('Inner View' × 'Enchanted Empress') × 'Holiday Frills'. DAVID KIRCHHOFF

'Hail Mary' (Steve Moldovan 1984). Dormant. Scape 24 in. (61.0 cm); flower 5.5 in. (14.0 cm). Early. A pink blend with silver highlights, a deeper pink halo, and a lemon watermark above a yellow-green throat. Tetraploid. ('Water Bird' × 'Queens Castle') × 'Love Goddess'. STEVE MOLDOVAN

'Harbor Gate' (Kate Carpenter 1985). Dormant. Scape 26 in. (66.0 cm); flower 6 in. (15.2 cm). Early. A beautiful baby-ribbon-pink with a bluish lavender cast and a green throat. Diploid. Seedling × 'Wynnson'. PATRICK STAMILE

'Inherited Wealth' (Robert Carr 1998). Evergreen. Scape 28 in. (71.1 cm); flower 5 in. (12.7 cm). Early. A heavily ruffled light pink with folded petal edges over a green throat. Tetraploid. 'America's Most Wanted' × 'Victorian Collar'. ROBERT CARR

'Jedi Dot Pierce' (Dan Wedgeworth 1988). Semi-evergreen. Scape 20 in. (50.8 cm); flower 6 in. (15.2 cm). Early midseason. A large rose-pink with slightly darker rose halo and a green throat. Diploid. Parents unknown. TED L. PETIT & JOHN P. PEAT

'Jedi Free Spirit' (Dan Wedgeworth 1987). Semi-evergreen. Scape 25 in. (63.5 cm); flower 5.5 in. (14.0 cm). Midseason. A lightly ruffled pink with a chartreuse throat. Diploid. Parents unknown. JOHN EISEMAN

'Jedi Sue McCord' (Dan Wedgeworth 1988). Semi-evergreen. Scape 22 in. (55.9 cm); flower 5.5 in. (14.0 cm). Early. A lightly ruffled, clear pink self with a darker rose halo and a green throat. Diploid. Parents unknown. TED L. PETIT & JOHN P. PEAT

'Jedi Tom Wilson' (Dan Wedgeworth 1988). Semi-evergreen. Scape 22 in. (55.9 cm); flower 6 in. (15.2 cm). Early. A wide-petaled, large copper and cinnamon-pink blend with a green throat. Diploid. Parents unknown. JOHN EISEMAN

'Jolyene Nichole' (Spalding-Guillory 1984). Evergreen. Scape 14 in. (35.6 cm); flower 6 in. (15.2 cm). Midseason. A wide-petaled, looping-ruffled rose blend with a green throat. Diploid. Parents unknown. Award of Merit 1993. JOHN EISEMAN

'Jock Randall' (Virginia Peck 1970). Evergreen. Scape 29 in. (73.7 cm); flower 6 in. (15.2 cm). Midseason. A large rose self with a green-yellow throat. Tetraploid. Seedling × 'Tet. Sanders Walker'. Award of Merit 1976. CURTIS & LINDA SUE BARNES

'Just Infatuation' (Ted L. Petit 1996). Semi-evergreen. Scape 22 in. (55.9 cm); flower 5.5 in. (14.0 cm). Midseason. An orchid-pink with a cream watermark, pleated throat, and heavy gold ruffled edge. Tetraploid. Seedling × 'Wrapped in Gold'. TED L. PETIT

'Josephine Marina' (Jack Carpenter 1987). Dormant. Scape 21 in. (53.3 cm); flower 7.5 in. (19.1 cm). Late. A very large, lightly ruffled apricot-peach self with an olive-green throat. Diploid. Parents unknown. Award of Merit 1993. JOHN EISEMAN

'Juliette Matthis' (Ted L. Petit 1996). Semi-evergreen. Scape 22 in. (55.9 cm); flower 6.5 in. (16.5 cm). Midseason. An orchid-pink with a lighter watermark, green throat, and very ruffled gold edge. Tetraploid. ('Fred Ham' × seedling) × 'Ida's Magic'. TED L. PETIT

'Kate Carpenter' (R. W. Munson Jr. 1980). Evergreen. Scape 28 in. (71.1 cm); flower 6 in. (15.2 cm). Early midseason. A large, pale pink self with a large green throat. Tetraploid. ('Wilbur Harling' × 'Kecia') × 'Pagoda Goddess'. Honorable Mention 1981. TED L. PETIT & JOHN P. PEAT

'Kelly's Girl' (W. M. Spalding 1983). Evergreen. Scape 19 in. (48.3 cm); flower 5.75 in. (14.6 cm). Midseason. An interesting rose-pink and light pink bitone with a green throat. Diploid. Parents unknown. JOHN EISEMAN

'Kings and Vagabonds' (Ted L. Petit 1994). Evergreen. Scape 22 in. (55.9 cm); flower 6 in. (15.2 cm). Midseason. A gold-edged, heavily ruffled orchid-cream-pink with a cream watermark above a green throat. Tetraploid. 'Wrapped in Gold' × 'Desert Jewel'. TED L. PETIT

'Lake Norman Sunset' (Kate Carpenter 1979). Semi-evergreen. Scape 19 in. (48.3 cm); flower 6.3 in. (15.9 cm). Early midseason. A creped, triangular, classically formed pink with white midribs and a green throat. Diploid. 'Best of Friends' × seedling. Award of Merit 1986. TED L. PETIT & JOHN P. PEAT

'Laurel Stevenson' (Ted L. Petit 1998). Semi-evergreen. Scape 22 in. (55.9 cm); flower 6.5 in. (16.5 cm). Midseason. A very large, wide-petaled, circular, medium pink flower with a green throat. Tetraploid. ('French Pavilion' × 'Canton Harbor') × 'Shishedo'. TED L. PETIT

'Lauren Leah' (Charlie Pierce 1983). Dormant. Scape 18 in. (45.7 cm); flower 6 in. (15.2 cm). Early midseason. A creamy pink blend with a green throat. Diploid. Seedling × 'Beverly Ann'. TED L. PETIT & JOHN P. PEAT

'Lindan Toole' (Ted L. Petit 1994). Evergreen. Scape 22 in. (55.9 cm); flower 6 in. (15.2 cm). Early midseason. A salmon-pink with cream watermark and a green throat. Tetraploid. ('Ruffled Dude' × seedling) × 'Shishedo'.
TED L. PETIT

'Lorikeet Springs' (John P. Peat 1998). Semi-evergreen. Scape 30 in. (76.2 cm); flower 6.5 in. (16.5 cm). Midseason. A very deep rose-pink over a green throat. Warmer weather brings out a powder-pink edge. The bloom scape offers four- or five-way lateral branching. Tetraploid. 'Serenity in Lace' × 'Betty Warren Woods'. JOHN P. PEAT

'Mabel Nolen' (William Nolen 1984). Dormant. Scape 28 in. (71.1 cm); flower 6 in. (15.2 cm). Early midseason. A rose-pink self with a large green throat. Diploid. Parents unknown.
TED L. PETIT & JOHN P. PEAT

'Maggie McDowell' (Mort Morss 1987). Evergreen. Scape 26 in. (66.0 cm); flower 4.5 in. (11.4 cm). Early midseason. An ivory-cream and pink polychrome edged in yellow, with a yellow halo above a green throat. Tetraploid. 'Ming Porcelain' × 'Inner View'.
DAVID KIRCHHOFF

'Mariska' (Steve Moldovan 1984). Dormant. Scape 28 in. (71.1 cm); flower 6.5 in. (16.5 cm). Midseason. A tailored, pale cream-pink blend with a lemon-green throat. Tetraploid. 'Queens Castle' × 'Lilac Snow'. Award of Merit 1992.
TED L. PETIT & JOHN P. PEAT

'Matissee' (R. W. Munson Jr. 1984). Evergreen. Scape 24 in. (61.0 cm); flower 5.5 in. (14.0 cm). Midseason. A wide-petaled rose-pink blend with a large lighter watermark and a yellow-green throat. Tetraploid. Parents unknown.
JOHN EISEMAN

'Merry Witch' (R. W. Munson Jr. 1983). Evergreen. Scape 30 in. (76.2 cm); flower 6 in. (15.2 cm). Midseason. A classic rose-pink flower with a lighter watermark and lemon-cream throat. Tetraploid. Parents unknown. R. W. MUNSON JR

'Misty Memories' (Ted L. Petit 1995). Semi-evergreen. Scape 20 in. (50.8 cm); flower 5.5 in. (14.0 cm). A slightly creped, clear pink self with crimped and ruffled gold edges and a green throat. Tetraploid. 'Ida's Magic' × seedling. TED L. PETIT

'Morning Whispers' (Ted L. Petit 1994). Semi-evergreen. Scape 22 in. (55.9 cm); flower 5.5 in. (14.0 cm). Midseason. A very round, creped, medium pink with a cream eyezone above a green throat. Tetraploid. 'Majestic Morning' × 'Shishedo'. TED L. PETIT

'Mumbo Jumbo' (Lucille Guidry 1979). Semi-evergreen. Scape 21 in. (53.3 cm); flower 6.25 in. (15.9 cm). Early. A large rose-pink bitone with a darker rose halo and a green throat. Diploid. Parents unknown. JOHN EISEMAN

'New Testament' (Lucille Guidry 1981). Evergreen. Scape 18 in. (45.7 cm); flower 6 in. (15.2 cm). Extra early. A classically formed pink self with a green throat. Diploid. Parents unknown. CURTIS & LINDA SUE BARNES

'Nicole Cabrera' (Ted L. Petit 1998). Semi-evergreen. Scape 23 in. (58.4 cm); flower 5.5 in. (14.0 cm). Early midseason. A soft shell-pink to baby-ribbon-pink with ruffled gold edges and a green throat. Tetraploid. 'Something Wonderful' × 'Deanna's Gift'. TED L. PETIT

'Ocean Rain' (Curt Hanson 1987). Semi-evergreen. Scape 26 in. (66.0 cm); flower 6 in. (15.2 cm). Early midseason. A triangular orchid-pink blend with a green-yellow throat. Tetraploid. 'King Throne' × 'Enchanted Empress'. JOHN EISEMAN

'One Step Beyond' (John Benz 1995). Semi-evergreen. Scape 32 in. (81.3 cm); flower 6.5 in. (16.5 cm). Midseason. A lavender-rose-pink self with a lime-green throat and a ruffled, wire gold edge. Tetraploid. 'Trudy Harris' × 'Tet. Barbara Mitchell'. JOHN BENZ

'Palladian Pink' (Patrick Stamile 1996). Semi-evergreen. Scape 21 in. (53.3 cm); flower 5 in. (12.7 cm). Early midseason. A pristine, lightly ruffled pink self with a green throat. Tetraploid. (('Crystalline Pink' × 'Peach Whisper') × 'Silken Touch') × ('Cherry Berry' × 'Tet. Priscilla's Rainbow'). PATRICK STAMILE

'Pastel Classic' (Bryant Millikan and Clarence Soules 1985). Semi-evergreen. Scape 23 in. (58.4 cm); flower 6 in. (15.2 cm). Midseason. A triangular, clear pink and buff blend with a yellow-green throat. Diploid. 'Mysterious Veil' × 'Becky Lynn'. Award of Merit 1993. JAY TOMPKINS

'Patrician Splendor' (Patrick Stamile 1996). Dormant. Scape 26 in. (66.0 cm); flower 6.25 in. (15.9 cm). Early midseason. A large, wide-petaled cream-pink blend with a deep green throat. Tetraploid. (('Ming Porcelain' × ('Pink Scintillation' × seedling)) × 'Seminole Wind'. PATRICK STAMILE

'Pink Ambrosia' (Patrick Stamile 1994). Evergreen. Scape 28 in. (71.1 cm); flower 6.75 in. (17.2 cm). Early. A large, ruffled pink bitone with a green throat. Tetraploid. 'Best Kept Secret' × 'Tet. Barbara Mitchell'. PATRICK STAMILE

'Pink Corduroy' (Patrick Stamile 1984). Semi-evergreen. Scape 28 in. (71.1 cm); flower 5.5 in. (14.0 cm). Midseason. A textured, rich pink flower with a dark green center. Diploid. 'Mumbo Jumbo' × 'Martha Adams'. PATRICK STAMILE

'Pink Debutante' (Patrick Stamile 1997). Dormant. Scape 24 in. (61.0 cm); flower 7 in. (17.8 cm). Early midseason. A wide-petaled, clear baby-ribbon-pink self and a green throat. Tetraploid. Seedling × 'Tet. Barbara Mitchell'. PATRICK STAMILE

'Pink Flirt' (Margaret DeKerlegand 1987). Semi-evergreen. Scape 20 in. (50.8 cm); flower 6 in. (15.2 cm). Early. A scallop-ruffled, bright pink self with a green throat. Diploid. 'Blushing Parfait' × 'Morning Cheerfulness'. Award of Merit 1995. TED L. PETIT & JOHN P. PEAT

'Pink Gloss' (Charlie Pierce and Thomas Wilson 1988). Semi-evergreen. Scape 20 in. (50.8 cm); flower 6 in. (15.2 cm). Early midseason. A pretty, clear pink self with a large green throat. Diploid. Parents unknown. PATRICK STAMILE

'Pink Jubilation' (Charlie Pierce and Thomas Wilson 1988). Evergreen. Scape 24 in. (61.0 cm); flower 6.5 in. (16.5 cm). Early midseason. A triangular, classically formed pink blend with a gold throat. Diploid. Parents unknown. TED L. PETIT & JOHN P. PEAT

'Pink Monday' (Van Sellers 1981). Dormant. Scape 26 in. (66.0 cm); flower 5.5 in. (14.0 cm). Midseason. A triangular, light rose-pink self with a green throat. Tetraploid. Parents unknown. PATRICK STAMILE

'Pink Tranquility' (Edwin C. Brown 1990). Semi-evergreen. Scape 26 in. (66.0 cm); flower 5.5 in. (14.0 cm). Early midseason. A cool clear pink self with a large green throat. Diploid. Parents unknown.
PATRICK STAMILE

'Pride of Jersey' (Betty Harwood 1994). Semi-evergreen. Scape 26 in. (66.0 cm); flower 6.25 in. (15.9 cm). Midseason. A ruffled apricot-cream self with an olive-green throat. Diploid. 'Enchanting Blessing' × (seedling × 'Wynn').
BETTY HARWOOD

'Princess Ellen' (Clarence Crochet 1985). Evergreen. Scape 18 in. (45.7 cm); flower 5.5 in. (14.0 cm). Early midseason. A cream with a lightly ruffled amber-rose border and a green throat. Diploid. Parents unknown.
JOHN EISEMAN

'Proud Mary' (Jeff Salter 1992). Semi-evergreen. Scape 26 in. (66.0 cm); flower 6 in. (15.2 cm). Midseason. A large, vivid, clear medium pink self with a green throat. Tetraploid. 'Spanish Glow' × seedling. TED L. PETIT & JOHN P. PEAT

'Rahab' (Dave Talbott 1989). Evergreen. Scape 25 in. (63.5 cm); flower 5.5 in. (14.0 cm). Midseason. A flamingo-pink self with white midribs and a darker halo surrounding a green heart. Diploid. 'Becky Lynn' × ('Martha Adams' × 'Becky Lynn'). TED L. PETIT & JOHN P. PEAT

'Ronda' (Sarah Sikes 1981). Semi-evergreen. Scape 26 in. (66.0 cm); flower 6.5 in. (16.5 cm). Midseason. A very triangular, deep flesh-pink with lavender midribs and bright green throat. Diploid. 'Yesterday Memories' × 'Elizabeth Yancey'. TED L. PETIT & JOHN P. PEAT

'Rose' (Harrold Harris and John Benz 1984). Dormant. Scape 26 in. (66.0 cm); flower 6 in. (15.2 cm). Midseason. A large rose-pink self with a strong green throat. Tetraploid. 'Nuka' × tet. seedling from ('Iron Gate Glacier' × 'Julia Tanner'). PATRICK STAMILE

'Rose Emily' (Charlie Pierce 1982). Semi-evergreen. Scape 18 in. (45.7 cm); flower 5 in. (12.7 cm). Midseason. A softly ruffled rose self with a striking green throat. Diploid. Parents unknown. Award of Merit 1988. TED L. PETIT & JOHN P. PEAT

'Rose Fever' (Patrick Stamile 1996). Evergreen. Scape 25 in. (63.5 cm); flower 6 in. (15.2 cm). Early midseason. A large, wide-petaled, deep hot rose with a grass-green throat. Tetraploid. ('Crystalline Pink' × 'Only You') × 'Seminole Wind'. PATRICK STAMILE

'Rose Talisman' (Harrold Harris and John Benz 1987). Dormant. Scape 30 in. (76.2 cm); flower 5.5 in. (14.0 cm). Early midseason. A rose-pink self with a green throat. Tetraploid. (('Hadassah' × 'Heather Green') × 'Tet. Sudie') × 'Tet. Mavis Smith'. TED L. PETIT & JOHN P. PEAT

'Sabra Salina' (Thomas Wilson 1991). Dormant. Scape 22 in. (55.9 cm); flower 6 in. (15.2 cm). Early midseason. A soft pale pink with a gold halo above a green throat. Diploid. ('Beverly Ann' × seedling) × 'Codie Wedgeworth'. TED L. PETIT & JOHN P. PEAT

'Sadie Lou' (Elsie Spalding 1978). Evergreen. Scape 19 in. (48.3 cm); flower 5.5 in. (14.0 cm). Midseason. A cream-pink with a green throat. Diploid. Parents unknown. JAY TOMPKINS

'Second Thoughts' (Sarah Sikes 1987). Dormant. Scape 27 in. (68.6 cm); flower 5.75 in. (14.6 cm). Midseason. A pale cream-pink blend with a green-yellow throat. Diploid. 'Fairy Tale Pink' × (('Sophisticated Miss' × 'My Belle') × 'Blue Happiness'). TED L. PETIT & JOHN P. PEAT

'Secret Splendor' (Jeff Salter 1991). Evergreen. Scape 25 in. (63.5 cm); flower 6 in. (15.2 cm). Midseason late. A light lavender-rose with a yellow-green throat. Tetraploid. Parents unknown. JOHN EISEMAN

'Seminole Wind' (Patrick Stamile 1993). Semi-evergreen. Scape 23 in. (58.4 cm); flower 6.5 in. (16.5 cm). Early midseason. A wide-petaled, clear medium pink self with a green throat. Tetraploid. ('Love Goddess' × 'Crush on You') × 'Tet. Barbara Mitchell'. PATRICK STAMILE

'Serengeti' (R. W. Munson Jr. 1987). Evergreen. Scape 26 in. (66.0 cm); flower 6 in. (15.2 cm). Early midseason. A cream-peach, sand, and ivory blend with a yellow-green throat. Tetraploid. (('Tet. Sari' × 'Magnifique') × ('Tet. Pink Lightning' × 'Zenobia')) × 'Kate Carpenter'. PATRICK STAMILE

'Shades of Pale' (Ted L. Petit 1994). Evergreen. Scape 19 in. (48.3 cm); flower 6.25 in. (15.9 cm). Midseason. Pink with a gold edge and yellow-cream watermark above a green throat. Tetraploid. (('Fred Ham' × 'Love Goddess') × ('Love Goddess' × 'Alvatine Taylor')) × ('Betty Warren Wood' × seedling). TED L. PETIT

'Serenity Morgan' (Marjorie Tanner 1982). Semi-evergreen. Scape 22 in. (55.9 cm); flower 5 in. (12.7 cm). Early midseason. A cream-pink self with a deep, sculpted green throat. Diploid. 'Hope Diamond' × 'Zaidee Williams'. PATRICK STAMILE

'Shades of Pale' (Ted L. Petit 1994). Evergreen. Scape 15 in. (38.1 cm); flower 6 in. (15.2 cm). Midseason. An orchid-pink-cream with a gold-cream watermark above a green throat. Tetraploid. 'Court Magician' × 'Ida's Magic'. TED L. PETIT

'Shibui Splendor' (R. W. Munson Jr. 1974). Evergreen. Scape 20 in. (50.8 cm); flower 6 in. (15.2 cm). Early midseason. A large, creped, triangular pink self with a chartreuse throat. Diploid. 'Sari' × 'Moment of Truth'. Award of Merit 1982. TOM ROOD

'Shimmering Elegance' (Patrick Stamile 1994). Dormant. Scape 25 in. (63.5 cm); flower 6 in. (15.2 cm). Early midseason. A round, wide-petaled, lightly ruffled pink self with a green throat. Tetraploid. (seedling × 'Silken Touch') × 'Seminole Winds'. PATRICK STAMILE

'Silken Touch' (Patrick Stamile 1990). Dormant. Scape 23 in. (58.4 cm); flower 6 in. (15.2 cm). Early midseason. A wide-petaled, round rose-pink self with a green throat and a darker halo. Tetraploid. ('Ming Porcelain' × 'Love Goddess') × 'Tet. Martha Adams'. PATRICK STAMILE

'Smoky Mountain Autumn' (Lucille Guidry 1986). Dormant. Scape 18 in. (45.7 cm); flower 5.75 in. (14.6 cm). Early. A rose-pink blend with raised ruffles, rose-lavender halo, and olive-green throat. Diploid. Parents unknown. Award of Merit 1992. L. Ernest Plouf Award 1990. JOHN EISEMAN

'Smooth Flight' (Virginia Peck 1981). Dormant. Scape 28 in. (71.1 cm); flower 6 in. (15.2 cm). Midseason. A clear, lightly ruffled pink self with a green-yellow throat. Tetraploid. 'Sherry Fair' × 'Dance Ballerina Dance'. PATRICK STAMILE

'Southern Charmer' (Sarah Sikes 1983). Evergreen. Scape 26 in. (66.0 cm); flower 5 in. (12.7 cm). Midseason. A narrow-petaled rose-pink with a green-yellow throat and white midribs. Diploid. 'Janet Gayle' × 'Rose Swan'. TED L. PETIT & JOHN P. PEAT

'Spanish Glow' (Jeff Salter 1988). Evergreen. Scape 26 in. (66.0 cm); flower 5 in. (12.7 cm). Midseason late. A slightly ruffled warm peach self with a green throat. Tetraploid. Parents unknown. TED L. PETIT & JOHN P. PEAT

'Spray of Pearls' (David Kirchhoff 1986). Semi-evergreen. Scape 26 in. (66.0 cm); flower 4.75 in. (12.1 cm). Early. A pastel orchid-pink with a yellow-green throat and a darker, pencil-thin halo. Tetraploid. 'Shell Point' × ('Damascene' × 'Tet. Lullaby Baby'). JOHN EISEMAN

'Stop the Show' (Lee Gates 1986). Evergreen. Scape 24 in. (61.0 cm); flower 6.5 in. (16.5 cm). Early. A lavender-pink and yellow polychrome with a green chartreuse throat. Tetraploid. Parents unknown. JOHN EISEMAN

'Star' (Mac Carter 1996). Semi-evergreen. Scape 28 in. (71.1 cm); flower 6 in. (15.2 cm). Midseason. A wide-petaled, very ruffled golden peach self with a green throat. Tetraploid. 'Copper Dawn' × 'Moon Dust'. MAC CARTER

'Strawberry Cupcake' (R. W. Munson Jr. 1992). Evergreen. Scape 18 in. (45.7 cm); flower 5 in. (12.7 cm). Early midseason. A wide-petaled, ruffled rose-pink self with a green throat. Tetraploid. 'Shishedo' × 'Pink Granache'. R. W. MUNSON JR

'Strawberry Rose' (Virginia Peck 1980). Dormant. Scape 27 in. (68.6 cm); flower 6.5 in. (16.5 cm). Midseason. A large, triangular rose-pink self with a green throat. Tetraploid. Seedling × 'Dance Ballerina Dance'. JOHN EISEMAN

'Subtle Charm' (Ted L. Petit 1993). Evergreen. Scape 30 in. (76.2 cm); flower 5.25 in. (13.3 cm). Midseason. A pastel pink with a gold edge and a cream-yellow eyezone above a green throat. Tetraploid. 'Ida's Magic' × 'Queen's Cape'. TED L. PETIT

'Sue Rothbauer' (Kate Carpenter 1983). Semi-evergreen. Scape 20 in. (50.8 cm); flower 6.5 in. (16.5 cm). Early midseason. A rose self with a striking green throat. Diploid. (seedling × 'Rose Swan') × 'Martha Adams'. Award of Merit 1990. TED L. PETIT & JOHN P. PEAT

'Surprisingly Pink' (Charlie Pierce 1983). Semi-evergreen. Scape 18 in. (45.7 cm); flower 6 in. (15.2 cm). Early midseason. A textured pastel blend of more than one shade of pink, with a green throat. Diploid. Seedling × 'Beverly Ann'. JOHN EISEMAN

'Susan Weber' (Charles Branch 1989). Semi-evergreen. Scape 26 in. (66.0 cm); flower 5.75 in. (14.6 cm). Late. A light rose-pink edged in rose with a yellow-green throat. Diploid. 'Great Thou Art' × 'Fairy Tale Pink'. TED L. PETIT & JOHN P. PEAT

'Tani' (Charlie Pierce 1983). Semi-evergreen. Scape 24 in. (61.0 cm); flower 6 in. (15.2 cm). Early midseason. A large rose-pink lightly ruffled self with a green throat. Diploid. Seedling × 'Becky Lynn'. JOHN EISEMAN

'Temple Goddess' (R. W. Munson Jr. 1987). Evergreen. Scape 28 in. (71.1 cm); flower 7 in. (17.8 cm). Early midseason. A very large, pale flesh-salmon self with a yellow-green throat. Tetraploid. (('Tet. Shibui Splendor' × 'Chateau Blanc') × ('Kecia' × 'Judy Koltz')) × 'Kate Carpenter'. PATRICK STAMILE

'Touched by Magic' (Jeff Salter 1998). Semi-evergreen. Scape 26 in. (66.0 cm); flower 5 in. (12.7 cm). Midseason. A coral-rose and peach blend with a heavy gold edge. Tetraploid. 'Ida's Magic' × 'Wisest of Wizards'. TED L. PETIT & JOHN P. PEAT

'Trade Last' (Sarah Sikes 1988). Dormant. Scape 24 in. (61.0 cm); flower 4.75 in. (12.1 cm). Midseason. A wide-petaled, ruffled, deep clear pink blend with a green-yellow throat. Diploid. 'Fairy Tale Pink' × 'Southern Charmer'. TED L. PETIT & JOHN P. PEAT

'Uptown Girl' (Patrick Stamile 1993). Semi-evergreen. Scape 27 in. (68.6 cm); flower 5 in. (12.7 cm). Early midseason. A wide-petaled baby-ribbon-pink self with a green throat. Tetraploid. 'Crush on You' × 'Peach Whisper'. PATRICK STAMILE

'Velvet Rose' (Patrick Stamile 1992). Semi-evergreen. Scape 23 in. (58.4 cm); flower 5.5 in. (14.0 cm). Early midseason. A ruffled, bright rose-pink self with a green throat. Tetraploid. (seedling × ('Chicago Candy Cane' × 'Tet. Yesterday Memories')) × seedling. PATRICK STAMILE

'Venice is Sinking' (Ted L. Petit 1997). Semi-evergreen. Scape 24 in. (61.0 cm); flower 6 in. (15.2 cm). Midseason. A ruffled deep rose self with a green throat and a large pink watermark. Tetraploid. ('Court Magician' × 'Wayne Johnson') × ('Ida's Magic' × ('Queen's Cape' × 'Ida's Magic')). TED L. PETIT

'Venus de Milo' (R. W. Munson Jr. 1990). Evergreen. Scape 28 in. (71.1 cm); flower 5.5 in. (14.0 cm). Early midseason. A clear salmon-peach to baby-ribbon-pink self with a green throat. Tetraploid. 'Fred Ham' × ('Ming Temple' × 'Connie Jones'). R. W. MUNSON JR

'Vi Simmons' (Dave Talbott 1987). Evergreen. Scape 24 in. (61.0 cm); flower 6 in. (15.2 cm). Midseason. A ruffled pink self with a green throat. Diploid. 'Martha Adams' × 'Becky Lynn'. JOHN EISEMAN

'Vera Biaglow' (Steve Moldovan 1984). Dormant. Scape 28 in. (71.1 cm); flower 6 in. (15.2 cm). Midseason late. A bright rose-pink self edged in silver with a lemon green throat. Tetraploid. 'Houdini' × 'Sinbad Sailor'. Award of Merit 1993. JAY TOMPKINS

'Vision of Beauty' (Kate Carpenter 1985). Dormant. Scape 21 in. (53.3 cm); flower 6 in. (15.2 cm). Midseason. A very light pink with a lavender-pink halo and a green throat. Diploid. Parents unknown. CURTIS & LINDA SUE BARNES

'When Spirits Unite' (Jeff Salter 1995). Semi-evergreen. Scape 26 in. (66.0 cm); flower 6 in. (15.2 cm). Midseason late. Pink-lavender blend with green throat. Tetraploid. Parents unknown. TED L. PETIT & JOHN P. PEAT

'William Austin Norris' (Jeff Salter 1995). Semi-evergreen. Scape 28 in. (71.1 cm); flower 5.5 in. (14.0 cm). Midseason. A medium pink blend with a lighter watermark above a green throat. Tetraploid. Parents unknown. TED L. PETIT & JOHN P. PEAT

'Winter Roses' (Dave Talbott 1989). Evergreen. Scape 31 in. (78.7 cm); flower 6.5 in. (16.5 cm). Midseason. A clear, dark ashes-of-roses self with a darker halo above a green heart. Diploid. 'Timeless Fire' × seedling. JOHN EISEMAN

'Wrapped in Gold' (R. W. Munson Jr. 1992). Evergreen. Scape 24 in. (61.0 cm); flower 5 in. (12.7 cm). Early midseason. A rose-amber blend edged in ruffled yellow-gold with a green-gold throat. Tetraploid. 'Desert Jewel' × 'Ida's Magic'. PATRICK STAMILE

'Xia Xiang' (Oliver Billingslea 1988). Semi-evergreen. Scape 22 in. (55.9 cm); flower 6 in. (15.2 cm). Midseason. A wide-petaled, clear deep pink self with a green throat. Diploid. 'Fairy Tale Pink' × 'While Angels Sing'. JOHN EISEMAN

'Zazu Pitts' (Mac Carter 1995). Evergreen. Scape 34 in. (86.4 cm); flower 7 in. (17.8 cm). Early midseason. A very ruffled, large coral-pink self with green throat. Tetraploid. 'Ruffled Elegante' × 'Avante Garde'. MAC CARTER

'Zenith Carter' (Mac Carter 1998). Semi-ever-green. Scape 26 in. (66.0 cm); flower 5.5 in. (14.0 cm). Early midseason. A ruffled, rose-pink, wide-petaled flower with a green throat. Tetraploid. 'Alda' × 'Shishedo'. MAC CARTER

LAVENDER (lavender to purple)

'All American Magic' (Jeff Salter 1994). Semi-evergreen. Scape 26 in. (66.0 cm); flower 5.5 in. (14.0 cm). Midseason. A lavender-purple with a lighter watermark, gold edge, and green throat. Tetraploid. Parents unknown.
TED L. PETIT & JOHN P. PEAT

'Arabian Magic' (Jeff Salter 1992). Semi-ever-green. Scape 28 in. (71.1 cm); flower 5 in. (12.7 cm). Midseason. A purple self with a lighter watermark, a silver-white edge, and a green heart. Tetraploid. Parents unknown.
JAY TOMPKINS

'Asian Sky' (R. W. Munson Jr. 1994). Evergreen. Scape 30 in. (76.2 cm); flower 6 in. (15.2 cm). Early Midseason. A lavender-lilac bitone with large lime-green throat below a slate-blue halo. Tetraploid. 'Dunedin' × 'Silver Ice'.
R. W. MUNSON JR

'Azure Violets' (Jean Duncan 1995). Evergreen. Scape 29 in. (73.7 cm); flower 5.25 in. (13.3 cm). Early. A medium blue-violet with gold edges and a broad ivory-cream eyezone. Tetraploid. 'Court Magician' × 'Ida's Magic'. JEAN DUNCAN

'Bamboo Blackie' (Dalton Durio 1988). Dormant. Scape 24 in. (61.0 cm); flower 5.5 in. (14.0 cm). Midseason. A tailored, deep red-black self with green-chartreuse throat. Tetraploid. ('Zorro' × 'Total Eclipse') × 'Spades'. TED L. PETIT & JOHN P. PEAT

'Banquet at Versailles' (Ted L. Petit 1998). Semi-evergreen. Scape 22 in. (55.9 cm); flower 5 in. (12.7 cm). Midseason. A medium lavender with heavy gold edge and a lighter watermark above a green throat. Tetraploid. 'Silver Sprite' × 'Ida's Magic'. TED L. PETIT

'Barbara Frum' (Henry Lorrain and Douglas Lycett 1996). Dormant. Scape 31 in. (78.7 cm); flower 6 in. (15.2 cm). Midseason late. A burgundy-purple blend with a wine-pink watermark above a green throat. Tetraploid. 'Royal Strut' × 'Michelle Reid'. HENRY LORRAIN & DOUGLAS LYCETT

'Beguiled Again' (Jeff Salter 1994). Semi-evergreen. Scape 26 in. (66.0 cm); flower 5.5 in. (14.0 cm). Midseason. A light lavender with a gold edge, lighter watermark, and a green center. Tetraploid. Parents unknown. TED L. PETIT & JOHN P. PEAT

'Bela Lugosi' (Curt Hanson 1995). Semi-evergreen. Scape 33 in. (83.8 cm); flower 6 in. (15.2 cm). Midseason. A dark, deep purple self with a green throat. Tetraploid. (seedling × 'Nairobi Night') × 'Tet. Grand Masterpiece'. CURT HANSON

'Benchmark' (R. W. Munson Jr. 1980). Evergreen. Scape 30 in. (76.2 cm); flower 6 in. (15.2 cm). Midseason. A lightly ruffled, lavender self with a cream throat. Tetraploid. Parents unknown. Award of Merit 1987. PATRICK STAMILE

'Big Blue' (Patrick Stamile 1995). Dormant. Scape 24 in. (61.0 cm); flower 6.5 in. (16.5 cm). Midseason. A wide-petaled lavender self with a green center. Tetraploid. 'White Zone' × 'Tet. Barbara Mitchell'. PATRICK STAMILE

'Black Ambrosia' (Jeff Salter 1991). Semi-evergreen. Scape 28 in. (71.1 cm); flower 5 in. (12.7 cm). Midseason. A black-purple self with a green throat. Tetraploid. Seedling × 'Quest for Excalibur'. TED L. PETIT & JOHN P. PEAT

'Blueberry Frost' (Patrick Stamile 1997). Evergreen. Scape 28 in. (71.1 cm); flower 5 in. (12.7 cm). Midseason. A slightly recurved and ruffled blue-purple blend with a green throat. Tetraploid. ('Winter Mint Candy' × 'Admiral's Braid') × 'Ida's Magic'. PATRICK STAMILE

'China Lake' (R. W. Munson Jr. 1982). Semi-evergreen. Scape 28 in. (71.1 cm); flower 6 in. (15.2 cm). Early midseason. A large plum-rose-lilac flower with a lighter watermark and a cream throat. Tetraploid. 'Benchmark' × 'Royal Heritage'. PATRICK STAMILE

'Chaleur' (R. W. Munson Jr. 1989). Evergreen. Scape 24 in. (61.0 cm); flower 6 in. (15.2 cm). Midseason. A triangular orchid-lilac self with a cream throat and green heart. Tetraploid. 'Simply Grand' × 'China Lake'. TED L. PETIT & JOHN P. PEAT

'Chateau Defleur' (R. W. Munson Jr. 1991). Evergreen. Scape 26 in. (66.0 cm); flower 5.5 in. (14.0 cm). Early midseason. Lavender with a large ivory watermark and a green throat. Tetraploid. ('Royal Heritage' × 'Winter Reverie') × ('Asian Emperor' × 'Benchmark'). R. W. MUNSON JR

'Chris Salter' (Jeff Salter 1993). Semi-evergreen. Scape 26 in. (66.0 cm); flower 6 in. (15.2 cm). Midseason. A ruffled, medium lavender self with a gold edge and a green throat. Tetraploid. Parents unknown. TED L. PETIT & JOHN P. PEAT

'Clothed in Glory' (Larry Grace 1996). Evergreen. Scape 18 in. (45.7 cm); flower 7 in. (17.8 cm). Midseason. A lavender-mauve with a lavender eyezone, a yellow-green throat, and a very heavy gold edge. Tetraploid. 'Collector's Choice' × 'Admiral's Braid'. LARRY GRACE

'China Veil' (R. W. Munson Jr. 1989). Evergreen. Scape 30 in. (76.2 cm); flower 6 in. (15.2 cm). Early midseason. A lightly ruffled lilac-pink self with a green throat below a lighter watermark. Tetraploid. ('Royal Heritage' × 'Nile Flower') × 'Royal Saracen'. R. W. MUNSON JR

'Court Magician' (R. W. Munson Jr. 1987). Evergreen. Scape 26 in. (66.0 cm); flower 5 in. (12.7 cm). Early midseason. A wide-petaled purple self with a chalky lilac eye and a yellow-green throat. Tetraploid. ('Asian Emperor' × 'Benchmark') × 'Royal Saracen'. Award of Merit 1994. R. W. MUNSON JR

'Courts of Europe' (Ted L. Petit 1996). Semi-evergreen. Scape 22 in. (55.9 cm); flower 6.5 in. (16.5 cm). Midseason. A large, ruffled lavender self with a large cream eyezone, gold edge, and a green center. Tetraploid. 'Grand Palais' × 'Ida's Magic'. TED L. PETIT

'Crayola Violet' (Patrick Stamile 1990). Dormant. Scape 27 in. (68.6 cm); flower 5 in. (12.7 cm). Midseason. A round, recurved violet-purple self with a green throat. Diploid. 'Christmas Story' × 'Super Purple'. PATRICK STAMILE

'Crystal Rapids' (Jean Duncan 1997). Evergreen. Scape 20 in. (50.8 cm); flower 5 in. (12.7 cm). Midseason late. A bubbly gold-edged lavender-pink with a lime-green center. Tetraploid. 'Wedding Band' × 'Ida's Magic'. JEAN DUNCAN

'Dark Castle' (R. W. Munson Jr. 1986). Semi-evergreen. Scape 26 in. (66.0 cm); flower 6 in. (15.2 cm). Early midseason. A dark burgundy-purple self with a yellow-green throat. Tetraploid. Parents unknown. PATRICK STAMILE

'Darker Shade' (Patrick Stamile 1992). Semi-evergreen. Scape 26 in. (66.0 cm); flower 5.5 in. (14.0 cm). Early midseason. A very dark purple self with striking green throat. Tetraploid. 'Nile Plum' × 'Still Night'. PATRICK STAMILE

'Divine Comedy' (Steve Moldovan 1996). Semi-evergreen. Scape 31 in. (78.7 cm); flower 6 in. (15.2 cm). Midseason. A rosy purple with a yellow watermark and a lemon to green throat. Tetraploid. 'Ida's Magic' × 'Salem Witch'. STEVE MOLDOVAN

'David Kirchhoff' (Jeff Salter 1992). Semi-evergreen. Scape 26 in. (66.0 cm); flower 5.5 in. (14.0 cm). Midseason late. A lavender blend with a green throat and heavy gold edge. Tetraploid. 'Tomorrow's Dream' × seedling. MELANIE MASON

'Druid Spell' (R. W. Munson Jr. 1993). Evergreen. Scape 20 in. (50.8 cm); flower 5.5 in. (14.0 cm). Early midseason. A deep burgundy-purple with a large chalky lemon-wine watermark above a green throat. Tetraploid. 'Cameroons' × 'Court Magician'. R. W. MUNSON JR

'Elizabeth's Magic' (Jeff Salter 1990). Semi-evergreen. Scape 24 in. (61.0 cm); flower 6 in. (15.2 cm). Midseason. A lavender-pink edged in deep gold with a green throat. Tetraploid. 'Fancy Filigree' × seedling. TED L. PETIT & JOHN P. PEAT

'Douglas Lycett' (R. W. Munson Jr. 1991). Evergreen. Scape 25 in. (63.5 cm); flower 6 in. (15.2 cm). Midseason. A lavender self with a slate-blue eyezone above a chartreuse throat. Tetraploid. ('Doge of Venice' × 'Royal Heritage') × 'Nivia Guest'. R. W. MUNSON JR

'Emperor Butterfly' (R. W. Munson Jr. 1986). Evergreen. Scape 28 in. (71.1 cm); flower 5 in. (12.7 cm). Early midseason. A violet-orchid-mauve blend with a yellow-violet eyezone and a yellow-green throat. Tetraploid. 'Corfu' × 'Royal Saracen'. TED L. PETIT & JOHN P. PEAT

'Eternity's Shadow' (Ted L. Petit 1996). Evergreen. Scape 21 in. (53.3 cm); flower 6 in. (15.2 cm). Midseason. A purple with a light purple eyezone and a green throat. Tetraploid. 'Wedding Band' × 'Secret Splendor'. TED L. PETIT

'Forbidden Desires' (Ted L. Petit 1998). Semi-evergreen. Scape 20 in. (50.8 cm); flower 6 in. (15.2 cm). Midseason. A large, dark grape-purple to plum-purple with a lighter watermark, green throat, and heavy gold edge. Tetraploid. 'Louis the Sixteenth' × 'Arabian Magic'. TED L. PETIT

'Fortune's Dearest' (Mort Morss 1994). Evergreen. Scape 25 in. (63.5 cm); flower 6 in. (15.2 cm). Early. A grape-purple with white shark's tooth edge, lighter grape-purple watermark ,and a chartreuse halo. Tetraploid. Parents unknown. DAVID KIRCHHOFF

'Franklin Edward League' (R. W. Munson Jr. 1995). Evergreen. Scape 26 in. (66.0 cm); flower 5.5 in. (14.0 cm). Early midseason. A clear, rich purple self with a very large and distinct lighter watermark above a green throat. Tetraploid. ('Court Magician' × 'Silver Sprite') × 'Snow Shadows'. R. W. MUNSON JR

'Heavenly Shades' (Dan Trimmer 1996). Dormant. Scape 26 in. (66.0 cm); flower 5.75 in. (14.6 cm). Early midseason. A deep lavender with a darker halo above a green throat. Tetraploid. 'Always Afternoon' × 'Tet. Neal Berrey'. DAN TRIMMER

'Ida's Magic' (Ida Munson 1988). Evergreen. Scape 28 in. (71.1 cm); flower 6 in. (15.2 cm). Early midseason. A lavender with a lighter watermark, gold edge, and a green throat. Extremely popular and important in breeding. Tetraploid. ('Royal Saracen' × 'Enchanted Empress') × 'Ruffled Dude'. R. W. MUNSON JR

'Ida's Braid' (Matthew Kaskel 1996). Evergreen. Scape 23 in. (58.4 cm); flower 5.25 in. (13.3 cm). Midseason late. A lavender self with yellow to green throat and a heavy gold ruffled edge. Tetraploid. 'Ida's Magic' × 'Admiral's Braid'. MATTHEW KASKEL

'Imperial Splendor' (Jeff Salter 1993). Semi-evergreen. Scape 27 in. (68.6 cm); flower 6 in. (15.2 cm). Midseason. A purple self with a green throat. Tetraploid. Seedling × 'Black Ambrosia'. TED L. PETIT & JOHN P. PEAT

'Irving Shulman' (Jeff Salter 1992). Semi-evergreen. Scape 24 in. (61.0 cm); flower 5.5 in. (14.0 cm). Midseason. A lavender blend with a large lighter watermark over a green center. Tetraploid. Parents unknown. JOHN EISEMAN

'Lavender Stardust' (Jack Carpenter 1991). Dormant. 26 in. (66.0 cm) scape; flower 5.5 in. (14.0 cm). Midseason late. A ruffled lavender blend with a small watermark above a green throat. Diploid. Parents unknown. TED L. PETIT & JOHN P. PEAT

'Kabuki Ballet' (R. W. Munson Jr. 1993). Evergreen. Scape 26 in. (66.0 cm); flower 6 in. (15.2 cm). Early midseason. A large, round claret-plum with claret-pink eyezone above a yellow-green throat. Tetraploid. 'Cameroons' × 'Respighi'. TED L. PETIT & JOHN P. PEAT

'Karla Kitamura' (Ted L. Petit 1996). Semi-evergreen. Scape 24 in. (61.0 cm); flower 5.5 in. (14.0 cm). Midseason. A lightly ruffled lavender and cream bitone with a cream eyezone above a green throat. Tetraploid. 'Silver Sprite' × 'Ida's Magic'. TED L. PETIT

'Lavender Tonic' (W. M. Spalding 1983). Evergreen. Scape 17 in. (43.2 cm); flower 5.25 in. (13.3 cm). Midseason. A wide-petaled lavender blend with a green throat and raised cream midribs. Diploid. Parents unknown.
JOHN EISEMAN

'Lexington Avenue' (R. W. Munson Jr. 1990). Evergreen. Scape 24 in. (61.0 cm); flower 6 in. (15.2 cm). Early midseason. A dark wine with light whitish wine eyezone and a green to yellow throat. Tetraploid. 'Nivia Guest' × 'Malaysian Monarch'. R. W. MUNSON JR

'Lifting Me Higher' (Larry Grace 1998). Evergreen. Scape 24 in. (61.0 cm); flower 6 in. (15.2 cm). Early midseason. Burgundy-rose with gold edge and watermark above a green throat. Tetraploid. Seedling × 'Clothed in Glory'. LARRY GRACE

'Light Years Away' (Ted L. Petit 1996). Dormant. Scape 20 in. (50.8 cm); flower 5 in. (12.7 cm). Midseason. A light lavender to orchid-pink flower with a green throat and a heavily ruffled gold edge. Tetraploid. 'Eternity Shadow' × 'Admiral's Braid'. TED L. PETIT

'Lilac Snow' (R. W. Munson Jr. 1977). Semi-evergreen. Scape 28 in. (71.1 cm); flower 6 in. (15.2 cm). Midseason. A pale lilac self with a lighter watermark above a green throat. Tetraploid. Seedling × 'Tet. Catherine Woodbery'. Honorable Mention 1981. R. W. MUNSON JR

'Lord of Rings' (Steve Moldovan 1996). Evergreen. Scape 28 in. (71.1 cm); flower 5.25 in. (13.3 cm). Midseason. A dark purple edged with a creamy violet etched band above a creamy lemon to green throat. Tetraploid. 'Court Magician' × 'Mountain Majesty'.
STEVE MOLDOVAN

'Louis the Sixteenth' (Ted L. Petit 1994). Semi-evergreen. Scape 20 in. (50.8 cm); flower 6 in. (15.2 cm). Midseason. A ruffled purple self with gold edge and green throat. Tetraploid. Seedling × (('Desert Jewel' × ('Queen's Cape' × 'Desert Jewel')). TED L. PETIT

'Mable Lewis Nelson' (R. W. Munson Jr. 1989). Evergreen. Scape 18 in. (45.7 cm); flower 7 in. (17.8 cm). Midseason late. A large lilac-cream self with a large cream watermark and a green throat. Tetraploid. 'Twilight Madonna' × 'Royal Saracen'. R. W. MUNSON JR

'Maestro Puccini' (Steve Moldovan 1989). Evergreen. Scape 28 in. (71.1 cm); flower 5.5 in. (14.0 cm). Midseason. A medium rose-purple with a lemon-lime throat. Tetraploid. 'Love Goddess' × 'Benchmark'. R. W. MUNSON JR

'Manhattan Night' (R. W. Munson Jr. 1989). Semi-evergreen. Scape 34 in. (86.4 cm); flower 5 in. (12.7 cm). Early midseason. A dark, rich purple self with a lighter watermark above a chartreuse throat. Tetraploid. Parents unknown. JOHN EISEMAN

'Magic Filigree' (Jeff Salter 1988). Semi-evergreen. Scape 24 in. (61.0 cm); flower 6 in. (15.2 cm). Midseason. A triangular lavender with a light amber halo, gold edge, and a yellow-green throat. Tetraploid. Parents unknown. TED L. PETIT & JOHN P. PEAT

'Malaysian Monarch' (R. W. Munson Jr. 1986). Semi-evergreen. Scape 24 in. (61.0 cm); flower 6 in. (15.2 cm). Early midseason. A burgundy-purple self with large cream-white watermark above a green heart. Tetraploid. Parents unknown. Award of Merit 1993. R. W. MUNSON JR

'Mary Ann Smith' (R. W. Munson Jr. 1993). Evergreen. Scape 24 in. (61.0 cm); 5 in. flower (12.7 cm). Midseason. A violet-plum with a large chalky watermark over a green throat. Tetraploid. 'Court Magician' × 'Porcelain Geisha'. R. W. MUNSON JR

'Mephistopheles' (Steve Moldovan 1990). Dormant. Scape 30 in. (76.2 cm); flower 5.75 in. (14.6 cm). Early midseason. Dark, intense velvet-violet-purple with a green throat. Tetraploid. 'Strutter's Ball' × 'Grand Masterpiece'. STEVE MOLDOVAN

'Michelle Reid' (Henry Lorrain and Douglas Lycett 1991). Semi-evergreen. Scape 23 in. (58.4 cm); flower 6 in. (15.2 cm). Early midseason. A wide-petaled soft lilac self with a large cream watermark above a green throat. Tetraploid. 'Benchmark × Mariska'. HENRY LORRAIN & DOUGLAS LYCETT

'Midnight Raider' (Patrick Stamile 1995). Evergreen. Scape 30 in. (76.2 cm); flower 6.5 in. (16.5 cm). Midseason. A lightly ruffled dark purple self with a green throat. Tetraploid. 'Darker Shade' × 'Dragon King'. BETH CREVELING

'Midnight Tango' (David Kirchhoff 1995). Evergreen. Scape 28 in. (71.1 cm); flower 5.25 in. (13.34 cm). Early midseason. A wine-purple with a lighter wine watermark above a yellow to green throat. Tetraploid. 'Afghan Pride' × 'Dragon King'. DAVID KIRCHHOFF

'Nivia Guest' (R. W. Munson Jr. 1984). Evergreen. Scape 24 in. (61.0 cm); flower 5 in. (12.7 cm). Midseason. A purple self with smaller watermark above a yellow-green throat. Tetraploid. 'Royal Heiress' × ('Tet. Betty Barnes' × 'Ethiopia'). JOHN EISEMAN

'Nordic Night' (Jeff Salter 1991). Semi-evergreen. Scape 24 in. (61.0 cm); flower 5 in. (12.7 cm). Early midseason. A dark purple with a chalky red-purple eyezone above a striking green throat. Tetraploid. Parents unknown. TED L. PETIT & JOHN P. PEAT

'Old King Cole' (Steve Moldovan 1995). Dormant. Scape 32 in. (81.3 cm); flower 5.5 in. (14.0 cm). Midseason. A medium lavender-purple and ivory bicolor with a lighter watermark and a green throat. Tetraploid. 'Flying Carpet' × 'Emperor Butterfly'. STEVE MOLDOVAN

'Prince Charming Returns' (Jeff Salter 1996). Semi-evergreen. Scape 28 in. (71.1 cm); flower 5 in. (11.4 cm). Midseason. A wide-petaled, dark, rich grape-purple self with a green center. Tetraploid. 'Taken by Storm' × 'Midnight Rambler'. TED L. PETIT & JOHN P. PEAT

'Purple Sky' (Mac Carter 1997). Dormant. Scape 30 in. (76.2 cm); flower 6 in. (15.2 cm). Midseason. A wide-petaled, dark purple self with a green throat. 'Mountain Majesty' × 'Ebony Fire'. MAC CARTER

'Prince of Midnight' (Jeff Salter 1990). Semi-evergreen. Scape 26 in. (66.0 cm); flower 6 in. (15.2 cm). Midseason. A dark royal purple with a green throat. Tetraploid. Parents unknown. TED L. PETIT & JOHN P. PEAT

'Purple Twilight Time' (R. W. Munson Jr. 1989). Semi-evergreen. Scape 28 in. (71.1 cm); flower 6 in. (15.2 cm). Midseason late. A violet-purple with a chalky lavender eyezone above a striking green throat. Tetraploid. 'Royal Saracen' × 'Strutter's Ball'. R. W. MUNSON JR

'Queen Priscilla' (Henry Lorrain and Douglas Lycett 1996). Dormant. Scape 26 in. (66.0 cm); flower 6 in. (15.2 cm). Midseason late. A recurved burgundy-purple with a wine-pink watermark and green throat. Tetraploid. 'Strutter's Ball' × seedling. HENRY LORRAIN & DOUGLAS LYCETT

'Queen's Cape' (R. W. Munson Jr. 1989). Evergreen. Scape 24 in. (61.0 cm); flower 6 in. (15.2 cm). Early midseason. A ruffled violet-lavender edged in gold with a chalky eyezone and a chartreuse throat. Tetraploid. Parents unknown. CURTIS & LINDA SUE BARNES

'Quest for Excalibur' (Jeff Salter 1989). Semi-evergreen. Scape 24 in. (61.0 cm); flower 6 in. (15.2 cm). Midseason. A wide-petaled, recurved, very dark purple self with a green throat. Tetraploid. Parents unknown. PATRICK STAMILE

'Reine de Violettes' (R. W. Munson Jr. 1992). Evergreen. Scape 26 in. (66.0 cm); flower 5.5 in. (14.0 cm). Early midseason. An orchid-lilac self with a lighter watermark above a cream-green throat. Tetraploid. ('Benchmark' × 'Asian Violet') × 'Royal Saracen'. R. W. MUNSON JR

'Rhythm and Blues' (Patrick Stamile 1994). Dormant. Scape 22 in. (55.9 cm); flower 6 in. (15.2 cm). Early midseason. A lightly ruffled, large lavender self with a green throat. Tetraploid. 'Lavender Memories' × 'Only You'. TED L. PETIT & JOHN P. PEAT

'Royal Heiress' (R. W. Munson Jr. 1982). Evergreen. Scape 24 in. (61.0 cm); flower 6 in. (15.2 cm). Early midseason. A large burgundy with a chalky cream-burgundy eyezone and a cream-green throat. Tetraploid. 'Siamese Royalty' × seedling. R. W. MUNSON JR

'Royal Heritage' (R. W. Munson Jr. 1978). Semi-evergreen. Scape 32 in. (81.3 cm); flower 6 in. (15.2 cm). Midseason. A triangular violet-plum with a chalky violet eyezone and a lemon-green throat. Tetraploid. ('Stasbourg' × 'Chicago Regal') × 'Empress Seal'. R. W. MUNSON JR

'Royal Saracen' (R. W. Munson Jr. 1982). Evergreen. Scape 26 in. (66.0 cm); flower 6 in. (15.2 cm). Early midseason. A medium purple self with a lighter watermark above a cream chartreuse throat. Tetraploid. 'Royal Heritage' × 'Winter Reverie'. R. W. MUNSON JR

'Ruffian's Apprentice' (Ted L. Petit 1994). Evergreen. Scape 18 in. (45.7 cm); flower 5.5 in. (14.0 cm). Early midseason. Lavender with a gold edge and a light lavender watermark above a green throat. Tetraploid. (('Fred Ham' × 'Love Goddess') × ('Love Goddess' × 'Alvatine Taylor')) × 'Ida's Magic'. TED L. PETIT

'Sebastian' (June Williams 1978). Evergreen. Scape 20 in. (50.8 cm); flower 5.5 in. (14.0 cm). Early midseason. A purple self with a lime-green throat. Diploid. Parents unknown. Award of Merit 1987. PATRICK STAMILE

'Shinto Etching' (R. W. Munson Jr. 1989). Evergreen. Scape 26 in. (66.0 cm); flower 5.5 in. (14.0 cm). Early midseason. A peach-mauve over cream-yellow and lemon-ivory bicolor with a pencil-thin mauve eyezone above a yellow-green throat. Tetraploid. (('Benchmark × ('Tet. Catherine Woodbery' × 'Water Bird')) × (('Knave' × 'Chicago Royal') × 'Water Bird')) × ('Ruffles Elegante × Sir Oliver'). R. W. MUNSON JR

'Silver Sprite' (R. W. Munson Jr. 1983). Evergreen. Scape 20 in. (50.8 cm); flower 5 in. (12.7 cm). Midseason. A lavender self with a large chalky watermark above a deep green throat. Tetraploid. Parents unknown. R. W. MUNSON JR

'Simply Heaven' (R. W. Munson Jr. 1992). Evergreen. Scape 28 in. (71.1 cm); flower 6 in. (15.2 cm). Midseason late. A peach-lavender with a gold ruffled edge and a cream watermark above a green throat. Tetraploid. 'Royal Saracen' × (('Royal Heritage' × 'High Lama') × ('Tet. Betty Barnes' × 'Waterbird')). R. W. MUNSON JR

'Silver Ice' (R. W. Munson Jr. 1983). Semi-evergreen. Scape 25 in. (63.5 cm); flower 5 in. (12.7 cm). Early midseason. A pale lavender self with a cream throat. Tetraploid. Parents unknown.
CURTIS & LINDA SUE BARNES

'Snow Blush' (R. W. Munson Jr. 1990). Evergreen. Scape 24 in. (61.0 cm); flower 5 in. (12.7 cm). Midseason late. A lightly ruffled ivory-cream-pink-lilac with a lighter watermark and green throat. Tetraploid. 'Enchanted Empress' × 'Winter Reverie'. R. W. MUNSON JR

'Spartacus Adorned' (Curt Hanson 1998). Semi-evergreen. Scape 36 in. (91.4 cm); flower 5.5 in. (14.0 cm). Midseason late. A deep purple with an ornate gilded edge and a large violet watermark. Tetraploid. 'Warrior Spirit' × 'Tupac Amaru'. CURT HANSON

'Sovereign Queen' (R. W. Munson Jr. 1983). Semi-evergreen. Scape 30 in. (76.2 cm); flower 6 in. (15.2 cm). Midseason. A bluish lavender triangular flower with a lighter watermark and a deep green throat. Tetraploid. Parents unknown. R. W. MUNSON JR

'Super Purple' (Bob Dove 1979). Semi-evergreen. Scape 27 in. (68.6 cm); flower 5.75 in. (14.6 cm). Midseason. A triangular, deep, rich purple self with a lime-green throat. Diploid. 'Sugar Time' × seedling. Award of Merit 1989. TED L. PETIT & JOHN P. PEAT

'Swirling Water' (Kate Carpenter 1978). Semi-evergreen. Scape 22 in. (55.9 cm); flower 6.5 in. (16.5 cm). Early midseason. A narrow-petaled lavender-purple with a lighter watermark above a green throat. Diploid. 'Talent Show' × 'Impresario'. TED L. PETIT & JOHN P. PEAT

'Ten to Midnight' (Jeff Salter 1992). Semi-evergreen. Scape 24 in. (61.0 cm); flower 6 in. (15.2 cm). Midseason late. A large, dark purple self with a green throat. Tetraploid. Seedling × 'Quest for Excalibur'. TED L. PETIT & JOHN P. PEAT

'Thunder and Lightning' (Robert Carr 1995). Evergreen. Scape 24 in. (61.0 cm); flower 5.5 in. (14.0 cm). Early midseason. A deep purple blend with a darker purple eye, gold edge, and green throat. Tetraploid. 'Study in Scarlet' × 'Special Effects'. TED L. PETIT & JOHN P. PEAT

'Timbavati Horizon' (John P. Peat 1998). Semi-evergreen. Scape 20 in. (50.8 cm); flower 6 in. (15.2 cm). Midseason. A large, deep lavender-purple with a lighter yellow watermark on a green throat. Tetraploid. 'Ida's Magic' × 'Silver Sprite'. JOHN P. PEAT

'Time Window' (Dave Talbott 1986). Evergreen. Scape 28 in. (71.1 cm); flower 6.5 in. (16.5 cm). Midseason. A very large lavender blend with a green throat. Diploid. 'Treasured Memory' × ('Lavender Illusion' × 'Agape Love'). JOHN EISEMAN

'Tomorrow's Dream' (Jeff Salter 1990). Semi-evergreen. Scape 28 in. (71.1 cm); flower 4.75 in. (12.1 cm). Midseason late. A medium lavender with a lighter watermark and a green throat. Tetraploid. 'Ruffles Elegante' × seedling. MELANIE MASON

'Tupac Amaru' (Curt Hanson 1995). Semi-evergreen. Scape 36 in. (91.4 cm); flower 6 in. (15.2 cm). Midseason. A rich royal purple with a wire white edge and a lighter watermark above a green throat. Tetraploid. 'Nosferatu' × 'Court Magician'. TED L. PETIT & JOHN P. PEAT

'Tuscawilla Blackout' (Ra Hansen 1992). Semi-evergreen. Scape 32 in. (81.3 cm); flower 5 in. (12.7 cm). Midseason late. A triangular, deep black-purple-rose blend with a chartreuse throat. Tetraploid. ('Eye of Lynx' × 'Vino De Notte') × ('Vintage Bordeaux' × 'Night Wings'). RA HANSEN

'Vino di Notte' (David Kirchhoff 1988). Evergreen. Scape 32 in. (81.3 cm); flower 5 in. (12.7 cm). Early. An imperial purple self with a lime-green throat. Tetraploid. 'Zinfandel' × 'Midnight Magic'. Award of Merit 1995.
DAVID KIRCHHOFF

'Victorian Principals' (Jeff Salter 1998). Semi-evergreen. Scape 26 in. (66.0 cm); flower 5.5 in. (14.0 cm). Early midseason. A bright lavender with a yellow watermark and a gold edge. Tetraploid. 'Untamed Glory' × seedling. TED L. PETIT & JOHN P. PEAT

'Water Goblin' (R. W. Munson Jr. 1986). Evergreen. Scape 24 in. (61.0 cm); flower 5 in. (12.7 cm). Midseason late. A lilac-cream blend with a very large watermark above a green heart. Tetraploid. Parents unknown. R. W. MUNSON JR

'Winter Reverie' (R. W. Munson Jr. 1980). Semi-evergreen. Scape 22 in. (55.9 cm); flower 5 in. (12.7 cm). Midseason. A pale lilac self with a large lighter watermark and a cream throat. Tetraploid. Parents unknown. PATRICK STAMILE

'Watership Down' (Steve Moldovan 1994). Semi-evergreen. Scape 26 in. (66.0 cm); flower 6 in. (15.2 cm). Early midseason. A concord-grape-purple blend edged in white and yellow with a green throat. Tetraploid. 'Abba' × 'Shaka Zulu'. STEVE MOLDOVAN

'With This Ring' (Jeff Salter 1995). Evergreen. Scape 26 in. (66.0 cm); flower 5 in. (12.7 cm). Midseason late. A lavender self with a yellow-green throat and heavy gold edge. Tetraploid. Parents unknown. JOHN EISEMAN

RED (red to black-red)

'Amadeus' (David Kirchhoff 1981). Semi-evergreen. Scape 26 in. (66.0 cm); flower 5.5 in. (14.0 cm). Early midseason. A tailored, triangular scarlet self with a yellow-green throat. Tetraploid. 'Scarlock' × (Sldg. × 'Tet. Cathay Caper'). PATRICK STAMILE

'American Revolution' (Allen Wild 1972). Dormant. Scape 28 in. (71.1 cm); flower 5.5 in. (14.0 cm). Midseason. A narrow-petaled black-red self with a green throat. Diploid. Parents unknown. JAY TOMPKINS

'Big Apple' (Van Sellers 1986). Evergreen. Scape 26 in. (66.0 cm); flower 5 in. (12.7 cm). Early midseason. A classic tailored cerise-red flower with a green throat. Diploid. 'When I Dream' × 'Super Purple'. Award of Merit 1992. JOHN EISEMAN

'Borgia Pope' (R. W. Munson Jr. 1991). Evergreen. Scape 26 in. (66.0 cm); flower 5 in. (12.7 cm). Early midseason. Claret-red with a light rose-pink eyezone above a green throat. Tetraploid. 'Cameroons' × 'Nivia Guest'. R. W. MUNSON JR

'Caribbean Frank League' (Dave Talbott 1993). Evergreen. Scape 24 in. (61.0 cm); flower 5 in. (12.7 cm). Midseason. A slightly ruffled near-black self with a simple emerald-green center. Tetraploid. 'Night Wings' × 'Midnight Magic'. TED L. PETIT & JOHN P. PEAT

'Central Park West' (Betty Harwood 1995). Dormant. Scape 27 in. (68.6 cm); flower 5 in. (12.7 cm). Midseason. A lightly ruffled bright claret-red self with a green throat. Diploid. 'Really Lizzie' × 'Catherine Neal'. BETTY HARWOOD

'Charles Johnston' (Lee Gates 1981). Semi-evergreen. Scape 24 in. (61.0 cm); flower 6 in. (15.2 cm). Early midseason. A narrow-petaled large cherry-red flower with a green throat. Tetraploid. Parents unknown. Award of Merit 1988. TED L. PETIT & JOHN P. PEAT

'Chinese Chariot' (Jeff Salter 1988). Semi-evergreen. Scape 28 in. (71.1 cm); flower 6 in. (15.2 cm). Midseason. A strongly recurved, bright red self with a very large, strong green center. Tetraploid. Parents unknown. TED L. PETIT & JOHN P. PEAT

'Crackling Burgundy' (John Benz 1996). Dormant. Scape 28 in. (71.1 cm); flower 5.5 in. (14.0 cm). Midseason. A dark burgundy-red self with a crunchy edge and a chartreuse throat. Tetraploid. 'Holiday Frills' × 'Serena Dancer'. JOHN BENZ

'Dominic' (June Williams 1984). Semi-evergreen. Scape 30 in. (76.2 cm); flower 5.5 in. (14.0 cm). Early midseason. A dark red, triangular, tailored flower with a light yellow throat. Tetraploid. 'Royal Ambassador' × 'Baja'. JOHN EISEMAN

'Dracula' (Mac Carter 1995). Dormant. Scape 28 in. (71.1 cm); flower 6.5 in. (16.5 cm). Midseason. A near-black-purple with a white edge and a green throat. Tetraploid. (seedling × 'Midnight Magic') × 'Harrods'. MAC CARTER

'Dragon King' (David Kirchhoff 1992). Evergreen. Scape 22 in. (55.9 cm); flower 5.5 in. (14.0 cm). Early. A solid mandarin-red self with a vivid green throat. Its heavy substance makes it important in breeding. Tetraploid. 'Study in Scarlet' × 'Anastasia'. TED L. PETIT & JOHN P. PEAT

'Ebony Jewel' (Patrick Stamile 1997). Evergreen. Scape 27 in. (68.6 cm); flower 5 in. (12.7 cm). Midseason. A wide-petaled, velvety black-red self with a chartreuse green throat. Tetraploid. 'Darker Shade' × 'Forever Red'. PATRICK STAMILE

'Edge of Eden' (Ted L. Petit 1994). Evergreen. Scape 22 in. (55.9 cm); flower 5.5 in. (14.0 cm). Midseason. An extremely popular black-red self with a heavy gold edge and a green throat. Tetraploid. 'Midnight Magic' × ('Ida's Magic' × 'Queen's Cape'). TED L. PETIT

'Firepower' (Edgar W. Brown 1984). Evergreen. Scape 25 in. (63.5 cm); flower 6 in. (15.2 cm). Early midseason. A deep barn-red, lightly ruffled flower with gold edging on the sepals and a gold-green throat. Tetraploid. 'Sir Prize' × seedling. JOHN EISEMAN

'Flames Over Africa' (R. W. Munson Jr. 1997). Evergreen. Scape 24 in. (61.0 cm); flower 7 in. (17.8 cm). Midseason late. A very large rose-red with a pinkish red eyezone and yellow to green throat. Tetraploid. 'Fred Ham' × 'Cesare Borgia'. TED L. PETIT & JOHN P. PEAT

'Frank Teele' (Jeff Salter 1994). Evergreen. Scape 26 in. (66.0 cm); flower 6 in. (15.2 cm). Midseason. A slightly ruffled, light burgundy-red self with a green throat. Tetraploid. Seedling × 'Quest for Excalibur'. TED L. PETIT & JOHN P. PEAT

'Greer Garson' (Mac Carter 1996). Dormant. Scape 22 in. (55.9 cm); flower 5.5 in. (14.0 cm). Midseason. An extremely wide-petaled, very ruffled red-orange blend with a green throat. Tetraploid. 'James Lewis' × 'Glory Days'. MAC CARTER

'Harrods' (R. W. Munson Jr. 1988). Semi-evergreen. Scape 24 in. (61.0 cm); flower 6 in. (15.2 cm). Early midseason. A deep burgundy ruffled red self with a gold-green throat. A time-honored paragon. Tetraploid. Seedling × 'Dance Ballerina Dance'. JOHN EISEMAN

'Highland Cranberry' (R. W. Munson Jr. 1983). Evergreen. Scape 28 in. (71.1 cm); flower 5 in. (12.7 cm). Early midseason. A red-plum with chalky plum eyezone and yellow-green throat. Tetraploid. Parents unknown. R. W. MUNSON JR

'Honky Tonk Dream' (David Kirchhoff 1991). Evergreen. Scape 30 in. (76.2 cm); flower 5 in. (12.7 cm). Midseason. A very pretty medium cardinal-red with pale red watermark above a chartreuse throat. Tetraploid. ('Amadeus' × ('Baja' × 'Saracen Silk')) × 'Study in Scarlet'. JOHN EISEMAN

'Hunter's Torch' (David Kirchhoff 1988). Evergreen. Scape 31 in. (78.7 cm); flower 6.5 in. (16.5 cm). Early midseason. A cardinal-red flower edged in wire gold with a green throat. Tetraploid. 'Sultans Ruby' × 'Vintage Bordeax'. DAVID KIRCHHOFF

'James Marsh' (James Marsh and Charles Klehm 1978). Dormant. Scape 28 in. (71.1 cm); flower 6.5 in. (16.5 cm). Early midseason. A long-time popular deep red self with lime-green heart. Tetraploid. Seedling × 'Chicago Cherry'. TED WHITE

'Jay Turman' (David Kirchhoff 1992). Evergreen. Scape 31 in. (78.7 cm); flower 6 in. (15.2 cm). Early. A beautifully formed, wide-petaled, dark red self with a large gold-green throat. Tetraploid. 'Ebony Fire' × 'Kent's Favorite Two'. BETH CREVELING

'Jovial' (Lee Gates 1986). Semi-evergreen. Scape 20 in. (50.8 cm); flower 5 in. (12.7 cm). Early. A wine-red self with a chartreuse-green throat. Tetraploid. Parents unknown. JOHN EISEMAN

'Kent's Favorite Two' (David Kirchhoff 1988). Evergreen. Scape 26 in. (66.0 cm); flower 5.25 in. (13.3 cm). Early. A bright red self with a bright yellow-green throat. Tetraploid. Seedling × (('Douglas Dale' × 'Plantagenet') × 'Ring of Change'). JOHN EISEMAN

'Lady of Madrid' (Ted L. Petit 1998). Semi-evergreen. Scape 20 in. (50.8 cm); flower 6 in. (15.2 cm). Extra early. A heavily budded, rich burgundy-red flower with a green heart and raised, ruffled edges. Tetraploid. ('Lindan Toole' × ('Betty Warren Woods' × 'Elizabeth Salter')) × 'Kings and Vagabonds'. TED L. PETIT

'Leonard Bernstein' (David Kirchhoff 1991). Evergreen. Scape 26 in. (66.0 cm); flower 5.5 in. (14.0 cm). Early midseason. A wonderfully formed bright red self with a green throat. Tetraploid. 'Vintage Bordeaux' × 'Kent's Favorite Two'. DAVID KIRCHHOFF

'Midnight Magic' (John Kinnebrew 1979). Evergreen. Scape 28 in. (71.1 cm); flower 5.5 in. (14.0 cm). Early midseason. A striking, deep black-burgundy self with a green throat. An all-time most popular daylily. Very fertile. Tetraploid. 'Ed Murray' × 'Kilimanjaro'. Award of Merit 1986. TED L. PETIT & JOHN P. PEAT

'Minstrel's Daughter' (Ted L. Petit 1998). Evergreen. Scape 24 in. (61.0 cm); flower 5 in. (12.7 cm). Midseason. A lavender-rose with a lighter watermark, a wire gold edge, and a green throat. Tetraploid. ('Study in Scarlet' × 'Ida's Magic') × 'Romeo is Bleeding'. TED L. PETIT

'Night Deposit' (Curt Hanson 1995). Semi-evergreen. Scape 28 in. (71.1 cm); flower 6 in. (15.2 cm). Midseason. A black-maroon self with a chartreuse green throat. Tetraploid. ('Velvet Underground' × 'Royal Heiress') × 'Nosferatu'. CURT HANSON

'Night Wings' (June Williams 1986). Evergreen. Scape 30 in. (76.2 cm); flower 6 in. (15.2 cm). Early. A triangular flower, extremely black-red in color with a yellow-green throat. Tetraploid. 'Dominic' × seedling. TED L. PETIT & JOHN P. PEAT

'Outback Red' (Jeff Salter 1998). Semi-evergreen. Scape 28 in. (71.1 cm); flower 7 in. (17.8 cm). Midseason late. A large, bright, smooth red flower with a bright green throat. Tetraploid. Seedling × 'Sultans Warrior'. TED L. PETIT & JOHN P. PEAT

'Passion District' (Robert Carr 1997). Evergreen. Scape 28 in. (71.1 cm); flower 5.75 in. (14.6 cm). Midseason. A ruffled red with a lighter red watermark and a green throat. Tetraploid. 'Midnight Magic' × 'Betty Warren Woods'. ROBERT CARR

'Passion for Red' (Patrick Stamile 1994). Semi-evergreen. Scape 27 in. (68.6 cm); flower 6.75 in. (17.2 cm). Early midseason. A scarlet-red self with a deep green throat. Tetraploid. (seedling × 'Tet. Super Purple') × (seedling × 'Tet. When I Dream'). JAY TOMPKINS

'Potion for Passion' (Robert Carr 1998). Evergreen. Scape 29 in. (73.7 cm); flower 5 in. (12.7 cm). Midseason. A crimson-red, very ruffled, with a white picotee. Tetraploid. 'Ida's Magic' × (('Harrod's' × 'Study in Scarlet') × 'Betty Warren Woods'). ROBERT CARR

'Radar Love' (John Benz 1993). Semi-evergreen. Scape 30 in. (76.2 cm); flower 5 in. (12.7 cm). Midseason. A raspberry-rose self with a lime-green throat and a wire white edge. Tetraploid. 'Trudy Harris' × 'Ruby Sentinel'. JOHN BENZ

'Rambo' (Ra Hansen 1989). Evergreen. Scape 22 in. (55.9 cm); flower 6.25 in. (15.9 cm). Early. A recurved, bright blood-red with a lime throat. Tetraploid. (('Charles Johnston' × 'Embassy') × 'Cherry Treat') × ('Embassy' × 'Charles Johnston'). RA HANSEN

'Ransom Note' (Robert Carr 1998). Evergreen. Scape 27 in. (68.6 cm); flower 5 in. (12.7 cm). Early midseason. Purple self with a gold wire edge and watermark. Tetraploid. 'Arabian Magic' 'Weddng Band'. ROBERT CARR

'Red Peacemaker' (Robert Carr 1997). Dormant. Scape 28 in. (71.1 cm); flower 4.5 in. (11.4 cm). Midseason. A dark garnet-red with white edge and a green throat. Tetraploid. 'Midnight Magic' × 'Angel's Smile'. ROBERT CARR

'Red Sangria' (R. W. Munson Jr. 1992). Evergreen. Scape 32 in. (81.3 cm); flower 7 in. (17.8 cm). Midseason late. A large burgundy-red self with a green throat. Tetraploid. 'Respighi' × (('Ethiopia' × 'Tet. Betty Barnes') × 'Royal Heiress')). R. W. MUNSON JR

'Restless Warrior' (Ted L. Petit 1998). Evergreen. Scape 18 in. (45.7 cm); flower 5 in. (12.7 cm). Midseason. A bright red flower with a green throat and gold edge. Tetraploid. 'Wrapped in Gold' × (seedling × 'Betty Warren Woods'). TED L. PETIT

'Richard Taylor' (R. W. Munson Jr. 1987). Semi-evergreen. Scape 20 in. (50.8 cm); flower 6 in. (15.2 cm). Midseason. A paragon flower. A large, deep red, opulently formed bloom with a yellow-green throat. Tetraploid. 'Warrior Prince' × ('Dance Ballerina Dance' × seedling). PATRICK STAMILE

'Riley Barron' (R. W. Munson Jr. 1977). Semi-evergreen. Scape 30 in. (76.2 cm); flower 6 in. (15.2 cm). Midseason. A red self with a green throat. Tetraploid. Parents unknown. Honorable Mention 1982. R. W. MUNSON JR

'Romeo is Bleeding' (Ted L. Petit 1996). Evergreen. Scape 23 in. (58.4 cm); flower 5.5 in. (14.0 cm). Midseason. A deep velvet, highly ruffled red with a crunchy wire gold edge and a green throat. Tetraploid. 'Ida's Magic' × 'Midnight Magic'. TED L. PETIT

'Royal Ambassador' (R. W. Munson Jr. 1976). Evergreen. Scape 26 in. (66.0 cm); flower 6 in. (15.2 cm). Early midseason. A tailored, triangular red self with a gold throat. Very popular. Tetraploid. 'Embassy' × 'Tet. Martin Standard'. PATRICK STAMILE

'Scarlet Orbit' (Lee Gates 1984). Evergreen. Scape 22 in. (55.9 cm); flower 6 in. (15.2 cm). Early. Among the most popular red daylilies, this has a chartreuse throat. Tetraploid. Seedling × 'Charles Johnston'. Award of Merit 1991. TED L. PETIT & JOHN P. PEAT

'Seductor' (Lee Gates 1983). Evergreen. Scape 18 in. (45.7 cm); flower 6 in. (15.2 cm). Extra early. A very early-blooming, apple-red self with a green throat. Tetraploid. 'Passionate Prize' × seedling. Award of Merit 1990. TED L. PETIT & JOHN P. PEAT

'Serena Dancer' (Bernice Marshall 1986). Dormant. Scape 28 in. (71.1 cm); flower 4.5 in. (11.4 cm). Midseason late. A dark rich red, slightly recurved, with a wire yellow edge and a green throat. Tetraploid. ('Fair Annet' × 'Tet. Edna Spalding') × 'Tet. Ed Murray'. PATRICK STAMILE

'Shaka Zulu' (Steve Moldovan 1992). Semievergreen. Scape 28 in. (71.1 cm); flower 6 in. (15.2 cm). Early midseason. A very dark grapepurple with white edging and a pale watermark above a green center. Tetraploid. 'Court Magician' × 'Mephistopheles'. STEVE MOLDOVAN

'Siloam Paul Watts' (Pauline Henry 1988). Dormant. Scape 18 in. (45.7 cm); flower 4.75 in. (12.1 cm). Midseason. A very bright, widepetaled, ruffled red self with a green throat. Very highly regarded. Diploid. Parents unknown. Award of Merit 1995. JOHN EISEMAN

'Startle' (Eugene Belden 1988). Dormant. Scape 26 in. (66.0 cm); flower 5 in. (12.7 cm). Midseason. A red bitone with a cream halo and a green throat. Very heavy gold edge. Tetraploid. 'Broadmore Red' × 'My Sunshine'. JOHN BENZ

'Street Urchin' (David Kirchhoff 1992). Evergreen. Scape 25 in. (63.5 cm); flower 5.5 in. (14.0 cm). Midseason. A bright red with wide almond edges and a green to yellow throat. Tetraploid. 'Whooperee' × 'Autumn Valentine'. DAVID KIRCHHOFF

'Study in Scarlet' (David Kirchhoff 1985). Evergreen. Scape 28 in. (71.1 cm); flower 5 in. (12.7 cm). Early. A deep blood-red self with a green throat. A time-honored favorite. Tetraploid. 'Midnight Magic' × 'Amadeus'. JOHN EISEMAN

'Suddenly It's Autumn' (Allen Wild 1979). Dormant. Scape 31 in. (78.7 cm); flower 5 in. (12.7 cm). Midseason late. A diamond-dusted orange-red with darker eyezone, ruffled with a greenish yellow throat. Diploid. Parents unknown. JOHN EISEMAN

'Sultans Warrior' (Jeff Salter 1991). Evergreen. Scape 23 in. (58.4 cm); flower 5 in. (12.7 cm). Midseason. A deep red self with a strong green center. Tetraploid. Seedling × 'Tet. Christmas'. JOHN EISEMAN

'Sultry Smile' (Ted L. Petit 1996). Evergreen. Scape 20 in. (50.8 cm); flower 5.5 in. (14.0 cm). Midseason. A raspberry-plum with chalky watermark and a tangerine-gold edge. Very important in breeding. Tetraploid. 'Ida's Magic' × 'Cherry Chapeau'. TED L. PETIT

'Thunderbird Feathers' (David Kirchhoff 1991). Evergreen. Scape 22 in. (55.9 cm); flower 5 in. (12.7 cm). Midseason. A garnet-red with a lighter watermark above a green throat. Tetraploid. Seedling × ('Ring of Change' × 'Scarlock'). DAVID KIRCHHOFF

'Time Lord' (R. W. Munson Jr. 1983). Evergreen. Scape 30 in. (76.2 cm); flower 6 in. (15.2 cm). Early midseason. A copper-rose-red with a large lighter watermark above a lime-gold throat. Tetraploid. Parents unknown. R. W. MUNSON JR

'Timeless Fire' (Lucille Guidry 1986). Evergreen. Scape 18 in. (45.7 cm); flower 5.25 in. (13.3 cm). Early midseason. A slightly recurved, deep red self with a yellow-green throat. Diploid. Parents unknown. JOHN EISEMAN

'Tippy Tippy Tin' (Mac Carter 1994). Semi-evergreen. Scape 24 in. (61.0 cm); flower 6 in. (15.2 cm). Midseason. Red with a yellow edge and a lighter watermark above a green throat. Tetraploid. ('Dominic' × 'Scarlet Orbit') × 'Malaysian Monarch'. MAC CARTER

'Tom Wise' (Enman R. Joiner 1980). Dormant. Scape 29 in. (73.7 cm); flower 7 in. (17.8 cm). Midseason. A narrow-petaled, large red with a yellow edge and a yellow-green throat. Tetraploid. Parents unknown. TED L. PETIT & JOHN P. PEAT

'Vesuvian' (John Benz 1992). Dormant. Scape 36 in. (91.4 cm); flower 5.5 in. (14.0 cm). Mid-season. A dark, rich, velvety ruby-red self with a green throat and a wire white edge. Heavily ruffled. Tetraploid. Seedling × 'Tet. Ed Murray'. JOHN BENZ

'Vintage Bordeaux' (David Kirchhoff 1986). Evergreen. Scape 27 in. (68.6 cm); flower 5.75 in. (14.6 cm). Early. A dark cherry-red with a chartreuse throat. Tetraploid. 'Amadeus' × seedling. Award of Merit 1994. JOHN EISEMAN

'When I Dream' (Clarke Yancey 1979). Semi-evergreen. Scape 28 in. (71.1 cm); flower 6.5 in. (16.5 cm). Early midseason. A tailored and tri-angular blood-red self with a very large yellow-green throat. Diploid. (seedling × 'Prairie Warrior') × ('Stephen Fleishel' × (seedling × 'Cherry Festival')). Award of Merit 1986. JAY TOMPKINS

'Whooperee' (Lee Gates 1986). Evergreen. Scape 24 in. (61.0 cm); flower 6.5 in. (16.5 cm). Early. A rose-red with a darker eyezone and a chalky green throat. Tetraploid. Parents unknown. JOHN EISEMAN

CHAPTER FIVE
Eyed and Patterned Daylilies

The eyes of daylilies developed from members of the species that had dark eyes in the flowers. Since then, hybridizers have made remarkable and dramatic changes in eyezone characteristics. Along the way, they have altered other details of the flower to create fascinating patterns within the bloom.

The size of the eye ranges from a very narrow band to covering most of the petal. The shape of the eye has been altered, creating triangular or chevron-shaped as well as square eyes. Eye color has also been modified until many different eyezone colors now exist. In fact, the only blue color currently found in the daylily exists within the eyezone. The colors of the eye have also been intensified to make striking, dark, saturated near-blacks as well as vivid blood-reds. Efforts to clarify the background color of the petal self have complemented the intensified colors of the eye, increasing the contrast within the flower.

In addition to the solid eyes, hybridizers have worked toward increasing the complexity of the flower by forming patterns within the eyezone or elsewhere in the flower. Some hybrids break the eye into separate bands, either of the same color or differing colors. Other complex eyes encompass different colored veining within the eye. Some seem to bleed out into the petal self. Many patterns have a washed or faded appearance within the eye. The array of complex patterns emerging within modern daylilies seems to be never-ending.

The eyezone colors have also been painted along the petal edges to create a pattern called picotee. These picotee edges first appeared as a small wire of color extending from the eyezone as it touched the petal edge. Hybridizing efforts gradually pushed the eyezone color increasingly further around the petal edge, until it formed an edge of dark contrasting color completely surrounding the flower petals. The vast majority of daylilies with picotee edges have eyes that match the picotee color, but a few hybrids contain a darker edge without an eye. These picotee edges without an accompanying eye are currently not as dark, dramatic, or contrasting as those found on flowers with eyes. Hybridizers are striving to create flowers with more dramatic contrasting picotee edges without a dark eyezone.

Picotee edges have been increased in width, and more recently they have been surrounded by secondary edges of silver, gold, and white. This complexity has created a stunning and sometimes shocking effect in the modern hybrids. In some the eyes have become so large and the edges so wide that little petal self remains visible. Stippled or plicata eyes have also begun to appear in several hybridizing programs. These daylilies have petal color made of dots or splotches rather than a solid color. Stippling or plicata patterns are most commonly darker dots or splotches on a lighter petal background color. Stippling can cover the entire petal or can be confined to the eyezone. Hybridizers also have spent efforts on altering the color of the petal edges and throats. Darker (or picotee) petal edges are very popular, but a number of cultivars have lighter petal edges, particularly reds with lighter rose or pink edges. An iridescent cast, sometimes referred to as applique, has been developed in the throat.

The following daylilies are divided into those with solid eyes, followed by those containing a pattern within the flower.

EYES

'Alaqua' (Patrick Stamile 1996). Evergreen. Scape 23 in. (58.4 cm); flower 5.25 in. (13.3 cm). Midseason. A yellow-cream with a burgundy eye and picotee over a green throat. Tetraploid. ('Dewberry Candy' × 'Pirate's Patch') × 'Creative Edge'. PATRICK STAMILE

'All American Tiger' (Patrick Stamile 1995). Evergreen. Scape 24 in. (61.0 cm); flower 5.5 in. (14.0 cm). Midseason. A deep burnt-orange with a red eye and picotee edge above a green throat. Tetraploid. 'Tigger' × 'Pirate's Patch'. PATRICK STAMILE

'All Fired Up' (Patrick Stamile 1996). Evergreen. Scape 20 in. (50.8 cm); flower 6 in. (15.2 cm). Early. A peachy orange with a large red eye and picotee edge above a green throat. Tetraploid. ('Eye Declare' × ('Wineberry Candy' × 'Tet. Priscilla's Rainbow')) × 'Regal Braid'. PATRICK STAMILE

'All the Trimmings' (Mort Morss 1993). Evergreen. Scape 24 in. (61.0 cm); flower 5.25 in. (13.3 cm). Early midseason. A salmon-amber-peach with a gold edge, purple eye, and yellow throat. Tetraploid. 'Heavenly Dragon' × 'Fantasy Finish'. DAVID KIRCHHOFF

'Awakening Dream' (Patrick Stamile 1995). Evergreen. Scape 26 in. (66.0 cm); flower 5 in. (12.7 cm). Early midseason. A cream-yellow self with a burgundy-purple eye and picotee above a green throat. Tetraploid. 'Creative Edge' × 'Pirate's Patch'. PATRICK STAMILE

'Bayou Bride' (Jeff Salter 1995). Semi-evergreen. Scape 25 in. (63.5 cm); flower 5 in. (12.7 cm). Midseason. A cream-peach with a purple eye-zone and a green throat. Tetraploid. Parents unknown. JOHN EISEMAN

'Baracuda Bay' (Jeff Salter 1996). Semi-evergreen. Scape 26 in. (66.0 cm); flower 6 in. (15.2 cm). Midseason. A red to coral rust with a darker eye and a prominent white-toothed edge. Tetraploid. 'Mask of Time' × 'Mort's Masterpiece'. TED L. PETIT & JOHN P. PEAT

'Bengal Bay' (Jeff Salter 1996). Semi-evergreen. Scape 28 in. (71.1 cm); flower 6 in. (15.2 cm). Mid-season. A cream flower with a black-purple eyezone and a green throat. Tetraploid. Parents unknown. TED L. PETIT & JOHN P. PEAT

'Bette Davis Eyes' (David Kirchhoff 1982). Ever-green. Scape 23 in. (58.4 cm); flower 5.25 in. (13.34 cm). Early. A lavender with a grape-purple eyezone and intense lime-green throat. Diploid. 'Lhasa' × 'Agape Love'. Award of Merit 1991. Don C. Stevens Award 1986.
DAVID KIRCHHOFF

'Black Eye' (Alfred Goldner 1984). Dormant. Scape 30 in. (76.2 cm); flower 5 in. (12.7 cm). Midseason. A lavender to pink flower with a dark burgundy-pink eye and green throat. Tetraploid. Parents unknown. JOHN EISEMAN

'Blackthorne' (Dan Trimmer 1996). Evergreen. Scape 26 in. (66.0 cm); flower 4.5 in. (11.4 cm). Early midseason. A lightly ruffled cream with a very large black-purple eye and a dark green throat. Tetraploid. 'Always Afternoon' × 'Tet. Dragons Eye'. DAN TRIMMER

'Border Bride' (Jeff Salter 1995). Semi-evergreen. Scape 26 in. (66.0 cm); flower 5.5 in. (14.0 cm). Early midseason. A near-white with purple eye and picotee above a green throat. Tetraploid. Seedling × 'Daring Dilemma'. TED L. PETIT & JOHN P. PEAT

'Bull Durham' (Robert Elliott 1983). Semi-evergreen. Scape 18 in. (45.7 cm); flower 7 in. (17.8 cm). Early midseason. A classic orange-yellow self with a large magenta-purple eye. Diploid. ('Commanders Wing' × 'Edna Spalding Memorial') × 'Duke of Durham'. PATRICK STAMILE

'Burning Desire' (J. L. Cruse 1977). Evergreen. Scape 24 in. (61.0 cm); flower 5 in. (12.7 cm). Early midseason. A bright red with darker cherry eyezone, and a green throat. Diploid. 'Gypsy Maiden' × seedling. PATRICK STAMILE

'Cherry Eyed Pumpkin' (David Kirchhoff 1991). Semi-evergreen. Scape 28 in. (71.1 cm); flower 5.75 in. (14.6 cm). Extra early. An orange self with a red eye above a gold throat. Tetraploid. (seedling × 'Dance Ballerina Dance') × 'Yuma'. DAVID KIRCHHOFF

'Cimarron Knight' (Jeff Salter 1990). Evergreen. Scape 22 in. (55.88 cm); flower 6 in. (15.2 cm). Midseason. A burnt sienna with a black-plum eye and a green throat. Tetraploid. Parents unknown. PATRICIA LOVELAND

'Cindy's Eye' (Jeff Salter 1994). Semi-evergreen. Scape 30 in. (76.2 cm); flower 6 in. (15.2 cm). Midseason. An ivory cream with a large, dramatic medium purple eye and picotee. Tetraploid. Parents unknown. TED L. PETIT & JOHN P. PEAT

'Cinnamon Sunrise' (Nita Copenhaver and Donald Copenhaver 1991). Semi-evergreen. Scape 25 in. (63.5 cm); flower 6.5 in. (16.5 cm). Midseason. A cinnamon-orange with a large burgundy eye and orange midribs. Diploid. 'Pumpkin Kid' × seedling. TED L. PETIT & JOHN P. PEAT

'Comanche Eyes' (Lucille Guidry 1985). Evergreen. Scape 30 in. (76.2 cm); flower 6 in. (15.2 cm). Extra early. A large, wide, full-formed cream flower with a rose eye. Diploid. Parents unknown. PATRICK STAMILE

'Corinthian Pink' (Patrick Stamile 1996). Dormant. Scape 26 in. (66.0 cm); flower 7.25 in. (18.4 cm). Early midseason. A deep rose-pink with a distinct darker rose-pink eye. Tetraploid. ((seedling × 'Love Goddess') × (seedling × 'Tet. Martha Adams')) × 'Seminole Wind'. PATRICK STAMILE

'Creative Edge' (Patrick Stamile 1993). Semi-evergreen. Scape 23 in. (58.4 cm); flower 6 in. (15.2 cm). Midseason. A breakthrough flower with a double edge. Cream-lavender with a purple eye and a purple and gold picotee. Tetraploid. ('Plum Candy' × 'Wintermint Candy') × 'Admiral's Braid'. PATRICK STAMILE

'Daring Deception' (Jeff Salter 1994). Semi-evergreen. Scape 24 in. (61.0 cm); flower 5 in. (12.7 cm). Early midseason. A pale lavender-pink flower with a black-purple edge and matching eyezone. Tetraploid. 'Daring Dilemma' × seedling. TED L. PETIT & JOHN P. PEAT

'Daring Dilemma' (Jeff Salter 1992). Semi-evergreen. Scape 24 in. (61.0 cm); flower 5 in. (12.7 cm). Midseason. A cream to light pink with a plum edge and eyezone above a green throat. Tetraploid. Parents unknown. TED L. PETIT & JOHN P. PEAT

'Dark and Handsome' (Jack Carpenter 1990). Semi-evergreen. Scape 20 in. (50.8 cm); flower 5.75 in. (14.6 cm). Midseason. A smoky pink with a dark maroon eye above a yellow and green throat. Diploid. Parents unknown. JOHN EISEMAN

'Designer Jeans' (Sarah Sikes 1983). Dormant. Scape 34 in. (86.4 cm); flower 6.5 in. (16.5 cm). Midseason. A lavender with dark lavender edge and eyezone, and yellow-green throat. Tetraploid. ('Pink Mystique' × 'Chicago Knobby') × ('Medea' × 'Chicago Knobby'). Award of Merit 1991. JOHN EISEMAN

'Desperado Love' (Patrick Stamile 1994). Semi-evergreen. Scape 26 in. (66.0 cm); flower 5 in. (12.7 cm). Midseason. A golden yellow with a large plum-purple eye and picotee surrounding a green throat. Tetraploid. 'El Desperado' × 'Pirate's Patch'. PATRICK STAMILE

'Destiny's Child' (Jeff Salter 1989). Semi-evergreen. Scape 26 in. (66.0 cm); flower 6 in. (15.2 cm). Midseason. A peach-pink with striking red eyezone and a green throat. Tetraploid. ('Jade Lady' × 'Suva') × ('Ming Porcelain' × seedling). JOHN EISEMAN

'Didgeridoo' (John P. Peat 1998). Semi-evergreen. Scape 24 in. (61.0 cm); flower 5 in. (12.7 cm). Midseason. A lavender-purple with a purple eye and picotee surrounded by a wire gold edge. Tetraploid. ('Misty Memories' × 'Daring Dilemma') × 'Mardi Gras Ball'. JOHN P. PEAT

'Driving Me Wild' (Patrick Stamile 1992). Evergreen. Scape 26 in. (66.0 cm); flower 5.5 in. (14.0 cm). Early midseason. Lavender with a gold edge and deeper lavender eye. Tetraploid. 'Wineberry Candy' × ((seedling × 'Pink Monday') × 'Tet. Martha Adams'). PATRICK STAMILE

'Druid's Chant' (Patrick Stamile 1993). Semievergreen. Scape 23 in. (58.4 cm); flower 6.5 in. (16.5 cm). Early midseason. A deep lavender with a large dark purple eye and wide picotee and a large green throat. Tetraploid. ('El Bandito' × 'Plum Candy') × 'Admiral's Braid'. PATRICK STAMILE

'Duke of Durham' (Robert Elliott 1977). Dormant. Scape 29 in. (73.7 cm); flower 6 in. (15.2 cm). Midseason late. A copper-brown self with a large burgundy-purple eyezone and a green throat. Diploid. 'Sea Warrior' × 'Chocolate Pudding'. CURTIS & LINDA SUE BARNES

'Edge of Darkness' (Patrick Stamile 1997). Evergreen. Scape 25 in. (63.5 cm); flower 5 in. (12.7 cm). Early midseason. A deep lavender-purple with a prominent dark purple eye and wide edge. Tetraploid. 'Festive Art' × 'Druid's Chant'. PATRICK STAMILE

'Elsie Spalding' (W. M. Spalding 1985). Evergreen. Scape 14 in. (35.6 cm); flower 6 in. (15.2 cm). Midseason. A large ivory bloom blushed pink and with a light pink halo above a strong lime-green throat. Diploid. Parents unknown. Award of Merit 1990. JOHN EISEMAN

'Emperor's Dragon' (R. W. Munson Jr. 1988). Evergreen. Scape 26 in. (66.0 cm); flower 5 in. (12.7 cm). Midseason. A silvery mauve with a raisin-plum eye and a chartreuse-yellow throat. Tetraploid. ('Chicago Knobby' × 'Water Bird') × ('Benchmark' × 'Caliphs Robe'). JOHN EISEMAN

'Empress of Bagdad' (R. W. Munson Jr. 1987). Evergreen. Scape 28 in. (71.1 cm); flower 5.5 in. (14.0 cm). Midseason late. An ivory-pink and lilac blend with a rose-beige eye above a green throat. Tetraploid. 'Elizabeth Anne Hudson' × ('Royal Heritage' × 'Chicago Knobby'). R. W. MUNSON JR

'Eye Catching' (Patrick Stamile 1997). Evergreen. Scape 23 in. (58.42 cm); flower 5 in. (12.7 cm). Early midseason. A cream pink flower with a very large dramatic purple eye and matching wide picotee. Tetraploid. 'Festive Art' × ('Cherry Drop' × 'Royal Braid'). PATRICK STAMILE

'Eye on America' (Jeff Salter 1996). Semi-evergreen. Scape 26 in. (66.0 cm); flower 5.5 in. (12.7 cm). Early midseason. A yellow-cream with a large, dramatic black-plum eye with matching picotee and a green throat. Tetraploid. 'Tet. Burning Desire' × ((('Tet. Lady Mischief' × seedling) × 'Daring Dilemma') × 'Border Bride'). TED L. PETIT & JOHN P. PEAT

'Fantasy Finish' (Mort Morss 1987). Evergreen. Scape 26 in. (66.0 cm); flower 5 in. (12.7 cm). Early. A pastel cream with a small purple eye that bleeds out onto the petals. Tetraploid. (((('Disraeli' × ('Kings Cloak' × 'Meadow Mystic')) × 'Chicago Two Bits') × 'Chicago Picotee Queen') × 'Sharks Tooth'. TED L. PETIT & JOHN P. PEAT

'Femme Fatale' (Dave Talbott 1985). Semi-evergreen. Scape 21 in. (53.3 cm); flower 5 in. (12.7 cm). Early. A creamy tangerine self with a purple eye and tangerine midribs. Diploid. ('Homeward Bound' × 'Apparition') × ('Homeward Bound' × 'Apparition'). JOHN EISEMAN

'Festive Art' (Patrick Stamile 1995). Evergreen. Scape 30 in. (76.2 cm); flower 5 in. (12.7 cm). Early midseason. A pale cream-pink blossom with a purple eye and picotee. Tetraploid. ('Joe Marinello' × 'Admiral's Braid') × 'Pirate's Patch'. PATRICK STAMILE

'Five O'clock Shadow' (Matthew Kaskel 1996). Semi-evergreen. Scape 26 in. (66.0 cm); flower 5.5 in. (14.0 cm). Early midseason. A parchment-colored bloom with a muted rose eye and an olive throat. Tetraploid. ('Paper Butterfly' × seedling) × 'Bit More Class'. MATTHEW KASKEL

'Flamboyant Eyes' (Jack Carpenter 1993). Dormant. Scape 26 in. (66.0 cm); flower 5 in. (12.7 cm). Midseason. Flesh-pink flower with a flamboyant raspberry-red eye above a green throat. Diploid. Parents unknown. TED L. PETIT & JOHN P. PEAT

'Flamingo Flight' (John P. Peat 1998). Semi-evergreen. Scape 28 in. (71.1 cm); flower 5.5 in. (14.0 cm). Midseason. A bright pink self with a dark rose-pink eye, matching picotee, and gold diamond-dusted edge. Tetraploid. ('Misty Memories' × ('Sylvan Delight' × 'Tet. Siloam Virginia Henson')) × 'Mardi Gras Ball'. JOHN P. PEAT

'Fooled Me' (Ann Hein 1990). Evergreen. Scape 24 in. (61.0 cm); flower 5.5 in. (14.0 cm). Early midseason. A golden yellow flower edged burgundy-red with a deep burgundy-red eye. Tetraploid. Parents unknown. TED L. PETIT & JOHN P. PEAT

'Graceful Eye' (W. M. Spalding 1981). Evergreen. Scape 21 in. (53.3 cm); flower 6 in. (15.2 cm). Early. A rose-lavender bloom with a purple eye surrounding a dark green throat. Diploid. Parents unknown. Award of Merit 1988. JOHN EISEMAN

'Gay Cravat' (Virginia Peck 1976). Dormant. Scape 27 in. (68.6 cm); flower 6 in. (15.2 cm). Midseason. A cream-pink with a wine-red eyezone and ivory-green throat. Tetraploid. Seedling × 'Crispin'. PATRICK STAMILE

'Graceland' (Mort Morss 1987). Evergreen. Scape 28 in. (71.1 cm); flower 6 in. (15.2 cm). Early. A pastel lavender to cream-pink with a darker halo eye above a patterned green throat. Tetraploid. 'Zinfandel' × ('Inner View' × 'Ming Porcelain'). PATRICK STAMILE

'Heady Wine' (Virginia Peck 1981). Semi-evergreen. Scape 22 in. (55.9 cm); flower 5.5 in. (14.0 cm). Midseason. A cream-peach with a burgundy-wine eye and a green throat. A very popular classic. Tetraploid. 'June Wine' × 'Dance Ballerina Dance'. CURTIS & LINDA SUE BARNES

'Imperial Edge' (Patrick Stamile 1993). Semi-evergreen. Scape 22 in. (55.9 cm); flower 5 in. (12.7 cm). Early midseason. A soft cream-pink, wide-petaled flower with a rose-pink picotee, gold edge, and rose-pink eyezone. Tetraploid. ('Wineberry Candy' × 'Wintermint Candy') × 'Admiral's Braid'. PATRICK STAMILE

'Indigo Moon' (Patrick Stamile 1987). Semi-evergreen. Scape 24 in. (61.0 cm); flower 6.5 in. (16.5 cm). Early midseason. A dark burgundy-purple with a burgundy-black eyezone and striking green throat. Tetraploid. 'In the Purple' × 'Tet. Olivier Monette'. PATRICK STAMILE

'Jambalaya' (Marjorie Soules 1981). Dormant. Scape 21 in. (53.3 cm); flower 7.25 in. (18.4 cm). Midseason. A blend of bronze and tan-orange with darker orange-brown eye. Tetraploid. (seedling × 'Paprika Velvet') × 'Viracocha'. JOHN EISEMAN

'Jan Johnson' (Thomas Wilson 1991). Dormant. Scape 24 in. (61.0 cm); flower 6 in. (15.2 cm). Early midseason. A cream-lavender-pink with darker lavender eye. Diploid. 'Codie Wedgeworth' × 'Jedi Rose Frost'. TED L. PETIT & JOHN P. PEAT

'Jedi Codie Wedgeworth' (Dan Wedgeworth 1990). Semi-evergreen. Scape 26 in. (66.0 cm); flower 6 in. (15.2 cm). Early midseason. A cream-lavender-pink with a maroon eyezone and a green throat. Diploid. Parents unknown. TED L. PETIT & JOHN P. PEAT

'Jerome' (Elsie Spalding 1979). Evergreen. Scape 22 in. (55.9 cm); flower 6.75 in. (17.2 cm). Early midseason. A yellow to orange triangular flower with a deeper eye. Diploid. Parents unknown. Award of Merit 1987. JOHN EISEMAN

'Joe Marinello' (Patrick Stamile 1989). Dormant. Scape 21 in. (53.3 cm); flower 5 in. (12.7 cm). Early. A cream-pink with a beautiful deep wine-purple eye above a green center. Tetraploid. 'Paper Butterfly' × 'Tet. Siloam Virginia Henson'. Award of Merit 1997. PATRICK STAMILE

'Jolly Lad' (Elsie Spalding 1980). Evergreen. Scape 17 in. (43.2 cm); flower 6 in. (15.2 cm). Early midseason. An apricot flower with an orange halo surrounding a very large lime-green throat. Diploid. Parents unknown. JOHN EISEMAN

'King George' (George Rasmussen 1991). Semi-evergreen. Scape 30 in. (76.2 cm); flower 7 in. (17.8 cm). Midseason. An extremely large, deep yellow flower with a wine-red eye. Tetraploid. Seedling × 'Tet. Top Honors'. CURTIS & LINDA SUE BARNES

'Kyoto Garden' (Ted L. Petit 1994). Evergreen. Scape 17 in. (43.2 cm); flower 5.5 in. (14.0 cm). Midseason. An orchid-pink with a lavender eye and very large green throat. Tetraploid. 'Silver Sprite' × ('Ida's Magic' × seedling). TED L. PETIT

'Lambada' (David Kirchhoff 1990). Evergreen. Scape 30 in. (76.2 cm); flower 6.5 in. (16.5 cm). Midseason. A medium orange flower, edged burgundy, with a burgundy eye. Tetraploid. ('Ring of Change' × 'Tet. Elysian Field') × 'Atlanta Cover Girl'. DAVID KIRCHHOFF

'Least Expected' (John P. Peat 1998). Semi-evergreen. Scape 30 in. (76.2 cm); flower 5 in. (12.7 cm). Early midseason. A peach-burgundy with dark burgundy eye and picotee with burgundy midribs and a green throat. Tetraploid. ('Heady Wine' × 'Ida's Magic') × 'Mardi Gras Ball'. JOHN P. PEAT

'Leebea Orange Crush' (Lee Gates 1978). Semi-evergreen. Scape 18 in. (45.7 cm); flower 6 in. (15.2 cm). Early midseason. A classically formed cream-orange flower with a red eyezone and yellow-green throat. Tetraploid. Parents unknown. JOHN EISEMAN

'Lin Wright' (Mort Morss 1991). Evergreen. Scape 24 in. (61.0 cm); flower 6 in. (15.2 cm). Midseason. A ivory-cream flower edged in wine with a wine eyezone above a green throat. Tetraploid. (('Zinfandel' × 'Tet. Sebastian') × ('Your Song' × 'Meadow Mystic')) × (seedling × ('Zinfandel' × 'Chicago Picotee Queen')). JOHN EISEMAN

'Lonesome Dove' (Ema Harvey and David Kirchhoff 1991). Semi-evergreen. Scape 28 in. (71.1 cm); flower 6 in. (15.2 cm). Early. A cream-yellow with a subtle eyezone above a green throat. Tetraploid. 'Paper Butterfly' × 'Kate Carpenter'. TED L. PETIT & JOHN P. PEAT

'Making Whoopee' (Lee Gates 1989). Evergreen. Scape 20 in. (50.8 cm); flower 6 in. (15.2 cm). Early. A silver-burgundy-purple with a dark burgundy-purple eye and a large green throat. Diploid. Parents unknown. JOHN EISEMAN

'Lipstick Traces' (Matthew Kaskel 1994). Evergreen. Scape 22 in. (55.9 cm); flower 5 in. (12.7 cm). Early midseason. A beautifully formed light yellow with a distinct red eyezone above yellow-green throat. Tetraploid. (('Altamira' × seedling) × 'Elsie Spalding') × 'Stairway to Heaven'. MATTHEW KASKEL

'Mardi Gras Ball' (Ted L. Petit 1996). Semi-evergreen. Scape 23 in. (58.4 cm); flower 6 in. (15.2 cm). Midseason. A lavender-purple with darker purple eye and picotee and a heavy gold edge. Tetraploid. ('Tet. Siloam Virginia Henson' × 'Ida's Magic') × 'Admiral's Braid'. TED L. PETIT

'Marilyn Siwik' (David Kirchhoff 1994). Evergreen. Scape 29 in. (73.7 cm); flower 7 in. (17.8 cm). Extra early. A burnt orange with red-orange edge and intense, dark red eyezone above a gold to green throat. Tetraploid. 'Cherry Eyed Pumpkin' × 'Lambada'. DAVID KIRCHHOFF

'Mask of Time' (Jeff Salter 1993). Semi-evergreen. Scape 26 in. (66.0 cm); flower 6 in. (15.2 cm). Midseason late. An orange-rose with a black plum eyezone above a green throat. Tetraploid. Parents unknown. JOHN EISEMAN

'Merle Kent Memorial' (Jack Carpenter 1990). Evergreen. Scape 26 in. (66.0 cm); flower 7 in. (17.8 cm). Midseason. A cream-peach with a darker rose eyezone and a green center. Diploid. Parents unknown. MELANIE MASON

'Missouri Memories' (Ra Hansen 1992). Evergreen. Scape 26 in. (66.0 cm); flower 6 in. (15.2 cm). Late. A wide-petaled, ruffled, pale orchid-pink flower with a lavender-violet band above a green throat. Diploid. Parents unknown. RA HANSEN

'Molino Pink Loveliness' (Richard McCord 1992). Evergreen. Scape 18 in. (45.7 cm); flower 5.5 in. (14.0 cm). Early. A pastel pink with a rose halo surrounding a large chartreuse throat. Diploid. 'Pink Flirt' × 'Edith Anne'. JOHN EISEMAN

'Monterrey Jack' (Dan Trimmer 1996). Dormant. Scape 24 in. (61.0 cm); flower 5.5 in. (14.0 cm). Early. A cream-yellow with a wine-red eye above a green throat. Tetraploid. 'Tet. Siloam Gumdrop' × 'Tet. Wings of Chance'. DAN TRIMMER

'Moonlit Masquerade' (Jeff Salter 1992). Semi-evergreen. Scape 26 in. (66.0 cm); flower 5.5 in. (14.0 cm). Early midseason. An ivory-cream self with very dark purple eye and picotee. Tetraploid. Parents unknown. TED L. PETIT & JOHN P. PEAT

'Mort's Magic' (Mort Morss 1989). Dormant. Scape 26 in. (66.0 cm); flower 5.5 in. (14.0 cm). Early midseason. A medium mauve self with a purple picotee and eye. Tetraploid. ('Nile Flower' × 'Montage') × 'Holiday Frills'. DAVID KIRCHHOFF

'Mort's Masterpiece' (Mort Morss 1995). Evergreen. Scape 27 in. (68.6 cm); flower 6 in. (15.2 cm). Midseason late. An alabaster self with a grape eye and edge. Tetraploid. 'Song Without Words' × 'Lin Wright'. TED L. PETIT & JOHN P. PEAT

'Neon Rainbow' (Enman R. Joiner 1995). Semi-evergreen. Scape 30 in. (76.2 cm); flower 6 in. (15.2 cm). Early midseason. A large, triangular cream-yellow with a pale lavender eye surrounding a patterned throat. Tetraploid. Seedling × 'Court Magician'. TED L. PETIT & JOHN P. PEAT

'No Regrets' (Mort Morss 1994). Semi-evergreen. Scape 20 in. (50.8 cm); flower 5 in. (12.7 cm). Late. A pale yellow to peach-lavender with a gold edge and deeper yellow to peach-lavender halo. Tetraploid. 'Dream Express' × 'Angelus Angel'. DAVID KIRCHHOFF

'New Series' (Kate Carpenter 1982). Semi-evergreen. Scape 25 in. (63.5 cm); flower 7.5 in. (19.1 cm). Midseason. A clear light pink with a rose-red band and bright lime-green throat. Diploid. 'Arkansas Bright Eyes' × 'Shibui Splendor'. Award of Merit 1991. Don C. Stevens Award 1991. JOHN EISEMAN

'Only Believe' (Larry Grace 1998). Semi-evergreen. Scape 24 in. (61.0 cm); flower 7 in. (17.8 cm). Midseason. A medium creamy pink with a burgundy-red eye and large green throat. Tetraploid. 'Wedding Band' × 'Song Without Words'. LARRY GRACE

'Night Vision' (Jean Duncan 1997). Evergreen. Scape 36 in. (91.4 cm); flower 6 in. (15.2 cm). Early midseason. A medium lavender-grape with dark purple picotee and eyezone above a green throat. Tetraploid. 'Rhine Maiden' × 'Pirate's Patch'. JEAN DUNCAN

'Paige's Pinata' (Ra Hansen 1990). Semi-evergreen. Scape 26 in. (66.0 cm); flower 6 in. (15.2 cm). Early midseason. A peach-pink flower with a very large, bold fuchsia eye covering most of the petal area. Diploid. ('So Excited' × seedling) × 'Janice Brown'. Award of Merit 1997. RA HANSEN

'Pink Circle' (W. M. Spalding 1981). Semi-evergreen. Scape 16 in. (40.6 cm); flower 5.25 in. (13.3 cm). Midseason. A medium pink bloom with a dark rose-pink band and a large green center. Diploid. Parents unknown.
JOHN EISEMAN

'Pink Cotton Candy' (Patrick Stamile 1991). Dormant. Scape 23 in. (58.4 cm); flower 5 in. (12.7 cm). Midseason late. A very clear pink with a bright red eyezone surrounding a strong green throat. Tetraploid. 'Papillon' × 'Tet. Siloam Virginia Henson'. PATRICK STAMILE

'Prince Michael' (Ra Hansen 1990). Evergreen. Scape 28 in. (71.1 cm); flower 7 in. (17.8 cm). Midseason late. A very large violet-lavender with a magenta-purple eye surrounding a dramatic green throat. Diploid. 'Ra Hansen' × ('Ruffled Ivory' × 'Motor Mouth'). RA HANSEN

'Prince of Monaco' (Dave Talbott 1991). Evergreen. Scape 31 in. (78.7 cm); flower 6.5 in. (16.5 cm). Early midseason. A large flesh-pink triangular flower with a muted rose band. Diploid. 'Vi Simmons' × 'Elsie Spalding'.
JOHN EISEMAN

'Pug Yarborough' (Jack Carpenter 1990). Semi-evergreen. Scape 20 in. (50.8 cm); flower 6.5 in. (16.5 cm). Early. A large peach-pink with a round rose-red eye extending far into the petals. Diploid. Parents unknown. TED L. PETIT & JOHN P. PEAT

'Pumpkin Kid' (Elsie Spalding 1987). Evergreen. Scape 18 in. (45.7 cm); flower 5.5 in. (14.0 cm). Midseason. A dramatic, burnt orange, ruffled flower with a precise red band surrounding a shocking green throat. Diploid. Parents unknown. Award of Merit 1992. Don C. Stevens Award 1992. JOHN EISEMAN

'Radiant Ruffles' (Edwin C. Brown 1987). Semi-evergreen. Scape 24 in. (61.0 cm); flower 4.75 in. (12.1 cm). Midseason. A cream-ivory with a burgundy-red eyezone above yellow halo and green throat. Diploid. 'Rosy Sunset' × 'Siloam Virginia Henson'. Award of Merit 1994. TED L. PETIT & JOHN P. PEAT

'Raspberry Candy' (Patrick Stamile 1989). Dormant. Scape 26 in. (66.0 cm); flower 4.75 in. (12.1 cm). Early. Cream with a deep raspberry-red eye punctuated by cream midribs. Tetraploid. Seedling × Tet. Siloam Virginia Henson'. L. Ernest Plouf Award 1997. PATRICK STAMILE

'Rave On' (Patrick Stamile 1995). Semi-evergreen. Scape 26 in. (66.0 cm); flower 5 in. (12.7 cm). Midseason late. A light ivory-cream-white with a dramatic dark-purple eyezone and matching picotee. Tetraploid. 'Raspberry Candy' × 'Pirate's Patch'. BETH CREVELING

'Regal Braid' (Patrick Stamile 1994). Dormant. Scape 12 in. (30.5 cm); flower 5.5 in. (14.0 cm). Midseason. A cream-lavender with a braided purple edge and purple eye. A much sought-after daylily. Tetraploid. 'Tropical Snow' × ('Chicago Candy Cane' × 'Tet. Yesterday Memories'). PATRICK STAMILE

'Rhapsody in Time' (Jeff Salter 1996). Semi-evergreen. Scape 28 in. (71.1 cm); flower 5 in. (12.7 cm). Early midseason. A lavender-rose with striking near-blue-violet eye. Tetraploid. ('Tet. Lady Violet Eyes' × 'Night Mist') × ('Tet. Little Print' × ('Night Mist' × ('Nivea Guest' × 'Corfu'))). TED L. PETIT & JOHN P. PEAT

'Rosy Sunset' (Edwin C. Brown 1982). Evergreen. Scape 25 in. (63.5 cm); flower 6 in. (15.2 cm). Early. A peach-rose with a faint rose eyezone and rose veining. Diploid. Parents unknown. PATRICK STAMILE

'Rouge and Lace' (Matthew Kaskel 1997). Evergreen. Scape 28 in. (71.1 cm); flower 5.25 in. (13.3 cm). Early midseason. A ruffled cream flower with a rouge-red eyezone. Tetraploid. (seedling × 'Tet. Siloam Virginia Henson') × (seedling × (seedling × 'Wedding Band')). MATTHEW KASKEL

'Rouged Talisman' (R. W. Munson Jr. 1978). Evergreen. Scape 26 in. (66.0 cm); flower 5 in. (12.7 cm). Early midseason. A peach-rose with a warm burgundy-rose eye over a yellow-green throat. Tetraploid. 'Great Expectations' × 'Elizabeth Ann Hudson'. R. W. MUNSON JR

'Royal Braid' (Patrick Stamile 1993). Semi-evergreen. Scape 25 in. (63.5 cm); flower 5 in. (12.7 cm). Midseason. A cream-lavender with silver edge and royal purple braid and eye above a green throat. Very important breeder. Tetraploid. 'Cherry Berry' × 'Admiral's Braid'. PATRICK STAMILE

'Rune Mark' (Mort Morss 1992). Evergreen. Scape 24 in. (61.0 cm); flower 6 in. (15.2 cm). Early. A pale peach flower with a grape and lavender-veined eye. Tetraploid. 'Paper Butterfly' × 'Fantasy Finish'. DAVID KIRCHHOFF

'Russian Easter' (David Kirchhoff 1991). Evergreen. Scape 30 in. (76.2 cm); flower 6 in. (15.2 cm). Midseason. A large yellow flower with prominent mauve-rose eye. Tetraploid. 'Scarlock' × 'Charles Johnston'. JOHN EISEMAN

'Russian Rhapsody' (R. W. Munson Jr. 1973). Semi-evergreen. Scape 30 in. (76.2 cm); flower 6 in. (15.2 cm). Midseason. Violet-purple self with a dark eye and a yellow throat. Tetraploid. 'Knave' × 'Chicago Royal'. Award of Merit 1979. Lenington All-American Award 1989. R. W. MUNSON JR

'Sabina Bauer' (Jeff Salter 1998). Semi-evergreen. Scape 25 in. (63.5 cm); flower 6 in. (15.2 cm). Early midseason. A dramatic ivory-cream flower with a bold black-purple eye and matching bubbly edge. Tetraploid. 'Daring Deception' × 'Cindy's Eye'. TED L. PETIT & JOHN P. PEAT

'Scandinavian Sky' (Dan Trimmer 1996). Evergreen. Scape 26 in. (66.0 cm); flower 6.5 in. (16.5 cm). Early midseason. A recurved, large lavender with pale midribs and a darker eye above a green throat. Tetraploid. 'Arctic Snow' × 'Tet. Priscilla's Rainbow'. DAN TRIMMER

'Seductress' (Lee Gates 1979). Evergreen. Scape 18 in. (45.7 cm); flower 5.5 in. (14.0 cm). Early midseason. A burnt lavender flower edged in darker lavender with a matching eye. Tetraploid. Parents unknown. Award of Merit 1986. PATRICIA LOVELAND

'Shark's Tooth' (Mort Morss 1986). Semi-evergreen. Scape 26 in. (66.0 cm); flower 6 in. (15.2 cm). Early. A violet self with darker violet eye. Flowers sometimes show a white toothy edge. Tetraploid. ('Charles Hamil' × ('Knave' × 'Bold Baron')) × 'Chicago Knobby'. DAVID KIRCHHOFF

'Siloam Merle Kent' (Pauline Henry 1984). Dormant. Scape 22 in. (55.9 cm); flower 5.5 in. (14.0 cm). Midseason. A bright orchid with deep burgundy-purple eyezone and green throat. Diploid. Parents unknown. Award of Merit 1990. Annie T. Giles Award 1992. TED L. PETIT & JOHN P. PEAT

'So Excited' (Ra Hansen 1986). Evergreen. Scape 26 in. (66.0 cm); flower 5.5 in. (14.0 cm). Early midseason. A deep rose-pink, recurved flower with a very large, dark raspberry eyezone and lime throat. Diploid. Seedling × 'Ann Crochet'. Award of Merit 1993. RA HANSEN

'Someone Special' (Sarah Sikes 1985). Dormant. Scape 26 in. (66.0 cm); flower 5 in. (12.7 cm). Midseason. A full-formed, ruffled cream-pink with deeper rose halo and a green throat banded yellow. Diploid. 'Blue Happiness' × 'Ann Blocher'. JOHN EISEMAN

'Song Without Words' (David Kirchhoff 1991). Evergreen. scape 28 in. (71.1 cm); flower 6.25 in. (15.9 cm). Early midseason. A very large pastel rose-pink with an orchid-rose eyezone above a yellow throat. Tetraploid. ('Tet. Elysian Field' × 'Ring of Change') × 'Atlanta Cover Girl'. DAVID KIRCHHOFF

'Spanish Masquerade' (R. W. Munson Jr. 1981). Evergreen. Scape 22 in. (55.9 cm); flower 7 in. (17.8 cm). Early midseason. A cream-yellow with russet-plum eyezone and cream throat. Diploid. 'Shibui Splendor' × 'Sabie'. TED L. PETIT & JOHN P. PEAT

'Splendid Touch' (Patrick Stamile 1994). Evergreen. Scape 26 in. (66.0 cm); flower 5.75 in. (14.6 cm). Early midseason. A very round, strikingly pink flower with a small rose eyezone above a deep green throat. Very heavy substance. Tetraploid. 'Silken Touch' × Tet. Barbara Mitchell'. PATRICK STAMILE

'Stairway to Heaven' (Matthew Kaskel 1994). Evergreen. Scape 26 in. (66.0 cm); flower 5.5 in. (14.0 cm). Early midseason. A beautifully formed cream-yellow with a wine-red eyezone above a yellow-green throat. Tetraploid. (seedling × 'Sun's Magic') × 'Tet. Elsie Spalding'. MATTHEW KASKEL

'Strawberry Lace' (Jeff Salter 1998). Semi-evergreen. Scape 26 in. (66.0 cm); flower 5 in. (12.7 cm). Midseason. A pale ivory-cream with a bright rose eye and picotee below a gold edge. Throat small and yellow-green. Tetraploid. 'Daring Deception' × 'Wisest of Wizards'. TED L. PETIT & JOHN P. PEAT

'Swashbuckler Bay' (Jeff Salter 1998). Semi-evergreen. Scape 28 in. (71.1 cm); flower 5 in. (12.7 cm). Midseason. A bright salmon-coral with large, triangular, deep black eye and bold black edge. Very dramatic. Tetraploid. ('Tet. Burning Desire' × seedling) × 'Mask of Time'. TED L. PETIT & JOHN P. PEAT

'Texas Gal' (Ra Hansen 1988). Semi-evergreen. Scape 24 in. (61.0 cm); flower 5 in. (12.7 cm). Early midseason. A wide-petaled flesh-pink with a large rose band and a chartreuse throat. Diploid. ('Martha Adams' × 'So Excited') × 'Martha Adams'. RA HANSEN

'Tiger's Eye' (Jack Carpenter 1990). Dormant. Scape 22 in. (55.9 cm); flower 6.5 in. (16.5 cm). Midseason. A large burnt orange flower with a dramatic, triangular, dark maroon eyezone and yellow-green throat. Diploid. Parents unknown. PATRICK STAMILE

'Tivoli Nightingale' (Jean Duncan 1995). Evergreen. Scape 20 in. (50.8 cm); flower 5 in. (12.7 cm). Midseason. A lavender-purple with a darker purple eye and picotee surrounded by a gold edge. Tetraploid. 'Matthew Louis' × 'Marble Faun'. JEAN DUNCAN

'Tropical Heat Wave' (David Kirchhoff 1992). Evergreen. Scape 28 in. (71.1 cm); flower 5.25 in. (13.3 cm). Early. An orange with a red eyezone above a yellow throat. Tetraploid. 'Calistoga Sun' × 'Cherry Eyed Pumpkin'. TED L. PETIT & JOHN P. PEAT

'True Grit' (Patrick Stamile 1992). Dormant. Scape 21 in. (53.3 cm); flower 5 in. (12.7 cm). Midseason late. A cream-pink bloom with a small, dark wine eyezone above a green throat. Tetraploid. 'Papillon' × Tet. Siloam Virginia Henson'. PATRICK STAMILE

'Twenty Twenty' (Spalding-Guillory 1987). Evergreen. Scape 14 in. (35.6 cm); flower 6.5 in. (16.5 cm). Midseason. A light peach flower with a lavender-rose eye above a green throat. Diploid. Parents unknown. TED L. PETIT & JOHN P. PEAT

'Unconditional Love' (Dan Trimmer 1996). Dormant. Scape 26 in. (66.0 cm); flower 5.5 in. (14.0 cm). Early midseason. A wide-petaled, ruffled lavender with a wine halo and a green throat. Tetraploid. 'Always Afternoon' × 'Tet. Neal Berrey'. DAN TRIMMER

'Violet Explosion' (Patrick Stamile 1991). Dormant. Scape 25 in. (63.5 cm); flower 6.5 in. (16.5 cm). Early midseason. A large, ruffled cream-yellow with a deep violet-purple eye on both petals and sepals. Diploid. 'Salt Lake City' × 'Priscilla's Rainbow'. PATRICK STAMILE

'Way Over Yonder' (Matthew Kaskel 1996). Evergreen. Scape 28 in. (71.1 cm); flower 4.5 in. (11.4 cm). Early. A cream-yellow with a purple eyezone and a yellow to green throat. Tetraploid. Seedling × 'Etched Eyes'. MATTHEW KASKEL

'Well of Souls' (Jeff Salter 1988). Semi-evergreen. Scape 26 in. (66.0 cm); flower 6 in. (15.2 cm). Midseason. A cream-peach-pink and lavender blend with a burgundy-purple eye. Tetraploid. Parents unknown. TED L. PETIT & JOHN P. PEAT

'Wide Eyed Wanderer' (Ted L. Petit 1994). Evergreen. Scape 20 in. (50.8 cm); flower 6 in. (15.2 cm). Extra early. A ruffled tangerine-cream flower with rose-red eye over a green throat. Tetraploid. 'Betty Warren Woods' × 'Booger'. TED L. PETIT

'Wild Mustang' (Patrick Stamile 1995). Dormant. Scape 23 in. (58.4 cm); flower 5.5 in. (14.0 cm). Midseason late. A ruffled cream-pink with deep red eyezone and green throat. Tetraploid. 'Cherry Drop' × ('Wineberry Candy' × 'Tet. Priscilla's Rainbow'). BETH CREVELING

'Wineberry Candy' (Patrick Stamile 1990). Dormant. Scape 22 in. (55.9 cm); flower 4.75 in. (12.1 cm). Early midseason. A clear pink bloom with a red-purple eyezone and green throat. Tetraploid. 'Tet. Siloam Virginia Henson' × 'Paper Butterfly'. Award of Merit 1997.
PATRICK STAMILE

'Wings of Chance' (W. M. Spalding 1985). Evergreen. Scape 16 in. (40.6 cm); flower 5.5 in. (14.0 cm). Midseason. A deep yellow with wide rose-red band and green throat. Diploid. Parents unknown. Award of Merit 1993.
JOHN EISEMAN

'Wisest of Wizards' (Jeff Salter 1994). Semi-evergreen. Scape 26 in. (66.0 cm); flower 5.5 in. (14.0 cm). Early midseason. An ivory-peach with gold-rose edge and pale rose eyezone. Tetraploid. Parents unknown. TED L. PETIT & JOHN P. PEAT

'Without Warning' (John P. Peat 1998). Semi-evergreen. Scape 28 in. (71.1 cm); flower 5 in. (12.7 cm). Early. A peach-cream-orange with burgundy-rose eye and picotee. Opens very well following extremely cool nights. Tetraploid. ('Heddy Wine' × 'Ida's Magic') × 'Mardi Gras Ball'. JOHN P. PEAT

PATTERNS

'Alien Encounter' (Patrick Stamile 1997). Evergreen. Scape 27 in. (68.6 cm); flower 6 in. (15.2 cm). Early. A cream-lavender with multicolored, complex, layered eye accentuated by a deep green throat. Tetraploid. 'Witch Stitchery' × 'Rainbow Eyes'. PATRICK STAMILE

'Altered State' (Robert Carr 1997). Evergreen. Scape 28 in. (71.1 cm); flower 5.5 in. (14.0 cm). Early midseason. Cherry-red with a darker red eyezone patterned cherry red and a pink-red, patterned border. Tetraploid. 'Whooperee' × 'Purely Exotic'. TED L. PETIT & JOHN P. PEAT

'Avante Garde' (Steve Moldovan 1986). Dormant. Scape 26 in. (66.0 cm); flower 5.5 in. (14.0 cm). Early midseason. An orange-amber bitone with a patterned, lighter edge, a red-orange eye, and a yellow-green throat. Tetraploid. 'House of Lords' × 'Pirates Cove'. STEVE MOLDOVAN

'Bertie' (Elizabeth H. Salter 1998). Semi-evergreen. Scape 26 in. (66.0 cm); flower 3 in. (7.6 cm). Early midseason. A pale lemon-cream with a green throat. Eye is a wash of pale violet-blue etched with a darker edge. Tetraploid. 'Tet. Little Print' × 'Witches Wink'. TED L. PETIT & JOHN P. PEAT

'Blue Moon Rising' (Elizabeth H. Salter 1991). Semi-evergreen. Scape 24 in. (61.0 cm); flower 3 in. (7.6 cm). Midseason. A pale ivory-peach with blue-violet eyezone surround by a thin rose-burgundy mascara band. Diploid. Parents unknown. JOHN EISEMAN

'Borgia Queen' (R. W. Munson Jr. 1986). Evergreen. Scape 26 in. (66.0 cm); flower 5 in. (12.7 cm). Midseason late. A silver-lavender-mauve with a chalky slate-blueish eye surrounded by a thinner burgundy band. Tetraploid. (('Astarte' × ('Chicago Regal' × 'Knave')) × (('Silver Veil' × 'Mountain Violet') × 'Changeable Silk')) × ('Tet. Catherine Woodbery' × 'Waterbird'). PATRICK STAMILE

'Child of Fortune' (Elizabeth H. Salter 1987). Evergreen. Scape 15 in. (38.1 cm); flower 3 in. (7.6 cm). Midseason. A pale pink with chalky lavender and washed violet eyezone surrounded by a darker band of burgundy. Diploid. (seedling × ('Garden Elf' × 'Little Grappette')F2) × seedling. PATRICK STAMILE

'Chinese Cloisonne' (R. W. Munson Jr. 1974). Evergreen. Scape 24 in. (61.0 cm); flower 5 in. (12.7 cm). Midseason. A classic peach-mauve with mauve-violet-veined eye surrounded by a burgundy-violet band. Tetraploid. 'Chittagong' × 'Devils Magic'. PATRICK STAMILE

'Chinese Temple Flower' (Ida Munson 1980). Evergreen. Scape 24 in. (61.0 cm); flower 5 in. (12.7 cm). Early midseason. A lilac-lavender with an iridescent throat surrounded by a deep purple eyezone. Tetraploid. Parents unknown. R. W. MUNSON JR

'Crintonic Shadowlands' (Curt Hanson 1995). Evergreen. Scape 34 in. (86.4 cm); flower 5.5 in. (14.0 cm). Early midseason. An orchid-rose with a bluish halo above an iridescent center and a green throat. Tetraploid. Seedling × ('Benchmark' × 'Elegant One'). CURT HANSON

'Damascene' (R. W. Munson Jr. 1974). Semi-evergreen. Scape 32 in. (81.3 cm); flower 5 in. (12.7 cm). Midseason. A pale lavender-mauve with light violet, complex eye over a green throat. Tetraploid. Seedling × 'Mountain Violet'. Honorable Mention 1977. R. W. MUNSON JR

'Devil's Footprint' (Elizabeth H. Salter 1992). Semi-evergreen. Scape 18 in. (45.7 cm); flower 3.25 in. (8.3 cm). Early midseason. A cream-yellow with a multiple-banded burgundy-purple to charcoal-gray eyezone layered above green throat. Diploid. 'Alpine Mist' × 'Highland Mystic'. JOHN EISEMAN

'Elfin Etching' (Elizabeth H. Salter 1992). Semi-evergreen. Scape 20 in. (50.8 cm); flower 3 in. (7.6 cm). Midseason late. An ivory-cream with a complex-veined, soft lavender-violet eyezone above a green throat. Diploid. 'Enchanter's Spell' × 'Janice Brown'. JOHN EISEMAN

'Dragon Dreams' (Elizabeth H. Salter 1991). Semi-evergreen. Scape 25 in. (63.5 cm); flower 3 in. (7.6 cm). Midseason late. Lavender with a washed light violet-blue eyezone above a yellow-green throat. Diploid. 'Enchanter's Spell' × 'Janice Brown'. PATRICIA LOVELAND

'Enchanter's Spell' (Elizabeth H. Hudson 1982). Semi-evergreen. Scape 18 in. (45.7 cm); flower 3 in. (7.6 cm). Midseason. An ivory self with a dark burgundy-purple washed eye bleeding into the petals and sepals. Throat lime-green. Diploid. Parents unknown. Award of Merit 1992. Annie T. Giles Award 1991.
JOHN EISEMAN

'Elfin Illusion' (Elizabeth H. Salter 1995). Semi-evergreen. Scape 22 in. (55.9 cm); flower 3.5 in. (8.9 cm). Midseason. A dark purple kaleido-scope flower with washed lavender eyezone, lighter petal edges, and patterned sepals. Diploid. Parents unknown. TED L. PETIT & JOHN P. PEAT

'Enchanted Rainbow' (Patrick Stamile 1997). Evergreen. Scape 28 in. (71.1 cm); flower 6 in. (15.2 cm). Early midseason. A cream-yellow flower with multiple purple to slate bands surrounding a green throat. Tetraploid. 'Peach Candy' × 'Awakening Dream'. PATRICK STAMILE

'Exotic Echo' (Van Sellers 1984). Dormant. Scape 16 in. (40.6 cm); flower 3 in. (7.6 cm). Midseason. A cream-pink blend with a washed burgundy to charcoal eye and green throat. Sometimes double. Diploid. Parents unknown. Award of Merit 1994. Annie T. Giles Award 1993. TED L. PETIT & JOHN P. PEAT

'Expanding Universe' (Ted L. Petit 1998). Semi-evergreen. Scape 26 in. (66.0 cm); flower 5.5 in. (14.0 cm). Midseason. A bright cream flower with cinnamon stippling and darker stippled eye above a green throat. Tetraploid. ('Midnight Magic' × 'Shinto Etching') × ('Ida's Magic' × 'Wrapped in Gold'). TED L. PETIT

'Faces of a Clown' (Jeff Salter 1998). Semi-evergreen. Scape 26 in. (66.0 cm); flower 6 in. (15.2 cm). Early midseason. A bright gold-yellow with a washed magenta, violet-patterned eye surrounding a green throat. Tetraploid. 'Sacred Drummer' × 'Winter Masquerade'. TED L. PETIT & JOHN P. PEAT

'Fairy Firecracker' (Elizabeth H. Hudson 1984). Evergreen. Scape 15 in. (38.1 cm); flower 2.75 in. (7.0 cm). Midseason. A red-orange self with lighter petal edges and lighter eye surrounded by a darker band. Diploid. Parents unknown. PATRICK STAMILE

'Hiding the Blues' (Ted L. Petit 1998). Semi-evergreen. Scape 20 in. (50.8 cm); flower 5 in. (12.7 cm). Midseason. A cream-peach with a green throat and an eye patterned in silver-slate and lavender. Tetraploid. ('Wedding Band' × 'Paper Butterfly') × ('Heady Wine' × 'Ida's Magic'). TED L. PETIT

'Highland Mystic' (Elizabeth H. Salter 1988). Semi-evergreen. Scape 18 in. (45.7 cm); flower 3 in. (7.6 cm). Early midseason. A pale lavender with a washed lavender eyezone edged rose-purple above a lime-green throat. Diploid. 'Enchanter's Spell' × seedling. JOHN EISEMAN

'Inner View' (Mort Morss 1982). Evergreen. Scape 26 in. (66.0 cm); flower 6.5 in. (16.5 cm). Extra early. A lavender-cream triangular flower with an iridescent throat edged in darker lavender. Tetraploid. 'Silver Veil' × 'Zinfandel'. PATRICK STAMILE

'Jason Salter' (Elizabeth H. Salter 1987). Evergreen. Scape 18 in. (45.7 cm); flower 2.75 in. (7.0 cm). Early midseason. A deep yellow with washed lavender-purple eye edged in deep purple. Diploid. 'Enchanter's Spell' × ('Enchanted Elf' × 'Cosmic Hummingbird'). Award of Merit 1995. Donald Fischer Memorial Cup 1993. Don C. Stevens Award 1994. PATRICK STAMILE

'Kabuki Plus' (Mort Morss 1996). Evergreen. Scape 28 in. (71.1 cm); flower 5.5 in. (14.0 cm). Early. An ivory-flesh with veined lavender eye edged red-violet above an olive-green throat. Tetraploid. Seedling × 'Lonesome Dove'. DAVID KIRCHHOFF

'Little Print' (Elizabeth H. Salter 1992). Semi-evergreen. Scape 16 in. (40.6 cm); flower 2.75 in. (7.0 cm). Midseason. A light ivory-cream with a strongly washed eye of violet-magenta edged in a deeper magenta. Diploid. 'Lady Jinx' × 'Enchanter's Spell'. TED L. PETIT & JOHN P. PEAT

'Little Witching Hour' (Elizabeth H. Salter 1988). Semi-evergreen. Scape 18 in. (45.7 cm); flower 3.25 in. (8.3 cm). Midseason. A rose-lavender with a washed light lavender-rose eyezone edged dark purple above a green throat. Diploid. 'Enchanter's Spell' × seedling. JOHN EISEMAN

'Magnificent Rainbow' (Patrick Stamile 1995). Dormant. Scape 17 in. (43.2 cm); flower 6 in. (15.2 cm). Late. A lavender bicolor with a gray-blue eye with charcoal bands edged in burgundy. Tetraploid. 'Always Afternoon' × 'Tet. Priscilla's Rainbow'. PATRICK STAMILE

'Morrie Otte' (Elizabeth H. Salter 1996). Semi-evergreen. Scape 18 in. (45.7 cm); flower 2.75 in. (7.0 cm). Midseason. A mauve-lavender with a silver-frost washed eye on petals and sepals over a large green throat. Diploid. Parents unknown. TED L. PETIT & JOHN P. PEAT

'Mystical Rainbow' (Patrick Stamile 1996). Dormant. Scape 25 in. (63.5 cm); flower 5.5 in. (14.0 cm). Early midseason. A clear pink with multiple-banded rose-raspberry, charcoal, and yellow eyezone above a green throat. Tetraploid. 'Exotic Candy' × 'Rainbow Eyes'. PATRICK STAMILE

'Navy Blues' (Elizabeth H. Salter 1993). Evergreen. Scape 16 in. (40.6 cm); flower 2.5 in. (6.4 cm). Early midseason. A light lavender with an etched eye of navy blue above a green throat. Diploid. ((seedling × 'Enchanter's Spell') × 'Janice Brown') × 'Morrie Otte'. TED L. PETIT & JOHN P. PEAT

'Paper Butterfly' (Mort Morss 1983). Semi-ever-green. Scape 24 in. (61.0 cm); flower 6 in. (15.2 cm). Early. A cream-peach-pink with a rose-violet blended and veined eye bleeding into the petals. Tetraploid. ((((seedling × 'Chicago Two Bits') × 'Thais') × ('Silver Veil' × ('Knave' × 'Chicago Mist'))) × 'Chicago Mist'. Award of Merit 1990. Don C. Stevens Award 1987.
JAY TOMPKINS

'Patchwork Puzzle' (Elizabeth H. Salter 1990). Dormancy unknown. Scape 18 in. (45.7 cm); flower 2.75 in. (7.0 cm). Early midseason. A cream-lemon with a washed lavender-purple eyezone banded in burgundy above a deep green throat. Tetraploid. Parents unknown. Donald Fischer Memorial Cup 1995.
JOHN EISEMAN

'Pharaoh's Treasure' (R. W. Munson Jr. 1988). Evergreen. Scape 24 in. (61.0 cm); flower 5 in. (12.7 cm). Early midseason. A grape-purple with an iridescent yellow halo over a lime-green throat. Tetraploid. 'Doge of Venice' × ('Archduke' × ('Violet Jade' × 'Silver Veil')).
PATRICK STAMILE

'Priscilla's Rainbow' (Spalding-Guillory 1985). Evergreen. Scape 22 in. (55.9 cm); flower 6.25 in. (15.9 cm). Midseason. A pink-lavender with rainbow halo edged in burgundy-rose above a green throat. Diploid. Parents unknown. Award of Merit 1991. JOHN EISEMAN

'Rainbow Candy' (Patrick Stamile 1996). Dormant. Scape 28 in. (71.1 cm); flower 4.25 in. (10.8 cm). Early midseason. An ivory-cream with deep, veined, purple-lavender-gray eyezone edged purple above a green throat. Tetraploid. 'Blueberry Candy' × 'Tet. Little Print'.
PATRICK STAMILE

'Rainbow Eyes' (Patrick Stamile 1994). Dormant. Scape 21 in. (53.3 cm); flower 6.75 in. (17.2 cm). Early. A cream-orchid-pink with a veined, layered charcoal, gray, and lavender eyezone. Tetraploid. 'Always Afternoon' × 'Tet. Priscilla's Rainbow'. PATRICK STAMILE

'Sacred Drummer' (Jeff Salter 1996). Evergreen. Scape 29 in. (73.7 cm); flower 6 in. (15.2 cm). Midseason. A pale pink with a blue-violet eyezone and green throat. Tetraploid. Parents unknown. TED L. PETIT & JOHN P. PEAT

'Silent Sentry' (Jeff Salter 1992). Semi-evergreen. Scape 24 in. (61.0 cm); flower 5.5 in. (14.0 cm). Early midseason. A purple self with a lighter eye and an iridescent throat above a green heart. Tetraploid. Parents unknown. MELANIE MASON

'Siloam David Kirchhoff' (Pauline Henry 1986). Dormant. Scape 16 in. (40.6 cm); flower 3.5 in. (8.9 cm). Early midseason. An orchid-pink with a cerise pencil-lined and washed eyezone and a green throat. Diploid. Parents unknown. Award of Merit 1993. Annie T. Giles Award 1995. Don C. Stevens Award 1996. TED L. PETIT & JOHN P. PEAT

'Sings the Blues' (Ra Hansen 1990). Semi-evergreen. Scape 26 in. (66.0 cm); flower 6 in. (15.2 cm). Midseason late. A medium lavender-rose with a variegated violet-blue and charcoal eyezone and an emerald throat. Diploid. 'Surf' × 'Ruffled Ivory'. RA HANSEN

'Spell Fire' (Elizabeth H. Salter 1988). Semi-evergreen. Scape 20 in. (50.8 cm); flower 3.5 in. (8.9 cm). Midseason. A cream-yellow with bleeding, bright red eyezone and small green throat. Diploid. ('Pyewacket' × 'Elf Witch') × 'Burning Desire'. PATRICK STAMILE

'Strange Eyes' (Jack Carpenter 1992). Evergreen. Scape 26 in. (66.0 cm); flower 5.5 in. (14.0 cm). Midseason. Yellow with a banded, gray and red eyezone above a green throat. Diploid. Parents unknown. TED L. PETIT & JOHN P. PEAT

'Teller of Tales' (Elizabeth H. Salter 1996). Evergreen. Scape 22 in. (55.9 cm); flower 3.5 in. (8.9 cm). Midseason late. Rose-pink with a dusty rose eyezone and green throat. Diploid. Parents unknown. JOHN EISEMAN

'True Blue Heart' (Elizabeth H. Salter 1993). Semi-evergreen. Scape 18 in. (45.7 cm); flower 3.75 in. (9.5 cm). Early midseason. A pale ivory-rose with blue-washed-violet eye edged in burgundy-red above a green throat. Diploid. Parents unknown. JOHN EISEMAN

'Winds of Tide' (Ra Hansen 1992). Semi-evergreen. Scape 24 in. (61.0 cm); flower 4.75 in. (12.1 cm). Midseason late. A peach-pink with dark rose veins and bands surrounding a dark gray lavender-blue eyezone. Diploid. ('Whistling Dixie' × 'Surf') × ('Adam's Rib' × 'Surf'). RA HANSEN

'Witch Stitchery' (Mort Morss 1986). Semi-evergreen. Scape 26 in. (66.0 cm); flower 5.5 in. (14.0 cm). Extra early. A cream-yellow self with a veined lavender eyezone edged purple and bleeding out into the petal. Tetraploid. (seedling × 'Chicago Two Bits') × Paper Butterfly'. Award of Merit 1997. JOHN EISEMAN

 **CHAPTER SIX**
Doubles

Double daylilies are a passion for many gardeners and hybridizers. The extra petals and petaloids add a greater sense of fullness and depth to the flower, creating a beauty that has captured the imagination and hearts of flower lovers and breeders. Like double flowers of other genera, such large, full flower form adds a new dimension and gives a completely new look to the flower.

History of Doubles

Double daylilies are by no means a new flower form. Plants of the *Hemerocallis* species found growing wild in China included *H. fulva* var. *kwanso* and *H. fulva* 'Flore Pleno', both doubles. Unfortunately, these flowers are triploids, which are sterile, and could not be used in creating modern hybrids.

The hybrid double daylily was created from single daylilies that sometimes had double tissue. These doubles, often only semi-double, began as narrow-petaled flowers without ruffling. As hybridizers worked on improving the doubles, the new flowers emerged with wider petals and ruffles, giving them a more finished look. Through generation after generation of double breeding, the blooms became more consistently and fully double. During the 1980s and 1990s double tetraploid daylilies emerged, with heavier substance and clearer, brighter colors. Like tetraploid singles, initially there were no tetraploid doubles with which to work, which made the first efforts to produce tetraploid doubles arduous and slow. The pioneering efforts of hybridizers such as David Kirchhoff, Betty Hudson, and Ted Petit slowly created breeding lines. At the time of this writing, less than 100 double tetraploid daylilies are in commerce. Currently, hybridizers are interested in bringing some features of the modern single flower into the double lines, such as gold edging and heavily crimped ruffling. They have also attempted to produce double daylilies in all colors, as well as flowers with eyes, watermarks, and contrasting edges.

Form of Doubles

To simply appreciate the exquisite beauty of double flowers it is not necessary to know the intricacies of their form. However, an even greater appreciation of double daylilies will result from understanding the way they are made. The double daylily is somewhat complex and ever changing and is worth a few extra minutes spent to study its nature.

An attempt at understanding and classifying double daylily forms is not new, and different individuals use different terms to describe daylily types. In 1945 in *Herbertia*, A. B. Stout published a description of the forms of doubling he observed along with suggested names for those forms. Some of his terms are still used more than 50 years later, however, no standard method of classifying doubles has yet been agreed upon. The following paragraphs employ the most common terms in use among daylily hybridizers and enthusiasts.

Double daylilies are derived from single daylilies. The normal single daylily has three sepals, three petals, and six stamens (see the figure below). The daylily is made of four whorls or layers: (1) the sepals, (2) petals, (3) stamens, and (4) the pistil. The ideal way to form a double flower would be to add extra layers to the whorl of petals, creating multiple layers of petals. However, most double daylilies are formed by modifying the stamens.

Most double daylilies are created through the formation of petaloids. Though they look like extra petals, petaloids are stamens with extra tissue along their sides. Some flowers add tissue to only one side of the stamen—these petaloids are easy to recognize as modified stamens. Other flowers add tissue to both sides of the stamen—these resemble true petals, although the anther, or pollen sac, can generally be found on the petaloid. Sometimes, the anther becomes rudimentary or even non-existent, so that the petaloid looks like a perfectly normal petal. Since petaloids are formed from the stamen tissue and daylilies have only six stamens, six is the maximum number of petaloids that a daylily can have. If it has less than six petaloids, the remaining stamens will be normal, and the flower will appear semi-double. Double flowers of most other genera contain extra layers of true petals, not simply modified stamens, and typically contain many more than six extra petals. Daylilies, therefore, are quite different from other double flowers.

Some double daylily flowers add tissue at the midrib of the petaloid. This midrib tissue usually projects upward and outward from the center of the petaloid, resembling the wings of a butterfly. The form of midrib tissue can vary. Some petaloids contain only a single wing, many petaloids have two wings, and occasionally each individual wing can appear as two parallel layers of tissue. Midrib tissue gives the appearance of even more petals, giving the flower added fullness, particularly as this tissue becomes large and ruffled.

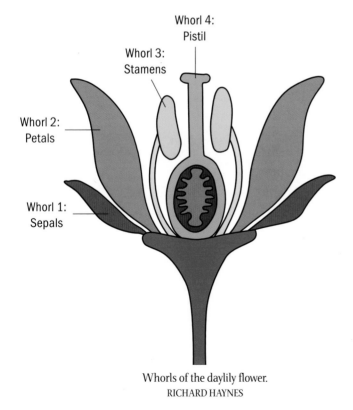

Whorl 4:
Pistil

Whorl 3:
Stamens

Whorl 2:
Petals

Whorl 1:
Sepals

Whorls of the daylily flower.
RICHARD HAYNES

Some "apparently single" daylilies, which contain only three true petals, also have extra tissue rising up from the midrib of the petals, similar to the extra tissue on petaloids. This formation has caused some disagreement as to whether these flowers should be classified as singles or doubles—currently they are referred to as "midrib doubles." Some people insist that these flowers are single since they have only three true petals. Others argue that if doubles can be produced by forming petaloid tissue from stamens, they can also be produced by forming petaloid tissue from petals. Midrib doubles, then, are flowers with only three true petals, with extra tissue generated from, or fused to, the midrib of those three true petals. This tissue is typically formed from the middle of the petal at 45- to 90-degree angles, resembling the two wings of a butterfly. The fact that midrib tissue can form on either the three regular petals of an otherwise single flower or on the midrib of petaloids indicates that this is an inherited characteristic in daylilies potentially separate and distinct from the production of extra petals or stamen-derived petaloids.

All of this is very different, however, from adding extra true petals. Flowers with extra true petals, called supernumerary doubles, or sometimes "super-doubles," are rare in daylilies. Supernumerary doubles stack on additional layers of petals and retain their normal stamens. They typically have nine petals, six extra, along with all six stamens. Since these doubles have their stamens intact, they have the potential to turn their stamens into petaloids. Such flowers would then have nine petals plus six petaloids, for a magnificent total of 15 colored segments.

Unlike petaloids, which are limited to six, the possible number of extra true petals seems to be unlimited. Theoretically, many layers of petals could be stacked, one on top of the other, to produce a double daylily with the number of petals of a rose or camellia. The sterile *Hemerocallis fulva* var. *kwanso* and *H. fulva* 'Flore Pleno' are supernumerary daylilies with many columns of true petals. Although most daylily enthusiasts feel that these species plants lack much of the beauty of modern hybrids, they do have a form as yet unachieved among modern daylilies. However, after many decades of work, hybridizers are beginning to produce supernumerary double daylilies, leading the way in an area for further daylily breeding.

Double daylilies can also be categorized according to the form of the extra petals or petaloids. The two primary groups are the hose-in-hose types and the peony types. Hose-in-hose are flowers in which the petals or petaloids lie flat in layers, resembling the look of extra true petals, as in the photograph of 'Blueberry Puff'. This gives the flower an appearance similar to a camellia or fully opened rose. Any petaloids are usually full, not half petaloids, and there is usually no midrib tissue.

In other doubles, the petaloids stick up in the center of the flower, pointing outward like stamens. This form is referred to as peony or cockatoo, as in the photograph of 'Double Amethyst'. The petaloids can be either half or full and may or may not have midrib tissue.

Flower petaloids. TED L. PETIT & JOHN P. PEAT

A hose-in-hose double. 'Blueberry Puff' (Jan Joiner 1997). Semi-evergreen. Scape 32 in. (81.3 cm); flower 6 in. (15.2 cm). Midseason. Mauve-orchid self with a green throat. Diploid. 'Jean Swann' × 'Peggy Bass'. TED L. PETIT & JOHN P. PEAT

Do not think too rigidly about double daylily forms. The double form of a day-lily can vary from day to day within an individual cultivar or even on a single plant, and new double forms are continuously emerging. Further, many cultivars that produce double flowers also produce single flowers, particularly early in the season. The degree of doubling appears to be temperature dependent—many of these cultivars produce single flowers in cool weather but bear more frequently double flowers as the weather warms.

A peony double. 'Double Amethyst' (David Kirchhoff 1994). Evergreen. Scape 30 in. (76.2 cm); flower 5.5 in. (14.0 cm). Early midseason. Rose-violet with a deeper watermark above a yellow to green throat. Tetraploid. (seedling × 'Tet. Enchanting Lady') × ('Tet. Cosmic Treasure' × 'Nagasaki'). PATRICK STAMILE

'Almond Puff' (Patrick Stamile 1990). Dormant. Scape 23 in. (58.4 cm); flower 6.5 in. (16.5 cm). Midseason. Beige-pink ruffled petals with a green throat. Diploid. 'Salt Lake City' × 'Barbara Mitchell'. Ida Munson Award 1997. PATRICK STAMILE

'Ambrosian Rhapsody' (Ted L. Petit 1994). Evergreen. Scape 24 in. (61.0 cm); flower 5.75 in. (14.6 cm). Midseason. Large, showy, warm pink with cream-pink watermark and green throat. Tetraploid. ('Wayne Johnson' × ('Ida's Magic' × 'Queen's Cape')) × seedling. TED L. PETIT

'Anasazi' (Patrick Stamile 1997). Evergreen. Scape 25 in. (63.5 cm); flower 6 in. (15.2 cm). Early midseason. Very deep, clear pink self with a green throat. Full modern-formed double. Tetraploid. (seedling × 'Poetic Voice') × 'Shimmering Elegance'. PATRICK STAMILE

'Artisan's Quilt' (Betty Hudson 1992). Semi-evergreen. Scape 30 in. (76.2 cm); flower 5 in. (12.7 cm). Early midseason. A rose-lavender self with lighter cream eyezone above yellow-green throat. Distinctive and unique. Tetraploid. 'Pastel Morning' × (('Royal Heritage' × 'Spring Intermezzo') × 'Asian Emperor'). BETTY HUDSON

'Bed of Clouds' (David Kirchhoff 1987). Evergreen. Scape 20 in. (50.8 cm); flower 5 in. (12.7 cm). Extra early. Pastel ivory, orchid, and pink polychrome with emerald-green throat. Diploid. 'Nathan Carroll' × 'Nagasaki'. JOHN EISEMAN

'Big Kiss' (Enman R. Joiner 1991). Dormant. Scape 28 in. (71.1 cm); flower 5.5 in. (14.0 cm). Midseason. Light peach-pink with a darker rose eyezone above a light green throat. Diploid. 'Dublin Elaine' × 'Frances Joiner'). TED L. PETIT & JOHN P. PEAT

'Bogie and Becall' (Ra Hansen 1992). Semi-evergreen. Scape 21 in. (53.3 cm); flower 5 in. (12.7 cm). Early midseason. Wide-petaled, medium pink with a cherry-red eyezone above a green throat. Diploid. Parents unknown. RA HANSEN

'Bombshell' (Enman R. Joiner 1993). Dormant. Scape 20 in. (50.8 cm); flower 6 in. (15.2 cm). Midseason late. Hose-in-hose, maize-yellow self with a pink blush over a light green throat. Diploid. 'Vanilla Fluff' × seedling. TED L. PETIT & JOHN P. PEAT

'Brent Gabriel' (Lucille Guidry 1981). Evergreen. Scape 20 in. (50.8 cm); flower 5.5 in. (14.0 cm). Extra early. Dramatic dark purple double with a green throat. Diploid. Parents unknown. Ida Munson Award 1992. JOHN EISEMAN

'Both Sides Now' (David Kirchhoff 1985). Evergreen. Scape 28 in. (71.1 cm); flower 5.75 in. (14.6 cm). Early midseason. Triangular, pastel peach-pink to coral with a large distinctive rosy red eyezone. Diploid. ('Siloam Double Rose' × 'Louise Mercer') × ('Double Love' × 'Nagasaki'). PATRICK STAMILE

'Bubbly' (Jan Joiner 1989). Semi-evergreen. Scape 20 in. (50.8 cm); flower 3 in. (7.6 cm). Midseason. Tailored cream to apricot self with green throat. Consistently double, small flowers. Diploid. 'Champagne Bubbles' × 'Fairies Pinafore'. TED L. PETIT & JOHN P. PEAT

'Cabbage Flower' (David Kirchhoff 1984). Evergreen. Scape 17 in. (43.2 cm); flower 4.5 in. (11.4 cm). Extra early. Pastel lemon-yellow double with a green throat. Very popular. Diploid. 'Twin Crown' × 'Nagasaki'. Ida Munson Award 1990. DAVID KIRCHHOFF

'Calypso Sunset' (Ted L. Petit 1994). Evergreen. Scape 29 in. (73.7 cm); flower 5.75 in. (14.6 cm). Midseason. A lavender to rose polychrome double with a lighter eyezone and a green throat. Tetraploid. 'Time Lord' × (('Royal Heritage' × 'Spring Intermezzo') × ('Asian Emperor × 'Pastel Morning')). TED L. PETIT

'Caribbean Reggae Moon' (Dave Talbott 1994). Evergreen. Scape 24 in. (61.0 cm); flower 6 in. (15.2 cm). Early midseason. A recurved tangerine double with a small red eye. Diploid. (seedling × 'Siloam Double Rose') × ('Rachael My Love' × seedling). JOHN EISEMAN

'Chinese Scholar' (Jeff Salter 1990). Semi-evergreen. Scape 22 in. (55.9 cm); flower 5 in. (12.7 cm). Midseason late. A bright red, consistently double flower. Tetraploid. Parents unknown. PATRICK STAMILE

'Clever Conversations' (John P. Peat 1998). Semi-evergreen. Scape 23 in. (58.4 cm); flower 5.5 in. (14.0 cm). Midseason. A clear yellow flower with a rose to burgundy eye. Tetraploid. 'Mango Coral' × 'Layers of Gold'. TED L. PETIT & JOHN P. PEAT

'Clovette Adams' (David Kirchhoff 1993). Evergreen. Scape 22 in. (55.9 cm); flower 6 in. (15.2 cm). Early. A salmon-red-orange self with a gold edge and a gold to green throat. Tetraploid. 'Layers of Gold' × ((seedling × 'Tet. Elysian Field') × 'Chestnut Mountain'). DAVID KIRCHHOFF

'Clouds Illusions' (Ted L. Petit 1998). Semi-evergreen. Scape 21 in. (53.3 cm); flower 5.5 in. (14.0 cm). Early. A peach- to orange-sherbet-cream and apricot blend, consistently double pompon flowers. Tetraploid. ('Wayne Johnson' × 'Mango Coral') × 'Rosetta Stone'. TED L. PETIT

'Codyted' (David Kirchhoff 1991). Evergreen. Scape 24 in. (61.0 cm); flower 3.5 in. (8.9 cm). Early. A peach flower edged gold with a rose-orange halo above a green throat. Diploid. 'Cotton Club' × 'Siloam Double Classic'. DAVID KIRCHHOFF

'Condilla' (Albert Grooms 1977). Dormant. Scape 20 in. (50.8 cm); flower 4.5 in. (11.4 cm). Early midseason. A classic, popular double of a deep gold color. Diploid. 'Whirling Skirt' × 'Chum'. Award of Merit 1985. Lenington All-American Award 1991. Ida Munson Award 1984. TED L. PETIT & JOHN P. PEAT

'Congo Coral' (David Kirchhoff 1990). Semi-evergreen. Scape 18 in. (45.7 cm); flower 4.75 in. (12.1 cm). Early midseason. A salmon-pink to coral self with a darker red eyezone and a yellow-green throat. Diploid. ('Nagasaki' × 'Arpeggio') × 'Siloam Double Rose'. PATRICK STAMILE

'Cotton Club' (David Kirchhoff 1985). Ever-green. Scape 20 in. (50.8 cm); flower 5 in. (12.7 cm). Early midseason. A popular, classic butter-cream self with a pink blush. Diploid. 'Double Pink Treasure' × 'Betty Woods'. PATRICK STAMILE

'Denali' (Patrick Stamile 1997). Evergreen. Scape 23 in. (58.4 cm); flower 8 in. (20.3 cm). Midseason late. A huge, pink, ruffled double with a green throat. Tetraploid. 'Victoria's Secret' × 'Big Blue'. PATRICK STAMILE

'Double Bold One' (John Miller 1981). Dormant. Scape 32 in. (81.3 cm); flower 6 in. (15.2 cm). Early midseason. An older style gold double with a burgundy-red eye. Diploid. 'Bold One' × 'Double Decker'. CURTIS & LINDA SUE BARNES

'Double Cranberry Ruffles' (Dave Talbott 1991). Semi-evergreen. Scape 19 in. (48.3 cm); flower 5 in. (12.7 cm). Midseason late. A bright cran-berry-red double. Diploid. 'Stroke of Midnight' × 'Siloam Double Rose'. JOHN EISEMAN

'Double Cutie' (Betty Brown 1972). Evergreen. Scape 13 in. (33.0 cm); flower 4 in. (10.2 cm). Early midseason. A cream-yellow, small-flow-ered double with a green throat. Diploid. (seedling × 'Roly Poly') × (((seedling × 'Double Chal-lenge') × (seedling × 'Double Eagle')) × 'Double Decker'). Award of Merit 1977. Ida Munson Award 1975. TED L. PETIT & JOHN P. PEAT

'Double Dandelion' (Betty Hudson 1985). Evergreen. Scape 28 in. (71.1 cm); flower 5.75 in. (14.6 cm). Early midseason. A pale dandelion-yellow self with a green throat. Tetraploid. ('Chateau Blanc' × 'Cream Brulee') × (seedling × 'Evening Bell'). BETTY HUDSON

'Doubly Delicious' (Jeff Salter 1998). Evergreen. Scape 28 in. (71.1 cm); flower 6.5 in. (16.5 cm). Early midseason. A very large, coral-pink, blended double with a darker halo eye. Tetraploid. 'John Kinnebrew' × seedling. TED L. PETIT & JOHN P. PEAT

'Fires of Fuji' (Betty Hudson 1990). Semi-evergreen. Scape 28 in. (71.1 cm); flower 5 in. (12.7 cm). Midseason. A red double with petals edged in orange to tan. Unusual and distinctive. Tetraploid. ('Palace Guard' × 'Troika') × 'Palace Guard'. BETTY HUDSON

'Forty Second Street' (David Kirchhoff 1991). Evergreen. Scape 24 in. (61.0 cm); flower 5 in. (12.7 cm). Midseason. A pastel pink with a bright rose eyezone above a yellow to green throat. Diploid. Parents unknown. DAVID KIRCHHOFF

'Frances Joiner' (Enman R. Joiner 1988). Dormant. Scape 24 in. (61.0 cm); flower 5.5 in. (14.0 cm). Midseason. Among the most popular doubles. A soft pink to rose blend. Diploid. Parents unknown. Award of Merit 1995. Ida Munson Award 1993. TED L. PETIT & JOHN P. PEAT

'Frills and Fancies' (Jan Joiner 1996). Evergreen. Scape 28 in. (71.1 cm); flower 5 in. (12.7 cm). Midseason. A very full double in a burnt orange blend. Diploid. Parents unknown. TED L. PETIT & JOHN P. PEAT

'Gladys Campbell' (Ted L. Petit 1994). Semi-evergreen. Scape 22 in. (55.9 cm); flower 6 in. (15.2 cm). Midseason. A hot coral-pink single with a lighter eyezone early in the season, softening to a warm pink double as the season progresses. Tetraploid. ('French Pavilion' × 'Canton Harbor') × 'Shishedo'. TED L. PETIT

'Gourmet Bouquet' (David Kirchhoff 1984). Evergreen. Scape 22 in. (55.9 cm); flower 4.75 in. (12.07 cm). Early. A medium red self with petals edged in a wire buff and a slightly darker red eye. Diploid. 'Cosmic Treasure' × 'Mozambique'. PATRICK STAMILE

'Grecian Sands' (Betty Hudson 1992). Evergreen. Scape 34 in. (86.4 cm); flower 6 in. (15.2 cm). Early midseason. A cream-yellow with a lavender to pink wash and a yellow watermark. Tetraploid. Parents unknown.
BETTY HUDSON

'Hampton Hocus Pocus' (Dan Trimmer 1994). Evergreen. Scape 26 in. (66.0 cm); flower 3.5 in. (8.9 cm). Early midseason. A cream double with a large, dramatic black-purple eye. Diploid. 'Roswitha' × seedling. DAN TRIMMER

'Hampton Magic' (Dan Trimmer 1993). Semi-evergreen. Scape 26 in. (66.0 cm); flower 5 in. (12.7 cm). Early midseason. A peachy pink-lavender with a pale plum eyezone. Tetraploid. 'Tet. Exotic Echo' × 'Tet. Nagasaki'. TED L. PETIT & JOHN P. PEAT

'Heather Harrington' (Enman R. Joiner 1991). Evergreen. Scape 30 in. (76.2 cm); flower 6 in. (15.2 cm). Early midseason. A ruffled light apricot-cream self. Diploid. 'Frances Joiner' × 'Double Pink Treasure'. TED L. PETIT & JOHN P. PEAT

'Holy Mackerel' (David Kirchhoff 1988). Evergreen. Scape 26 in. (66.0 cm); flower 5 in. (12.7 cm). Midseason. A bright cherry-red double edged in cream with a green throat. Diploid. 'Luke Senior Junior' × 'Imperial Dragon'. DAVID KIRCHHOFF

'Horizon Beyond' (David Kirchhoff 1994). Evergreen. Scape 20 in. (50.8 cm); flower 5 in. (12.7 cm). Midseason. An orchid-rose with a toothed edge and a lavender-peach watermark over a yellow to green throat. Tetraploid. (seedling × 'Pappy's Girl') × ((seedling × 'Jungle Tapestry') × seedling). DAVID KIRCHHOFF

'Highland Lord' (R. W. Munson Jr. 1983). Semi-evergreen. Scape 22 in. (55.9 cm); flower 5 in. (12.7 cm). Midseason late. A very popular and classic double of wine-red with a wire white edge on petals and petaloids. Tetraploid. Parents unknown. Ida Munson Award 1991. R. W. MUNSON JR

'Imperial Dragon' (David Kirchhoff 1980). Semi-evergreen. Scape 26 in. (66.0 cm); flower 6 in. (15.2 cm). Early. A classic dark red double with yellow petaloid edges. Diploid. 'Cosmic Treasure' × 'Mozambique'. JOHN EISEMAN

'Impetuous Fire' (Ted L. Petit 1993). Semi-evergreen. Scape 20 in. (50.8 cm); flower 5 in. (12.7 cm). Midseason. A bright red self with a green throat. Tetraploid. 'Wayne Johnson' × 'Court Magician'. TED L. PETIT

'Hussy' (Mac Carter 1998). Semi-evergreen. Scape 26 in. (66.0 cm); flower 5 in. (12.7 cm). Midseason. A peach-pink-rose double lightly ruffled with a green throat. Tetraploid. 'Tanglewood' × 'Hotsy Totsy'. MAC CARTER

'Jean Swann' (Enman R. Joiner 1993). Semi-evergreen. Scape 32 in. (81.3 cm); flower 6 in. (15.2 cm). Midseason late. A cream-ivory to yellow self with a green throat. Diploid. 'Frances Joiner' × 'Vanilla Fluff'. TED L. PETIT & JOHN P. PEAT

'John Kinnebrew' (Jeff Salter 1992). Semi-evergreen. Scape 24 in. (61.0 cm); flower 6 in. (15.2 cm). Midseason. A large, dramatic, consistently double, cream-yellow flower. Critical for breeding double tetraploids. Tetraploid. Seedling × 'Kathleen Salter'. TED L. PETIT & JOHN P. PEAT

'King Alfred' (Charles Reckamp 1975). Dormant. Scape 26 in. (66.0 cm); flower 5.5 in. (14.0 cm). Midseason. A popular older form double in light yellow. Tetraploid. 'Crown' × 'Divine Word'. Ida Munson Award 1978. JOHN EISEMAN

'King Kahuna' (Clarence Crochet 1994). Semi-evergreen. Scape 22 in. (55.9 cm); flower 6.5 in. (16.5 cm). Early midseason. A large cream to medium yellow self. Very showy presence. Diploid. 'Olin Frazier' × 'Ellen Christine'. TED L. PETIT & JOHN P. PEAT

'Land of Cotton' (Enman R. Joiner 1991). Semi-evergreen. Scape 30 in. (76.2 cm); flower 6 in. (15.2 cm). Midseason. A pale peachy pink to cream self. Diploid. 'Vanilla Fluff' × seedling. TED L. PETIT & JOHN P. PEAT

'Layers of Gold' (David Kirchhoff 1990). Evergreen. Scape 24 in. (61.0 cm); flower 5 in. (12.7 cm). Early midseason. An important tetraploid double of a medium gold color. Tetraploid. (('Czarina' × 'Ed Kirchhoff') × 'Inez Ways') × ('Double Jackpot' × ('King Alfred' × seedling)). PATRICK STAMILE

'Little Wildflower' (Grace Stamile 1996). Semi-evergreen. Scape 13 in. (33.0 cm); flower 2 in. (5.1 cm). Late. A very cute miniature red to coral blend with a green throat. Diploid. 'Bubbly' × 'You Angel You'. PATRICK STAMILE

'Madge Cayse' (Enman R. Joiner 1991). Dormant. Scape 24 in. (61.0 cm); flower 6 in. (15.2 cm). Midseason late. A dark apricot self with green throat, consistently double. Diploid. 'Tangerine Twist' × 'Frances Joiner'. TED L. PETIT & JOHN P. PEAT

'Lost in Love' (Jan Joiner 1995). Evergreen. Scape 30 in. (76.2 cm); flower 6 in. (15.2 cm). Midseason. A beautiful wide-petaled, soft shell-pink. Diploid. Seedling × 'Frances Joiner'. TED L. PETIT & JOHN P. PEAT

'Memories of Paris' (Ted L. Petit 1995). Evergreen. Scape 20 in. (50.8 cm); flower 5.5 in. (14.0 cm). Midseason. A soft coral-pink double with wire gold edges and a green throat. Tetraploid. Seedling × ('Betty Warren Woods' × 'Most Noble'). TED L. PETIT

'Merlot Rouge' (Ted L. Petit 1994). Evergreen. Scape 21 in. (53.3 cm); flower 5.75 in. (14.6 cm). Midseason. A richly colored, double, burgundy-red self. Tetraploid. ('Renaissance Queen' × 'Wayne Johnston') × ('Wayne Johnson' × 'Devaughn Hodges'). TED L. PETIT

'Moon Sent' (Enman R. Joiner 1997). Evergreen. Scape 24 in. (61.0 cm); flower 6 in. (15.2 cm). Midseason late. A darker edged, amber-rose blend with a green throat. Diploid. Seedling × 'Rebecca Marie'. TED L. PETIT & JOHN P. PEAT

'Moroccan Summer' (David Kirchhoff 1986). Evergreen. Scape 22 in. (55.9 cm); flower 4.75 in. (12.1 cm). Early midseason. An intensely colored yellow to gold double. Diploid. 'Nagasaki' × 'Betty Woods'. TED L. PETIT & JOHN P. PEAT

'Nagasaki' (David Kirchhoff 1978). Evergreen. Scape 19 in. (48.3 cm); flower 4.5 in. (11.4 cm). Early midseason. A cream to pink-lavender blend with a dark green throat. Diploid. ((seedling × 'Dorothy Lambert') × 'Double Cutie') × 'Keith Kennon'. JOHN EISEMAN

'Nebuchadnezzar's Furnace' (Dave Talbott 1988). Evergreen. Scape 22 in. (55.9 cm); flower 5 in. (12.7 cm). Midseason. A fiery red blend with black-red eyezone and a green throat. Diploid. ('Siloam Double Rose' × 'Stroke of Midnight') × ('Rachael My Love × 'Luke Senior Junior'). JOHN EISEMAN

'Ode' (Mac Carter 1996). Evergreen. Scape 24 in. (61.0 cm); flower 5 in. (12.7 cm). Midseason. A pastel pink double with a rose eyezone and a green throat. Tetraploid. 'Talking Picture' × (('Most Noble' × seedling) × 'Love Goddess'). MAC CARTER

'Oh Danny Boy' (David Kirchhoff 1994). Semi-evergreen. Scape 28 in. (71.1 cm); flower 6.5 in. (16.5 cm). Midseason. A mauve-lavender self with a yellow to green throat. Diploid. Seedling × (seedling × 'Double Breakthrough'). DAVID KIRCHHOFF

'Pappy's Girl' (David Kirchhoff 1991). Evergreen. Scape 24 in. (61.0 cm); flower 5 in. (12.7 cm). Early. A pastel salmon-cream double. Tetraploid. 'Champagne Chilling' × 'Mango Coral'. TED L. PETIT & JOHN P. PEAT

'Pat Neumann' (Dan Trimmer 1998). Dormant. Scape length unknown. Flower 6 in. (15.2 cm). Bloom season unknown. A double pink and cream blend with a green throat. Diploid. 'Almond Puff' × 'Francis Joiner'. DAN TRIMMER

'Peach Magnolia' (Enman R. Joiner 1986). Dormant. Scape 32 in. (81.3 cm); flower 5.5 in. (14.0 cm). Midseason late. A peach-pink self with a green throat. Diploid. Parents unknown. TED L. PETIT & JOHN P. PEAT

'Peggy Bass' (Enman R. Joiner 1993). Semi-evergreen. Scape 26 in. (66.0 cm); flower 7 in. (17.8 cm). Midseason. An attractive shell-pink double. Diploid. Parents unknown. TED L. PETIT & JOHN P. PEAT

'Peggy Jeffcoat' (Jan Joiner 1995). Dormant. Scape 18 in. (45.7 cm); flower 6.5 in. (16.5 cm). Midseason late. A large, pristine cream-white double with a pink blush. Diploid. 'Jean Swann' × 'Rebecca Marie'. TED L. PETIT & JOHN P. PEAT

'Piglet and Roo' (John P. Peat 1998). Semi-evergreen. Scape 18 in. (45.7 cm); flower 3.5 in. (8.9 cm). Midseason. A small-flowered, double, peach-pink self. Tetraploid. 'Memories of Paris' × (('Wayne Johnson' × 'Renaissance Queen') × 'Merlot Rouge'). TED L. PETIT & JOHN P. PEAT

'Pink Pompon' (Patrick Stamile 1987). Evergreen. 22 in. (55.9 cm) scape; flower 5 in. (12.7 cm). Early midseason. A very popular coral-pink double with a green throat. Tetraploid. ('Chartwell' × 'Violet Hour') × 'Pa Pa Gulino'. PATRICK STAMILE

'Plum Plume' (David Kirchhoff 1996). Evergreen. Scape 32 in. (81.3 cm); flower 5 in. (12.7 cm). Early midseason. Plum-violet self with a purple halo and a yellow to green throat. Edged in gold. Tetraploid. ((seedling × 'Tet. Enchanting Lady') × 'Inner View') × (('Ming Porcelain' × 'Inner View') × ('Zinfandel' × seedling)). TED L. PETIT & JOHN P. PEAT

'Pojo' (Elna Winniford 1972). Semi-evergreen. Scape 19 in. (48.3 cm); flower 3 in. (7.6 cm). Early. A small, dark yellow self. Diploid. Parents unknown. Award of Merit 1980. Ida Munson Award 1977. PATRICK STAMILE

'Rachael My Love' (Dave Talbott 1983). Evergreen. Scape 18 in. (45.7 cm); flower 5 in. (12.7 cm). Early midseason. A showy golden yellow double. Diploid. 'Janet Gayle' × 'Twin Masterpiece'. Award of Merit 1991. Ida Munson Award 1989. PATRICK STAMILE

'Reba My Love' (Dave Talbott 1990). Evergreen. Scape 28 in. (71.1 cm); flower 6 in. (15.2 cm). Early midseason. A large, soft pink double. Diploid. 'Rachael My Love' × 'Siloam Double Rose'. JOHN EISEMAN

'Rebecca Marie' (Enman R. Joiner 1992). Evergreen. Scape 24 in. (61.0 cm); flower 5 in. (12.7 cm). Early midseason. A slightly darker-edged pink to light rose double self. Diploid. 'Frances Joiner' × 'Double Pink Treasure'. TED L. PETIT & JOHN P. PEAT

'Red Explosion' (Van Sellers 1986). Dormant. Scape 26 in. (66.0 cm); flower 5.5 in. (14.0 cm). Early midseason. A bright red double with a strong yellow to green throat. Tetraploid. Parents unknown. PATRICK STAMILE

'Renaissance Queen' (Betty Hudson 1985). Evergreen. Scape 26 in. (66.0 cm); flower 5.5 in. (14.0 cm). Early midseason. A double, diamond-dusted, soft pink and cream blend. Tetraploid. ('Chateau Blanc' × 'Creme Brulee') × (('Chateau Blanc' × 'White Crane') × (seedling × 'Zenobia')). BETTY HUDSON

'Rose Doubloon' (Lucille Guidry 1991). Evergreen. Scape 22 in. (55.9 cm); flower 6.5 in. (16.5 cm). Extra early. A large, consistently double, rose self with yellow throat. Diploid. Parents unknown. JOHN EISEMAN

'Roswitha' (Dan Trimmer 1992). Dormant. Scape 14 in. (35.6 cm); flower 3.25 in. (8.3 cm). Early midseason. A small, medium peach double with a large, dramatic, dark purple eye. Diploid. 'Exotic Echo' × 'Janice Brown'. TED L. PETIT & JOHN P. PEAT

'Royal Eventide' (David Kirchhoff 1985). Evergreen. Scape 28 in. (71.1 cm); flower 5 in. (12.7 cm). Early. A medium violet flower edged in lavender with deeper halo and citron-green throat. Diploid. ('Alice Hammond × 'Dorothy Lambert')F2 × ('Cosmic Treasure' × 'Nagasaki'). DAVID KIRCHHOFF

'Ruby Knight' (Jeff Salter 1993). Semi-evergreen. Scape 25 in. (63.5 cm); flower 5.5 in. (14.0 cm). Early midseason. A velvety, dark blood-red self. Among the best red double tetraploids. Tetraploid. Parents unknown. JOHN EISEMAN

'Ruffled Double Frills' (Edwin C. Brown 1986). Semi-evergreen. Scape 24 in. (61.0 cm); flower 5 in. (12.7 cm). Early midseason. A very double greenish yellow self with a deeper green throat. Diploid. 'Double Pink Treasure' × 'Betty Woods'. PATRICK STAMILE

'Sanford Double Violet' (David Kirchhoff 1988). Evergreen. Scape 22 in. (55.9 cm); flower 5 in. (12.7 cm). Early. A burgundy to violet double with white midribs. Diploid. 'Double Breakthrough' × 'Desdemona'. JOHN EISEMAN

'Sanford Show Girl' (David Kirchhoff 1989). Evergreen. Scape 28 in. (71.1 cm); flower 6 in. (15.2 cm). Early. A pastel peach-mauve with wine-red eyezone and a gold throat. Diploid. 'Both Sides Now' × 'Bette Davis Eyes'. DAVID KIRCHHOFF

'Savannah Explosion' (Enman R. Joiner 1991). Semi-evergreen. Scape 26 in. (66.0 cm); flower 5.5 in. (14.0 cm). Midseason. An apricot-cream self with an apricot throat. Diploid. 'Savannah Debutante' × 'Frances Joiner'. TED L. PETIT & JOHN P. PEAT

'Savannah Knockout' (Enman R. Joiner 1991). Dormant. Scape 24 in. (61.0 cm); flower 7 in. (17.8 cm). Midseason. A soft peach-pink to melon double with a green throat. Diploid. 'Ivory Cloud' × seedling. TED L. PETIT & JOHN P. PEAT

'Savannah Sunburst' (Jan Joiner 1996). Dormant. Scape 26 in. (66.0 cm); flower 6.5 in. (16.5 cm). Midseason late. A peach to sunburst-yellow self with a green throat. Diploid. 'Jean Swann' × 'Rebecca Marie'. TED L. PETIT & JOHN P. PEAT

'Scatterbrain' (Enman R. Joiner 1988). Semi-evergreen. Scape 32 in. (81.3 cm); flower 6 in. (15.2 cm). Midseason. An extremely popular light peach-pink self with a light green throat. Diploid. 'Ivory Cloud' × seedling. Award of Merit 1996. TED L. PETIT & JOHN P. PEAT

'Schnickel Fritz' (David Kirchhoff 1996). Dormant. Scape 16 in. (40.6 cm); flower 5 in. (12.7 cm). Early midseason. A near white self with a green throat. Diploid. 'Chardonnay' × ('Nagasaki' × 'Siloam Double Classic').
DAVID KIRCHHOFF

'Scoop of Vanilla' (Mac Carter 1993). Evergreen. Scape 26 in. (66.0 cm); flower 6 in. (15.2 cm). Early midseason. An ivory to cream-white self with a green throat. Tetraploid. 'Ivory Velvet' × 'Mykonos'. MAC CARTER

'Seychelle Sands' (Ted L. Petit 1994). Evergreen. Scape 24 in. (61.0 cm); flower 6 in. (15.2 cm). Early. A large coral-pink polychrome with darker peach highlights. Dramatic. Tetraploid. ('Renaissance Queen' × 'Mango Coral') × ('Betty Warren Woods' × 'Most Noble').
TED L. PETIT

'Siloam Double Coral' (Pauline Henry 1983). Dormant. Scape 26 in. (66.0 cm); flower 5.5 in. (14.0 cm). Midseason. A coral-pink self with a green throat. Diploid. Parents unknown.
JOHN EISEMAN

'Siloam Double Dazzler' (Pauline Henry 1988). Dormant. Scape 16 in. (40.6 cm); flower 5.5 in. (14.0 cm). Midseason. A wide-petaled, ruffled, bright rose double with a green throat. Diploid. Parents unknown. PATRICK STAMILE

'Siloam Double Fringe' (Pauline Henry 1986). Dormant. Scape 30 in. (76.2 cm); flower 5 in. (12.7 cm). Early midseason. A ruffled, fringy, ivory to cream self with a green throat. Diploid. Parents unknown. TED L. PETIT & JOHN P. PEAT

'Siloam Double Frost' (Pauline Henry 1984). Dormant. Scape 18 in. (45.7 cm); flower 6 in. (15.2 cm). Early midseason. A wide-petaled, large cream self with a small green heart. Diploid. Parents unknown. PATRICK STAMILE

'Siloam Glory Bee' (Pauline Henry 1987). Dormant. Scape 18 in. (45.7 cm); flower 5.5 in. (14.0 cm). Midseason. A medium pink self with a green throat. Diploid. Parents unknown. JOHN EISEMAN

'Siloam Olin Frazier' (Pauline Henry 1990). Dormant. Scape 22 in. (55.9 cm); flower 5.25 in. (13.3 cm). Early. A very ruffled, hot rose-pink self. Diploid. Parents unknown. Award of Merit 1997. Ida Munson Award 1997. TED L. PETIT & JOHN P. PEAT

'Spotted Fever' (Collier Brown 1995). Semi-evergreen. Scape 22 in. (55.9 cm); flower 3.75 in. (9.5 cm). Midseason. A stippled tan to rose-peach blend in peony form with a lime-green throat. Diploid. Parents unknown. JOHN EISEMAN

'Spring Rite' (Kenneth Durio 1989). Semi-evergreen. Scape 28 in. (71.1 cm); flower 4.5 in. (11.4 cm). Midseason. A dark, rich red-purple with a green to yellow throat. Diploid. 'Gato' × 'Tet. Double Grapette'. CURTIS & LINDA SUE BARNES

'Staci Cox' (Marjorie Tanner 1979). Semi-evergreen. Scape 22 in. (55.9 cm); flower 4.5 in. (11.4 cm). Early midseason. A small, consistently double, light yellow self. Diploid. Parents unknown.
TED L. PETIT & JOHN P. PEAT

'Stormy Affair' (Ted L. Petit 1994). Dormant. Scape 17 in. (43.2 cm); flower 5.5 in. (14.0 cm). Midseason. A purple double with a slightly darker eyezone. Tetraploid. 'Renaissance Queen' × (('Royal Heritage' × 'Spring Inter-mezzo') × ('Asian Emperor' × 'Pastel Morning')). TED L. PETIT

'Stroke of Midnight' (David Kirchhoff 1981). Evergreen. Scape 25 in. (63.5 cm); flower 5 in. (12.7 cm). Extra early. A classic, deep bordeaux-red self with a chartreuse throat. Diploid. ((('Blond Joanie' × 'Robert Way Schlumpf') × 'Karmic Treasure') × 'Double Razzle Dazzle') × 'Mozambique'. Ida Munson Award 1987.
JOHN EISEMAN

'Super Double Delight' (Vera McFarland 1978). Evergreen. Scape 30 in. (76.2 cm); flower 7.5 in. (19.1 cm). Midseason. A golden yellow double. Diploid. 'Double Eva' × seedling. TED L. PETIT & JOHN P. PEAT

'Tanglewood' (Betty Hudson 1993). Evergreen. Scape 20 in. (50.8 cm); flower 5 in. (12.7 cm). Early midseason. A chocolate-rose-terra-cotta and cream-terra-cotta bitone double with a yellow-green throat. Tetraploid. Parents unknown. BETTY HUDSON

'Three Tiers' (Albert Grooms 1971). Dormant. Scape 24 in. (61.0 cm); flower 5.5 in. (14.0 cm). Midseason late. A narrow-petaled, older formed, double, medium gold self. Diploid. ('Moonlight Sonata' × 'Flore Pleno') × 'Double Peach'. TED L. PETIT & JOHN P. PEAT

'Totally Awesome' (S. Glen Ward 1993). Evergreen. Scape 28 in. (71.1 cm); flower 7 in. (17.8 cm). Early midseason. A very large, dramatic, rose-pink double with lighter edges and midribs. Diploid. 'Double Pink Treasure' × 'Brent Gabriel'. JOHN EISEMAN

'Uninhibited' (Lee Gates 1992). Semi-evergreen. Scape 24 in. (61.0 cm); flower 6 in. (15.2 cm). Early. A large, unique, light marbled-pink blend with a green throat. Diploid. Parents unknown. CURTIS & LINDA SUE BARNES

'Vanilla Fluff' (Enman R. Joiner 1988). Dormant. Scape 34 in. (86.4 cm); flower 6 in. (15.2 cm). Midseason. A large ivory to cream self. Diploid. 'Ivory Cloud' × seedling. Award of Merit 1995. Ida Munson Award 1996. L. Ernest Plouf Award 1993. TED L. PETIT & JOHN P. PEAT

'Two Part Harmony' (Matthew Kaskel and Dan Trimmer 1996). Evergreen. scape 34 in. (86.4 cm); flower 4 in. (10.2 cm). Early. Straw-yellow with a wine-red eyezone and green throat. Tetraploid. ('One Fine Day' × (seedling × 'Ruby Sentinel')) × ('Fooled Me' × Tet. Janice Brown'). MATTHEW KASKEL

'Virginia Franklin Miller' (David Kirchhoff 1990). Evergreen. Scape 28 in. (71.1 cm); flower 6.5 in. (16.5 cm). Early midseason. A very large pink double. Diploid. (('Best of Friends' × 'Nagasaki') × (('Shibui Splendor' × 'Agape Love') × 'Siloam Double Rose')F2) × seedling. DAVID KIRCHHOFF

'Victoria's Secret' (Jeff Salter 1991). Semi-evergreen. Scape 28 in. (71.1 cm); flower 5.5 in. (14.0 cm). Midseason late. A cream-pink with a distinct gold edge and a lime-green throat. Tetraploid. Parents unknown. TED L. PETIT & JOHN P. PEAT

'Whispered Visions' (David Kirchhoff 1994). Evergreen. Scape 24 in. (61.0 cm); flower 5.5 in. (14.0 cm). Midseason. A pale peach double with a lavender watermark and dramatic lighter eye. Unusual and important. Tetraploid. (('Jungle Tapestry' × 'Graceland') × seedling) × (('Ring of Change' × 'Tiffany Palace') × 'Tet. Enchanting Lady'). DAVID KIRCHHOFF

'Wayne Johnson' (Betty Hudson 1984). Evergreen. Scape 28 in. (71.1 cm); flower 5.5 in. (14.0 cm). Midseason. An extremely important and popular double in cherry-red. Very famous. Tetraploid. ('Royal Ambassador' × seedling) × ('Royal Ambassador' × seedling). BETTY HUDSON

'Yazoo Jim Terry' (Ethel Smith and Earl Barfield 1992). Semi-evergreen. Scape 20 in. (50.8 cm); flower 6 in. (15.2 cm). Early midseason. Consistently double, large rose-pink self with a lemon to lime throat. Diploid. Parents unknown. CURTIS & LINDA SUE BARNES

'Yazoo Souffle' (W. H. Smith 1983). Semi-evergreen. Scape 26 in. (66.0 cm); flower 5.5 in. (14.0 cm). Early midseason. A very wide-petaled light apricot-pink self. Diploid. 'Yazoo Powder Puff' × 'Yazoo Powder Puff'. Award of Merit 1988. Ida Munson Award 1985.
JOHN EISEMAN

CHAPTER SEVEN

Spiders, Variants, and Unusual Forms

As the saying goes, everything old is new again. The daylily species first offered simple, narrow-petaled flowers. Then hybridizing began in earnest in the 1940s, and breeders invested more than 50 years toward widening the petals to create a full-formed, round flower. Narrow-petaled flowers definitely became passé. But styles change, and the narrow-petaled daylily is in fashion again—spiders are all the rage. However, the new spiders have a number of features that set them apart from the species. They are narrower than the original species, with longer petals, creating flowers that look like spiders, indeed. They are more open and flatter than the species and show little or no overlap in the throat. Again, hybridizers have had to start from scratch in their attempts to produce tetraploid spiders, a relatively new commodity. They are some of the most avidly sought-after daylilies—difficult to find and expensive to buy.

Some top hybridizers have been bitten by the bug; as Patrick Stamile commented, "They are the first things I make a bee-line for in the morning; they are so much fun." The spiders have grown more interesting in the last few years, getting larger and narrower, with new features such as ornate shark-toothed, tentacled, and gold-braided edges. They also have increased twisting and twirling and complex eyes and edges. Spiders even come in double and polytepal forms. In fact, every nuance existing in the modern daylily is being adopted into the spider, spider variant, and unusual form. Today's spiders have little or no resemblance to the early species, rather they reflect the continuing search for advancement and distinction. But with this increased interest in the spiders has come increased scrutiny. Many flowers can have narrow petals, but are they narrow enough to be considered a spider? Flowers that look like spiders, but are not quite narrow enough to actually be spiders, are called spider variants. To clarify this difference, the American Hemerocallis Society wrote a definition for spiders and spider variants. They concluded that a true spider must have a petal length-to-width ratio of 5:1 or higher. A spider variant must have a petal length-to-width ratio of at least 4:1, up to but not including 5:1.

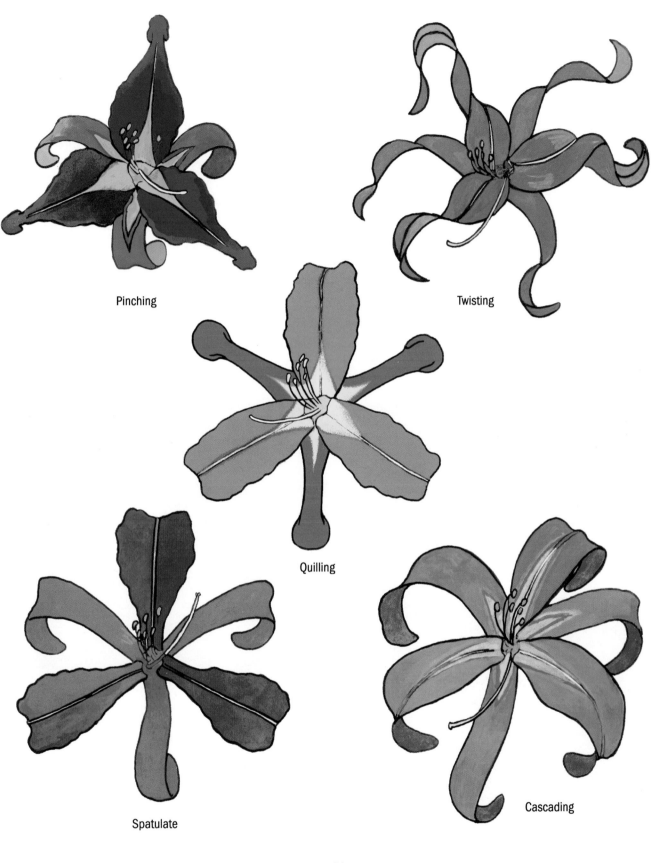

Pinching

Twisting

Quilling

Spatulate

Cascading

Unusual forms.
RICHARD HAYNES

Another group of daylilies at first glance might appear to be spiders or variants, but they have wider petals than spiders, and the floral segments appear to have consistent "movement." These are grouped under the designation "unusual forms" and have gained a following of their own. In response to the new interest in unusual forms, the American Hemerocallis Society developed a definition for them as well. Unusual form daylilies fit into three categories—crispate, cascading, and spatulate. The crispate category is further divided into three subcategories—pinching, twisting, and quilling. In flowers with crispate pinching, the floral segments have sharp folds giving a pinched or folded effect. Crispate flowers with twisting have floral segments with a corkscrew or pinwheel effect, and those with quilling have floral segments that turn upon themselves along their length to form a tubular shape. Cascading (or curling) flowers have narrow floral segments that display a pronounced curling, revolving upon themselves like wood shavings. Spatulate flowers have floral segments that are markedly wider at the end, like a kitchen spatula. Any daylily showing one or more of these categories or subcategories, known as movements, in their flower segments is qualified to be an unusual form daylily as long as it does not meet the official definition of a spider or spider variant.

'Aabache' (Raymond Cheetham 1957). Dormant. Scape 32 in. (81.3 cm); flower size unknown. Midseason late. A dark rust-ruby self with a yellow to green throat. A true spider with a length-to-width ratio of 7.5:1. Diploid. Parents unknown. MARY ANNE LEISEN

'All American Windmill' (Clarence Crochet 1995). Dormant. Scape 26 in. (66.0 cm); flower 7 in. (17.8 cm). Early midseason. A light orange polychrome unusual form with a darker orange, chevron eyezone and a green throat. Diploid. 'Copper Windmill' × 'Yellow Angel'. TED L. PETIT & JOHN P. PEAT

'Arachnephobia' (Jerry Dickerson 1991). Evergreen. Scape 20 in. (50.8 cm); flower 7 in. (17.8 cm). Early. A lightly ruffled, cream-pink, unusual-form self with a yellow-green throat. Diploid. Seedling × 'Kindly Light'. MARY ANNE LEISEN

'All American Chief' (Van Sellers 1994). Dormant. Scape 32 in. (81.3 cm); flower 9 in. (22.9 cm). Early midseason. An unusual-form, bright red self with a very large green center. Tetraploid. Parents unknown. TED L. PETIT & JOHN P. PEAT

'Black Plush' (Hooper P. Connell 1955). Evergreen. Scape 32 in. (81.28 cm); flower size unknown. Midseason. A velvet, dark black-red self with a large yellow-green center. A spider variant measuring 4.6:1. Diploid. Parents unknown. TED L. PETIT & JOHN P. PEAT

'Blakeway Spiderman' (Maureen Flanders 1989). Evergreen. Scape 28 in. (71.1 cm); 7 in. (17.8 cm) flower. Midseason. An ivory-near-white self with a green throat. Diploid. 'Chosen One' × ('Amazing Grace' × 'Snow Princess'). MARY ANNE LEISEN

'Boney Maroney' (Ken Kehl 1994). Semi-evergreen. Scape 36 in. (91.4 cm); flower 9 in. (22.9 cm). Early midseason. A deep yellow-gold self with a striking green heart. Tetraploid. 'Green Dolphin Street' × 'Tet. Kindly Light'. MARY ANNE LEISEN

'Cabaret Star' (Stanley Saxton 1977). Semi-evergreen. Scape 24 in. (61.0 cm); flower 5 in. (12.7 cm). Midseason late. A bright cherry-red self with a yellow-green throat. Diploid. Seedling × 'War Eagle'. MARY ANNE LEISEN

'Carolicolossal' (Loleta K. Powell 1968). Semi-evergreen. Scape 36 in. (91.4 cm); flower 10 in. (25.4 cm). Early. A deep yellow self with a green throat. A spider variant measuring 4.3:1. Diploid. 'Carolisurprise' × seedling. MARY ANNE LEISEN

'Carolispider' (Loleta K. Powell 1995). Dormant. Scape 30 in. (76.2 cm); flower 8 in. (20.3 cm). Early midseason. A medium lavender self with a large light center and a green throat. A true spider measuring 6.4:1. Diploid. 'Lavender Star' × 'Shadowed Pink'. MARY ANNE LEISEN

'Carrick Wildon' (Alfred Goldner 1987). Dormant. Scape 34 in. (86.4 cm); flower 7.5 in. (19.1 cm). Midseason late. A yellow-red variant blend with orange tips and yellow throat. Tetraploid. Parents unknown.
MARY ANNE LEISEN

'Cat's Cradle' (Ben Hager 1985). Evergreen. Scape 38 in. (96.5 cm); flower 8 in. (20.3 cm). Early midseason. Yellow with a bronze overtone and a green heart. A true spider measuring 5.8:1. Diploid. 'Carolicolossal' × 'Kindly Light'. Award of Merit 1993. Harris Olsen Spider Award 1991. JAY TOMPKINS

'Cerulean Star' (John R. Lambert 1982). Dormant. Scape 34 in. (86.4 cm); flower 5.5 in. (14.0 cm). Early midseason. A medium lavender-orchid self with a green star throat, measuring 4.4:1. Diploid. 'Louise Mercer' × 'Chum'.
MARY ANNE LEISEN

'Chesapeake Crablegs' (Margaret Reed 1994). Dormant. Scape 38 in. (96.5 cm); flower 6.5 in. (16.5 cm). Early midseason. A burnt orange with an orange-red, chevron eye above a gold to olive-green throat, measuring 4.0:1. Diploid. 'Smarty Pants' × 'Coral Crabs'.
MARY ANNE LEISEN

'Chin Whiskers' (Berneese McRae 1992). Dormant. Scape 20 in. (50.8 cm); flower 5 in. (12.7 cm). Early midseason. A lightly ruffled lavender-rose-pink blend with a large green throat. A true spider measuring 9.0:1. Diploid. Parents unknown. MARY ANNE LEISEN

'Christmas Ribbon' (Patrick Stamile 1991). Dormant. Scape 34 in. (86.4 cm); flower 8.5 in. (21.6 cm). Early. A deep Christmas-red self with a yellow throat. Tetraploid. 'Velvet Window' × 'Tet. Open Hearth'. PATRICK STAMILE

'Christmas Spider' (Bettie Jernigan 1988). Dormant. Scape 22 in. (55.9 cm); flower 7.5 in. (19.1 cm). Midseason late. A red-tipped, applegreen spider with a deeper green throat. Diploid. Parents unknown. PATRICK STAMILE

'Coburg Fright Wig' (Philip Brockington 1990). Dormant. Scape 33 in. (83.8 cm); flower 7.5 in. (19.1 cm). Early midseason. A burnt orangemaroon with a darker eye, lighter sepals, and a yellow throat. Diploid. 'Persian Pattern' × 'Lilly Dache'. MARY ANNE LEISEN

'Crimson Pirate' (Henry E. Sass 1951). Dormant. Scape 30 in. (76.2 cm); flower size unknown. Midseason. A deep red with cream midribs and a yellow-green throat. Measures 5.2:1. Diploid. 'Honey Redhead' × 'Queen Esther'. MARY ANNE LEISEN

'Crocodile Smile' (Dan Trimmer 1996). Evergreen. Scape 36 in. (91.4 cm); flower 8 in. (20.3 cm). Early midseason. A shark-tooth-edged mulberry and ivory bicolor with a triking cream-yellow-green throat. Very special. Tetraploid. 'Anastasia' × 'Tet. Spindazzle'. DAN TRIMMER

'Daisy' (Anna Glidden 1988). Evergreen. Scape 30 in. (76.2 cm); flower 8 in. (20.3 cm). Early midseason. A slightly ruffled, pale creamlavender-green with a large green throat. Diploid. 'Milady Greensleeves' × seedling. MARY ANNE LEISEN

'Dancing Lions' (Frederick Benzinger 1971). Dormant. Scape 28 in. (71.1 cm); flower 8 in. (20.3 cm). Early midseason. A clear goldyellow self with an olive-green throat. Tetraploid. 'Golden Surrey' × 'Tet. Hooper Connell'. MARY ANNE LEISEN

'Dark Gift' (John R. Lambert and James A. Whitacre 1997). Dormant. Scape 34 in. (86.4 cm); flower 7.5 in. (19.1 cm). Early midseason. A deep, dark purple self with a yellow-green throat. Diploid. 'Rigamarole' × 'Diabolique'. MARY ANNE LEISEN

'De Colores' (John Temple 1992). Evergreen. Scape 28 in. (71.1 cm); flower 8.5 in. (21.6 cm). Early. A stunning rose, tan, and yellow, 6.0:1 spider with a huge, triangular red-purple eye above a green throat. Diploid. 'Mountain Top Experience' × 'Garden Portrait'. TED L. PETIT & JOHN P. PEAT

'Divertissment' (Ben Hager 1990). Dormant. Scape 45 in. (114.3 cm); flower 6.5 in. (16.5 cm). Midseason late. A 4.8:1, light golden-yellow spider variant with a very pale reddish halo and a small green throat. Diploid. ('American Revolution' × 'Kindly Light') × 'Bold One'. MARY ANNE LEISEN

'Easy Ned' (Betty Brown 1987). Semi-evergreen. Scape 40 in. (101.6 cm); flower 6.5 in. (16.5 cm). Very late. A curled, yellow, 5.1:1 spider with a large green center. Diploid. 'Lady Fingers' × seedling. MARY ANNE LEISEN

'Dune Needlepoint' (Olive Pauley 1986). Dormant. Scape 29 in. (73.7 cm); flower 6 in. (15.2 cm). Midseason. A slightly creped cream-yellow with a pink-rose halo and a yellow throat. Diploid. 'Ouachita Beauty' × 'Yazoo Delta'. MARY ANNE LEISEN

'Emerald Jewel' (Betty Harwood 1997). Dormant. Scape 27 in. (68.6 cm); flower 8 in. (20.3 cm). Midseason. A very large, near-white, spider-looking flower with a striking green throat. Diploid. 'Jaunty Julie' × 'Grapeade'. BETTY HARWOOD

'Enduring Love' (Betty Brown 1986). Evergreen. Scape 23 in. (58.4 cm); flower 8 in. (20.3 cm). Early midseason. A recurved cream-yellow with a striking burgundy-purple eye and a large green throat. Diploid. Seedling × 'Persian Pattern'. MARY ANNE LEISEN

'Fellow' (Frank Childs 1975). Dormant. Scape 24 in. (61.0 cm); flower 7 in. (17.8 cm). Early midseason. A lavender-purple self with a lemon-green throat. Diploid. Parents unknown. TED L. PETIT & JOHN P. PEAT

'Fly Catcher' (John Miller 1978). Dormant. Scape 32 in. (81.3 cm); flower 7.5 in. (19.1 cm). Midseason late. A recurved, deep red with a green throat. Diploid. Seedling × 'Prairie Chief'. CURTIS & LINDA SUE BARNES

'Fol De Rol' (Hooper P. Connell 1953). Evergreen. Scape 40 in. (101.6 cm); Midseason late. A 6.7:1, floppy, brown to yellow blend with a darker triangular eye and a green throat. Diploid. Parents unknown. MARY ANNE LEISEN

'Green Tarantula' (L. Parker 1970). Evergreen. Scape 36 in. (91.4 cm); flower 7.5 in. (19.1 cm). Midseason. A ruffled, soft yellow-green self with a green throat. Diploid. 'Viola Parker' × 'Clarence Simon'. TED L. PETIT & JOHN P. PEAT

'Green Widow' (John Temple 1980). Evergreen. Scape 26 in. (66.0 cm); flower 6.5 in. (16.5 cm). Early. A 4.1:1, very dramatic yellow-green spider variant with a large, strong, dark green throat. Diploid. 'Celestial Light' × 'Green Avalanche'. MARY ANNE LEISEN

'Handsome Prince' (Geraldine Couturier 1993). Dormant. Scape 38 in. (96.5 cm); flower 7 in. (17.8 cm). Midseason. A pale yellow-orange with a large burgundy eye on petals and sepals above a chartreuse throat. Diploid. Parents unknown. MARY ANNE LEISEN

'Harbor Blue' (Sally Lake 1961). Evergreen. Scape 26 in. (66.0 cm); flower size unknown. Early midseason. A 4.3:1 lavender-violet self with a cream-green throat. Diploid. ('Lilac Time' × seedling) × 'Blue Horizon'. CURTIS & LINDA SUE BARNES

'Jan's Twister' (Jan Joiner 1991). Evergreen. Scape 28 in. (71.1 cm); flower 11.5 in. (27.9 cm). Early midseason. A twisted, cream-peach, unusual-form self with a green throat. Diploid. 'Jean Wise' × 'Kindly Light'. Award of Merit 1997. TED L. PETIT & JOHN P. PEAT

'Jaunty Julie' (Betty Harwood 1988). Dormant. Scape 32 in. (81.3 cm); flower 8 in. (20.3 cm). Early midseason. A very recurved, lavender bitone with a cream halo and a green throat. Diploid. 'Grape Ice' × 'Lilting Lavender'. MARY ANNE LEISEN

'Jazz' (Edith Sholar 1974). Dormant. Scape 34 in. (86.4 cm); flower 6 in. (15.2 cm). Early midseason. Rose-pink with a large chartreuse throat and spooning on the tips of the sepals. Diploid. 'Catherine Barks' × seedling. MARY ANNE LEISEN

'Jersey Spider' (Edward Grovatt 1973). Dormant. Scape 46 in. (114.3 cm); flower 8 in. (20.3 cm). Midseason late. A bright gold-orange self with a green throat. Diploid. 'Orange Marmalade' × 'President Rice'. MARY ANNE LEISEN

'Karen Burgoyne' (Betty Harwood 1998). Dormant. Scape 30 in. (76.2 cm); flower 5 in. (12.7 cm). Midseason. A lightly ruffled, deep burgundy with a green throat and twisting, spooned sepals. 'Damaskan Velvet' × 'Decatur Luminaria'. BETTY HARWOOD

'Kevin Michael Coyne' (Jerry Dickerson 1988). Evergreen. Scape 26 in. (66.0 cm); flower 9 in. (22.9 cm). Midseason. A bright, clear, recurved, yellow, 5.0:1 spider variant with a green throat. Diploid. Seedling × 'Kindly Light'. MARY ANNE LEISEN

'Kindly Light' (J. Bechtold 1950). Dormant. Scape 28 in. (71.1 cm); flower size unknown. Midseason. A very famous and popular, arching, bright yellow, 7.7:1 spider. Diploid. Parents unknown. Harris Olsen Spider Award 1989. MARY ANNE LEISEN

'Lacy Marionette' (Inez Tarrant 1987). Evergreen. Scape 26 in. (66.0 cm); flower 7 in. (17.8 cm). Early midseason. A 5.1:1 spider of bright yellow with a dark green throat. Diploid. 'Kindly Light' × seedling. MARY ANNE LEISEN

'Lady Fingers' (Virginia Peck 1967). Dormant. Scape 32 in. (81.3 cm); flower 6 in. (15.2 cm). Midseason. A light yellow-green, 4.8:1 spider variant with a strong green throat. Diploid. Parents unknown. Harris Olsen Spider Award 1990. PATRICK STAMILE

'Lady Neva' (J. Alexander and J. Moody 1970). Semi-evergreen. Scape 42 in. (106.7 cm); flower 9 in. (22.9 cm). Early midseason. A soft buff-yellow with a large, striking rose eye and a green throat. Diploid. Parents unknown. TED L. PETIT & JOHN P. PEAT

'Lake Norman Spider' (Kate Carpenter 1981). Dormant. Scape 28 in. (71.1 cm); flower 8 in. (20.3 cm). Midseason. A rose-pink blend with a lighter eyezone and large cream-green throat. Diploid. Parents unknown. MARY ANNE LEISEN

'Lavender Handlebars' (Ned Roberts 1994). Dormant. Scape 36 in. (91.4 cm); flower 8.5 in. (21.6 cm). Midseason. A lavender, 4.3:1 spider variant with a large yellow-green throat. Very pinched petals and sepals. Diploid. Parents unknown. CURTIS & LINDA SUE BARNES

'Lavender Spider' (Eula Harris and Joyce Reinke 1990). Dormant. Scape 32 in. (81.3 cm); flower 10 in. (25.4 cm). Early midseason. A light lavender, 5.2:1 spider with a darker halo, cream midribs, and a large yellow throat. Diploid. 'Kindly Light' × seedling. TED L. PETIT & JOHN P. PEAT

'Lemon Fellow' (Dan Trimmer 1998). Dormant. Scape 32 in. (81.3 cm); flower 11 in. (27.9 cm). Early midseason. A deep golden-yellow spider with curled segments and a green throat. Diploid. 'Spider Miracle' × 'Cat's Cradle'.
DAN TRIMMER

'Lines of Splendor' (John Temple 1993). Evergreen. Scape 25 in. (63.5 cm); flower 8.5 in. (21.6 cm). Early. A lightly ruffled, soft yellow-green, 5.2:1 spider with a soft rose-red eye above a green throat. Diploid. 'Green Widow' × 'Green Portrait'. MARY ANNE LEISEN

'Loch Ness Monster' (Geraldine Couturier 1992). Dormant. Scape 25 in. (63.5 cm); flower 7.5 in. (19.1 cm). Midseason. A 4.4:1 spider variant, ruffled, medium rose-lavender with a darker lavender halo above a yellow-green throat. Diploid. 'Lavinia Love' × seedling.
MARY ANNE LEISEN

'Lois Burns' (John Temple 1986). Evergreen. Scape 30 in. (76.2 cm); flower 8.5 in. (21.6 cm). Early. A curled, bright yellow-green, 4.0:1 spider variant with striking green throat. Diploid. Seedling × 'Grewen Widow'. Harris Olsen Spider Award 1995.
TED L. PETIT & JOHN P. PEAT

'Long Stocking' (Patrick Stamile 1997). Evergreen. Scape 46 in. (114.3 cm); flower 9.5 in. (24.1 cm). Early midseason. A bright Christmas-red, 4.0:1 spider variant with a green throat. Tetraploid. 'Christmas Ribbon' × 'Swirling Spider'. PATRICK STAMILE

'Long Tall Sally' (Dan Trimmer 1996). Dormant. Scape 38 in. (96.5 cm); flower 14 in. (35.6 cm). Early midseason. A 4.1:1, red spider variant with a yellow-green throat. Tetraploid. 'Spider Man' × 'Tet. Spindazzle'. DAN TRIMMER

'Mad Max' (Cindy Schott 1989). Dormant. Scape 46 in. (114.3 cm); flower 7 in. (17.8 cm). Midseason. A curly, rosy purple with a deep purple eyezone and a large, striking chartreuse throat. Diploid. Parents unknown. MARY ANNE LEISEN

'Marked by Lydia' (John Temple 1994). Semi-evergreen. Scape 29 in. (73.7 cm); flower 8.5 in. (21.6 cm). Early. A medium yellow, 5.3:1 spider with a very large, triangular purple eyezone above a green throat. Diploid. 'Mountain Top Experience' × 'Garden Portrait'. JOHN EISEMAN

'Mighty Highty Tighty' (Kenneth Cobb 1987). Semi-evergreen. Scape 28 in. (71.1 cm); flower 8 in. (20.3 cm). Midseason. A rose with lighter edges and a burgundy-wine halo above a yellow-green throat. Diploid. 'Limited Edition' × 'Lilting Lavender'. MARY ANNE LEISEN

'Miracle Worker' (Jerry Dickerson 1996). Dormant. Scape 25 in. (63.5 cm); flower 7 in. (17.8 cm). Early midseason. A pale yellow, 5.3:1 spider with a green throat. Tetraploid. Seedling × 'Tet. Kevin Michael Coyne'. MARY ANNE LEISEN

'Miss Jessie' (Julia Hardy 1956). Dormant. Scape 40 in. (101.6 cm); flower size unknown. Midseason. An orchid-mauve bicolor, 4.0:1 spider variant with a darker halo and a green throat. Diploid. ('Dorothea' × 'Su-Lin') × seedling. TED L. PETIT & JOHN P. PEAT

'Moon Creature' (Sally Birkholtz 1971). Dormant. Scape 28 in. (71.1 cm); flower 5 in. (12.7 cm). A recurved blend of yellow, pink, and green with a green throat. Diploid. Parents unknown. MARY ANNE LEISEN

'Mormon Spider' (R. Roberson 1982). Dormant. Scape 28 in. (71.1 cm); flower 8.5 in. (21.6 cm). Midseason. A lightly ruffled, bronze-edged, soft yellow with a gold throat. Diploid. 'Mormon' × 'Cashmere'. PATRICK STAMILE

'Morticia' (R. W. Munson Jr. 1994). Evergreen. Scape 38 in. (96.5 cm); flower 7 in. (17.8 cm). Midseason. A burgundy-purple with a creamy violet-plum-purple eyezone above a lime chartreuse throat. Tetraploid. 'Cameroons' × 'Respighi'. R. W. MUNSON JR

'Mountain Top Experience' (John Temple 1988). Evergreen. Scape 29 in. (73.7 cm); flower 7.5 in. (19.1 cm). Early. A 4.8:1, spider variant, yellow and rouge bicolor with a large burgundy eye and a green throat. Diploid. 'Rainbow Spangles' × 'Lois Burns'. MARY ANNE LEISEN

'Nona's Garnet Spider' (Nona Ford 1992). Semi-evergreen. Scape 36 in. (91.4 cm); flower 6.5 in. (16.5 cm). Midseason. A curled, 4.3:1 spider variant, garnet-red blend with a yellow throat. Diploid. Parents unknown. MARY ANNE LEISEN

'Old-Fashioned Maiden' (Geraldine Couturier 1993). Dormant. Scape 35 in. (88.9 cm); flower 6 in. (15.2 cm). Midseason. A 5.1:1, light red-orange spider with a wine, chevron eye above a gold-green throat. Diploid. Parents unknown. MARY ANNE LEISEN

'Orange Exotica' (Geraldine Couturier 1994). Dormant. Scape 33 in. (83.8 cm); flower 6.25 in. (15.9 cm). Early midseason. Burnt orange with a dark burnt orange eye above a gold-green throat. Diploid. 'Ice Carnival' × 'Beau Brummell'. CURTIS & LINDA SUE BARNES

'Orchid Corsage' (Stanley Saxton 1975). Dormant. Scape 32 in. (81.3 cm); flower 7.5 in. (19.1 cm). Midseason late. A lavender-pink unusual form with lighter midribs and a light yellow throat. Diploid. 'Lavender Touch' × 'Emperors Robe'. TED L. PETIT & JOHN P. PEAT

'Ostrich Plume' (Peter Fass 1962). Dormant. Scape 36 in. (91.4 cm); flower size unknown. Midseason. A 5.6:1 spider with curly petals of greenish yellow and a green throat. Diploid. 'Twinkle Curl' × 'Lily Curl'. MARY ANNE LEISEN

'Pale Moon Windmill' (Clarence Crochet 1996). Semi-evergreen. Scape 28 in. (71.1 cm); flower 6.5 in. (16.5 cm). Early. A cream blend, 4.0:1 spider variant with a light rose-lavender halo and a large, dark green throat. Diploid. 'Enduring Love' × seedling. CURTIS & LINDA SUE BARNES

'Parade of Peacocks' (William Oakes 1990). Dormant. Scape 36 in. (91.4 cm); flower 8 in. (20.3 cm). Midseason late. A rose-peach with a large, dramatic rose eye and a cream throat. Diploid. Parents unknown. TED L. PETIT & JOHN P. PEAT

'Peach Float' (Dorothy Warrell 1994). Dormant. Scape 35 in. (88.9 cm); flower 7.5 in. (19.1 cm). Midseason late. A lightly ruffled melon-peach self with light lavender midribs and a green to melon throat. Diploid. 'Sweet Charlotte' × 'Asiatic Pheasant'. MARY ANNE LEISEN

'Patsy Bickers' (Jerry Dickerson 1987). Semi-evergreen. Scape 20 in. (50.8 cm); flower 11 in. (27.9 cm). Midseason. A 5.5:1 beige-pink spider with a large, triangular brown-red eye and a green throat. Diploid. Seedling × 'Kindly Light'. CURTIS & LINDA SUE BARNES

'Peacock Maiden' (Kate Carpenter 1982). Evergreen. Scape 31 in. (78.7 cm); flower 9.5 in. (24.1 cm). Midseason. A dark purple unusual form with a creamy white eyezone and midribs and a large green throat. Diploid. ('Grape Arbor' × seedling) × seedling. JAY TOMPKINS

'Ping Pong' (Howard Hite 1995). Semi-evergreen. Scape 36 in. (91.4 cm); flower 8 in. (20.3 cm). Midseason. A dark red self with twisted petals and a very large yellow to green throat. Diploid. 'Mighty Highty Tighty' × 'Red Flag'. CURTIS & LINDA SUE BARNES

'Pink Super Spider' (Kate Carpenter 1982). Semi-evergreen. Scape 32 in. (81.3 cm); flower 10 in. (25.4 cm). Midseason. A lightly ruffled, rose-pink and pink-cream blend with a cream-green eyezone and a green throat. Diploid. Parents unknown. TED L. PETIT & JOHN P. PEAT

'Pink Windmill' (Clarence Crochet 1987). Semi-evergreen. Scape 24 in. (61.0 cm); flower 6 in. (15.2 cm). Early midseason. A clear, soft pink unusual form with a green throat. Diploid. Parents unknown. PATRICK STAMILE

'Prissy Frills' (Frank Childs 1981). Dormant. Scape 28 in. (71.1 cm); flower 7 in. (17.8 cm). Midseason. A dark lavender, unusual-form self with a lighter watermark and a green throat. Diploid. Parents unknown. PATRICK STAMILE

'Rainbow Spangles' (John Temple 1983). Evergreen. Scape 30 in. (76.2 cm); flower 7 in. (17.8 cm). Early midseason. A lavender and chartreuse bicolor, 4.4:1 spider variant with a purple eye and a green throat. Diploid. (('Lady Daphne' × 'Green Avalanche') × 'For Petes Sake') × 'Green Widow'. MARY ANNE LEISEN

'Red Rain' (Rosemary Whitacre 1988). Semi-evergreen. Scape 38 in. (96.5 cm); flower 5.5 in. (14.0 cm). Midseason. A bright cherry-red, 6.0:1 spider with a deep cherry-red eye and a yellow-green throat. Diploid. 'Garden Portrait' × 'Red Ribbons'. MARY ANNE LEISEN

'Red Suspenders' (Ruth Webster 1990). Dormant. Scape 32 in. (81.3 cm); flower 11 in. (27.9 cm). Midseason. A bright red, unusual-form, pinched-petaled self with a green-chartreuse throat. Tetraploid. 'Galaxy Rose' × 'Fire Arrow'. MARY ANNE LEISEN

'Red Thrill' (George Lenington 1964). Evergreen. Scape 40 in. (101.6 cm); flower 6 in. (15.2 cm). Midseason. A 4.2:1, cherry-red spider variant with a green throat. Diploid. 'Wanda' × seedling. MARY ANNE LEISEN

'Rope Dancer' (Berneese McRae 1989). Semi-evergreen. Scape 24 in. (61.0 cm); flower 8 in. (20.3 cm). Midseason. A red, pinched-petaled unusual form with a large green-gold throat. Diploid. Parents unknown. MARY ANNE LEISEN

'Ruby Spider' (Patrick Stamile 1991). Dormant. Scape 34 in. (86.4 cm); flower 9 in. (22.9 cm). Early. A ruby-red, unusual-formed self with a yellow throat. Tetraploid. 'Velvet Widow' × 'Tet. Open Hearth'. TED L. PETIT & JOHN P. PEAT

'Satan's Curls' (Nell Crandall 1987). Evergreen. Scape 29 in. (73.7 cm); flower 6 in. (15.2 cm). Early midseason. A red, very twisted and curved, unusual form with a large, striking green throat. Diploid. 'Prairie Satan' × 'Whirling Fury'. MARY ANNE LEISEN

'Shirley Temple Curls' (John Temple 1996). Evergreen. Scape 24 in. (61.0 cm); flower 10 in. (25.4 cm). Early midseason. A very curly, extremely large, 5.6:1, light yellow-burgundy spider with a burgundy eye and a deep green throat. Diploid. ('Lines of Splendor' × 'Garden Portrait') × ('Rainbow Spangles' × 'Lois Burns'). TED L. PETIT & JOHN P. PEAT

'Slender Lady' (Nell Crandall 1987). Evergreen. Scape 29 in. (73.7 cm); flower 7 in. (17.8 cm). Early midseason. A cream-yellow, 5.0:1 spider variant with a faint cinnamon eye and a very green throat. Diploid. 'Green Widow' × 'Kindly Light'. MARY ANNE LEISEN

'Snickerdoodle' (Berneese McRae 1989). Dormant. Scape 28 in. (71.1 cm); flower 9 in. (22.9 cm). Midseason. A very light rose-pink with a large, dramatic burgundy eye above a green throat. Diploid. Parents unknown. MARY ANNE LEISEN

'Spider Breeder' (John Miller 1978). Dormant. Scape 34 in. (86.4 cm); flower 10 in. (25.4 cm). Midseason late. A deep lemon-yellow, 4.8:1 spider variant with a green-yellow throat. Diploid. Seedling × 'Kindly Light'. MARY ANNE LEISEN

'Spider Man' (Kenneth Durio 1982). Dormant. Scape 24 in. (61.0 cm); flower size unknown. Early midseason. A bright red self with a chartreuse throat. Tetraploid. 'Douglas Dale' × 'Howard Goodson'. TED L. PETIT & JOHN P. PEAT

'Spider Miracle' (W. Hendricks 1986). Dormant. Scape 32 in. (81.3 cm); flower 8.5 in. (21.9 cm). Midseason. A yellow-green, recurved self with a large, strong green throat. Diploid. Parents unknown. Award of Merit 1996. TED L. PETIT & JOHN P. PEAT

'Spider Web' (Marjorie Tanner 1975). Evergreen. Scape 20 in. (50.8 cm); flower 11 in. (27.9 cm). Early midseason. A large, gold-yellow, lightly ruffled self with a green heart. Diploid. 'Eva Noble' × seedling. JOHN EISEMAN

'Spindazzle' (Thomas Wilson 1983). Semi-evergreen. Scape 26 in. (66.0 cm); flower 6 in. (15.2 cm). Midseason. A 4.4:1, gold-copper variant, veined red with red tips. Diploid. Seedling × 'Ferris Wheel'. TED L. PETIT & JOHN P. PEAT

'Spiral Charmer' (Margaret Dickson and Nell Crandall 1985). Semi-evergreen. Scape 36 in. (91.4 cm); flower 6.5 in. (16.5 cm). Midseason. A cream with pink overlay, 5.0:1 spider variant with a yellow-green throat. Diploid. Parents unknown. MARY ANNE LEISEN

'Star Spangled' (John R. Lambert 1965). Evergreen. Scape 24 in. (61.0 cm); flower 8 in. (20.3 cm). Evergreen. A lightly ruffled, grayish rose-pink blend, 5.4:1 spider. Diploid. Parents unknown. MARY ANNE LEISEN

'Strider Spider' (Kenneth Durio 1998). Semi-evergreen. Scape 24 in. (61.0 cm); flower 6.5 in. (16.5 cm). Early midseason. A curled, deep red, 4.7:1 spider variant with a large yellow-green throat. Tetraploid. 'Spider Man' × 'Tet. Red Thrill'. CURTIS & LINDA SUE BARNES

'Sunset' (Amos Perry 1931). Evergreen. Scape 34 in. (86.4 cm); flower size unknown. Midseason. A bright orange-red with a darker eye surrounding a green center. Diploid. 'Margaret Perry' × seedling. CURTIS & LINDA SUE BARNES

'Swirling Spider' (Howard Hite 1990). Semi-evergreen. Scape 34 in. (86.4 cm); flower 10 in. (25.4 cm). Midseason. A rose-red unusual form with white midribs and a yellow-green throat. Tetraploid. 'Twist of Lemon' × 'Samar Star Fire'. TED L. PETIT & JOHN P. PEAT

'Techny Spider' (Charles Reckamp and Charles Klehm 1987). Dormant. Scape 21 in. (53.3 cm); flower 7 in. (17.8 cm). Midseason late. A yellow-pink with crimped gold edges and a green throat. Tetraploid. Parents unknown. PATRICK STAMILE

'Toothpick' (Jerry Dickerson 1994). Dormant. Scape 28 in. (71.1 cm); flower 11 in. (27.9 cm). Midseason. A tan, melon, and orange polychrome, large, 7.0:1 spider with a darker halo and a green throat. Diploid. 'Arachnephobia' × 'Carolicolossal'. MARY ANNE LEISEN

'Twiggy' (Jerry Dickerson 1990). Dormant. Scape 18 in. (45.7 cm); flower 4 in. (10.2 cm). Midseason. A 6.3:1, bright burnt orange spider with a strong wine eye and a green throat. Diploid. Seedling × 'Kindly Light'. MARY ANNE LEISEN

'Tylwyth Teg' (Rosemary Whitacre 1988). Semi-evergreen. Scape 40 in. (101.6 cm); flower 8 in. (20.3 cm). Midseason. A pale cream-rainbow polychrome, 5.6:1 spider with a pale gold throat. Diploid. 'Sylph' × (('Satin Glass' × 'Frances Fay') × 'Arachne'). MARY ANNE LEISEN

'Velvet Widow' (Patrick Stamile 1988). Dormant. Scape 29 in. (73.7 cm); flower 8 in. (20.3 cm). Early midseason. A large, dark velvet-red self with a green throat. Tetraploid. (('Barbarossa' × 'Tet. Duddha') × 'Zorro') × 'Moonless Night'. PATRICK STAMILE

'Victorian Ribbons' (Bill Reinke 1992). Evergreen. Scape 40 in. (101.6 cm); flower 9 in. (22.9 cm). Midseason. A large, pale lavender unusual form with a darker halo above a green throat. Diploid. Parents unknown. TED L. PETIT & JOHN P. PEAT

'Watchyl Cyber Spider' (Mary Kreger 1995). Dormant. Scape 30 in. (76.2 cm); flower 14 in. (35.6 cm). Midseason. A very pale yellow with red eyezone and a green throat. Diploid. Parents unknown. TED L. PETIT & JOHN P. PEAT

'Whirling Fury' (L. Parker 1969). Semi-ever-green. Scape 26 in. (66.0 cm); flower 6 in. (15.2 cm). Early midseason. A bright green-yellow unusual form blend with a green throat. Diploid. 'Easter Greeting' × 'Green Dragon'. MARY ANNE LEISEN

'Wilson Spider' (William Oakes 1987). Dor-mant. Scape 28 in. (71.1 cm); flower 7.5 in. (19.1 cm). Midseason. A 4.6:1, lavender-purple spi-der variant with a chartreuse throat. Diploid. Parents unknown. Harris Olsen Spider Award 1994. MARY ANNE LEISEN

'Wind Frills' (Inez Tarrant 1978). Evergreen. Scape 34 in. (86.4 cm); flower 7 in. (17.8 cm). Early midseason. A cream-pink, lightly ruffled unusual form with a yellow-green throat. Dip-loid. 'Brazosport' × seedling. Award of Merit 1989. TED L. PETIT & JOHN P. PEAT

'Windmill Yellow' (Sarah Sikes 1992). Semi-evergreen. Scape 32 in. (81.3 cm); flower 8 in. (20.3 cm). Midseason. A clear lemon-yellow unusual form with a green center. Diploid. 'Green Widow' × 'Mynelle's Starfish'. TED L. PETIT & JOHN P. PEAT

'Wuthering Heights' (John R. Lambert 1966).
Evergreen. Scape 30 in. (76.2 cm); flower
7.25 in. (18.4 cm). Midseason. A dark ruby-
red with black overlay and a yellow-green
throat. Diploid. Parents unknown.
CURTIS & LINDA SUE BARNES

CHAPTER EIGHT
Polytepal Daylilies

The typical single daylily has three sepals and three petals. The sepals and petals together are known as tepals. Polytepals, therefore, are flowers that contain more than the typical number of tepals. It would be easier to think of the flowers in their proper perspective if botanists had reversed the letters and referred to these flowers as "polypetaled," a term most people would easily understand. Most people first notice that these flowers have more than the typical three petals.

As explained in chapter 6, the daylily flower is composed of four whorls: (1) sepals, (2) petals, (3) stamens, and (4) the pistil. Normally, each whorl has a characteristic number of segments: for example, the typical daylily has three sepals and three petals. Typically two stamens are associated with each petal, one attached to the center of the petal and the other attached to the edge, making six the usual number of stamens in the whorl. Every daylily has only one pistil, but upon close inspection you can see that it is divided into three parts. In short, the typical daylily is a three-part affair, with layers of flower parts all divisible by three.

The polytepal flower changes all this by increasing the basic number from three to four, five, or possibly even more. In cases in which the basic segments have been changed from three to four, each flower part exists in multiples of four. This results in four sepals and four petals. Since there are four petals, each with its characteristic two stamens, the flower has eight stamens instead of the usual six. The pistil also contains four chambers. It is difficult to see that the pistil has four, rather than three, chambers, but the seed pod will show it more clearly. If you pollinate the pistil, allow the flower to form a seed pod, and allow the seed pod to mature, you can clearly see that the seed pod has four seed chambers, rather than the typical three.

Though we have discussed the change from three to four components, the base number of segments does not appear to be limited. Four-petaled polytepal daylilies are most common, but several hybrids often produce five-petaled flowers. These also have five sepals, ten stamens, and a five-chambered pistil and seed pod. Evidence seems to indicate that the number of basic segments can be increased further, but we are not yet aware of any daylilies with more than five to six segments. Flowers of five or more segments are often referred to as super polytepals or superpolys.

People often confuse polytepal daylilies with double daylilies since both contain more than the normal number of petals. Look again at the diagram of the daylily in chapter 6, and consider the concept of flower whorls or layers. Double daylilies increase the number of petals or petaloids either by adding extra whorls or layers of petals or by modifying stamens. Each whorl of petals, however, still contains three petals. And the whorl of stamens still can only produce six petaloids. Polytepals, on the other hand, do something very different. First, no petaloid tissue is added to the stamens. Second, polytepals have only one layer of petals. Instead of adding layers, they change the number of petals within the single layer.

Polytepals are not universally loved. Many hybridizers see them as the ugly ducklings of daylilies. One daylily grower thought they were so ugly that whenever he saw a polytepal bloom he quickly picked it and threw it into the bushes before any garden visitor could see it. However, since hybridizers see "through" the flower into future generations, we see in the present polytepals the potential for great daylilies. Polytepals with four petals tend to look square, which has less of an aesthetic appeal for many people; however, we are in the infancy of this flower type. Most polytepals lack petal width and refinement, but such is typical of the early days of any breeding effort. Also, all commercially available polytepal cultivars thus far are diploid—with some exceptions, hybridizing efforts and breaks by serious hybridizers today occur at the tetraploid level. The lack of even a single readily available tetraploid polytepal has seriously hindered hybridizing efforts to date. However, several tetraploids occasionally throw polytepal blooms, and efforts are ongoing to convert diploid polytepals to tetraploid.

Many hybridizers hope to see polytepal flowers become more beautiful as modern daylily features are bred into them. One major goal is to breed five-petaled daylilies for the round and full look that five petals can impart. Increasing petal width has been a goal among normal single-daylily hybridizers in their work towards rounder flower form—five petals would instantly give an even rounder form to the flower. With additional petals, other features such as fancy edges become more dramatic. The possibilities for polytepal daylilies still can be only imagined: polytepal doubles would exponentially increase the number of flower petals and fullness of bloom, and polytepal spiders would have more hanging tendrils, looking more and more like spiders!

'Borg Invasion' (Bobby Baxter). Dormant. Scape 27 in. (68.6 cm); flower 5.5 in. (14.0 cm). Midseason. A pink polytepal with white midribs and a yellow throat. Diploid. 'Isolde' × 'Quad Eye'. BOBBY BAXTER

'Carolina Flying Poly Possum' (Bobby Baxter). Semi-evergreen. Scape 27 in. (68.6 cm); flower 8.5 in. (21.6 cm). Early midseason. A diamond-dusted pastel yellow with a large red eye and chartreuse throat. Diploid. Parents unknown. BOBBY BAXTER

'Dempsey Foursome' (Harrold Dempsey 1992). Dormant. Scape 24 in. (61.0 cm); flower 6 in. (15.2 cm). Early. Mauve-pink with purple eyezone above a chartreuse throat. Diploid. Parents unknown. BOBBY BAXTER

'Four Play' (Jeff Pansing 1998). Semi-evergreen. Scape 24 in. (61.0 cm); flower 5.5 in. (14.0 cm). Early midseason. A canary-yellow polytepal with a green throat. Diploid. Parents unknown. TED L. PETIT & JOHN P. PEAT

'Fuchsia Four' (Bill Reinke 1995). Semi-evergreen. Scape 22 in. (55.9 cm); flower 7 in. (17.8 cm). Midseason. A fuchsia self with large green center. Diploid. 'Open Hearth' × 'Chance'. BOBBY BAXTER

'Got No Goat' (Bobby Baxter). Evergreen. Scape 29 in. (73.6 cm); flower 6 in. (15.2 cm). Midseason. A high percentage polytepal with a faint eyezone and striking white midrib. Diploid. 'Quad Eye' × 'Isolde'. BOBBY BAXTER

'I'm Different' (E. Beckham 1981). Semi-evergreen. Scape 20 in. (50.8 cm); flower 7.5 in. (19.1 cm). Midseason. A cream-yellow self with a yellow-green throat. Diploid. 'White Doubloon' × 'Harry Barras'. BOBBY BAXTER

'Open Hearth' (John R. Lambert 1976). Dormant. Scape 26 in. (66.0 cm); flower 9 in. (22.9 cm). Midseason. Red and copper bitone with ruby halo and a green throat. Diploid. ('Droednoeth' × 'Lonnie') × 'Chocolate Pudding'. CURTIS & LINDA SUE BARNES

'Illusionary Horizon' (Bobby Baxter). Dormant. Scape 35 in. (88.9 cm); flower 6 in. (15.2 cm). Midseason. Watermelon polytepal with a darker eye above a yellow throat. Diploid. 'Queen of Diamonds' 'Quad Eye'.
BOBBY BAXTER

'Ruby Spider' (Patrick Stamile 1991). Dormant. Scape 34 in. (86.4 cm); flower 9 in. (22.9 cm). Early. A ruby-red, unusual-form self with a yellow throat. Tetraploid. 'Velvet Widow' × 'Tet. Open Hearth'. TED L. PETIT & JOHN P. PEAT

'Sallie Brown' (Bill Reinke 1994). Dormant. Scape 28 in. (71.1 cm); flower 7 in. (17.8 cm). Midseason. An amber-salmon blend with a green throat. Diploid. 'Open Hearth' × unknown. BILL & JOYCE REINKE

'Starry Day' (Philip Adams and Evelyn Adams 1991). Dormant. Scape 34 in. (86.4 cm); flower 5.5 in. (14.0 cm). Midseason. A clear yellow self with vibrant green throat. Diploid. Parents unknown. BOBBY BAXTER

'Tepaled Teddy' (Jack Carpenter 1995). Dormant. Scape 26 in. (66.0 cm); flower 6.5 in. (16.5 cm). Midseason. A buff-coral-peach blend with a bold mahogany-black eye and a yellow-green throat. Diploid. Parents unknown. BOBBY BAXTER

CHAPTER NINE
Small and Miniature Daylilies

The small-flowered daylily has its own intrinsic appeal and dedicated following. The very small flowers create charming and delightful bouquets of their own. They hold a special attraction, perhaps for the childlike, miniature world they seem to inhabit. The small-flowered daylily hybrids created by hybridizers are not simply smaller versions of large flowers. They have many characteristics that large-flower hybridizers wish to have in their lines.

Miniatures are flowers less than 3 in. (7.6 cm) across, and small flowers, or ponies, are those 3–4.5 in. (7.6–11.4 cm). Much of the work in small flowers has been carried out by the continuous efforts of hybridizers such as Elizabeth Salter, Pauline Henry, and Grace Stamile, who had to build an entire breeding line beginning from the large-flowered diploids. Each has left a personal stamp on the flowers she has created. Stamile has created a series of small-flowered diploids and has moved on to creating a tetraploid line that includes eyed, edged, and even small-flowered doubles. Henry has created the Siloam Series of small-flowered daylilies, concentrating exclusively at the diploid level. Many of her flowers have interesting eyes or patterns. Salter started hybridizing small-flowered daylilies in the late 1960s when she was still in her late teens. She initially created complex eyes in diploids and has moved toward boldly colored eyes and blue eyes at the tetraploid level. Many patterns found in her miniatures are unique to her flowers, and other hybridizers are making intense efforts to bring these features into large-flowered tetraploids. Other hybridizers working with miniatures are striving for doubles, spiders, and all sorts of dramatic forms. Small daylilies is one focus that certainly continues to move at a rapid pace.

'Addie Branch Smith' (Pauline Henry 1977). Dormant. Scape 20 in. (50.8 cm); flower 4 in. (10.2 cm). Midseason. A triangular orchid-rose with a purple eyezone and a green throat. Diploid. Parents unknown. TOM ROOD

'Angel's Smile' (Charles Reckamp and Charles Klehm 1985). Dormant. Scape 23 in. (58.4 cm); flower 4 in. (10.2 cm). Midseason. A pale cream-pink blend edged in yellow-gold with a green throat. Very important breeder. Tetraploid. Parents unknown. PATRICK STAMILE

'Baby Fresh' (Enman R. Joiner 1991). Evergreen. Scape 16 in. (40.6 cm); flower 3.5 in. (8.9 cm). Early midseason. A lightly ruffled, light peach self with a light green throat. Diploid. Seedling × 'My Pet'. TED L. PETIT & JOHN P. PEAT

'Beat the Barons' (Ra Hansen 1991). Evergreen. Scape 22 in. (55.9 cm); flower 3.75 in. (9.5 cm). Late. A round, bright yellow self with a striking, large, deep cherry eyezone above an emerald-green throat. Diploid. ('Ladybug's Louise' × 'Summer Echoes') × Janice Brown'. RA HANSEN

'Beloved Deceiver' (Jeff Salter 1996). Evergreen. Scape 24 in. (61.0 cm); flower 4.5 in. (11.4 cm). Mid-season late. A round, recurved, soft pink with a large, strong rose-red eye and a green throat. Tetraploid. Parents unknown. TED L. PETIT & JOHN P. PEAT

'Bibbity Bobbity Boo' (Elizabeth H. Salter 1992). Semi-evergreen. Scape 18 in. (45.7 cm); flower 2.75 in. (7.0 cm). Early midseason. A lavender-rose self with a dark grape-purple eye above a green center. Tetraploid. Seedling × Tet. Witch's Thimble'. JOHN EISEMAN

'Bird's Eye' (David Kirchhoff 1985). Evergreen. Scape 20 in. (50.8 cm); flower 3.5 in. (8.9 cm). Extra early. A pale ivory-cream with a very small, precise, rose-pink band surrounding a striking green center. Tetraploid. 'Chick Pink' × 'Nagasaki'. JOHN EISEMAN

'Black Lace' (Mac Carter 1997). Dormant. Scape 14 in. (35.6 cm); flower 4 in. (10.2 cm). Midseason. A near-black self with white edges and a green throat. Tetraploid. 'Rhapsody in Black' × 'Misty Night'. MAC CARTER

'Black Eyed Stella' (R. Roberson 1989). Dormant. Scape 13 in. (33.02 cm); flower 3 in. (7.6 cm). Early. A golden yellow with dark rose eyezone and a yellow-gold throat. Used heavily in landscaping. Diploid. 'Stella de Oro' × 'Little Celena'. TED L. PETIT & JOHN P. PEAT

'Bold Tiger' (Patrick Stamile 1990). Dormant. Scape 28 in. (71.1 cm); flower 4.25 in. (10.8 cm). Midseason. A bright orange self with a bold red eye and a green throat. Tetraploid. 'Hot Town' × 'Tet. Siloam Virginia Henson'. PATRICK STAMILE

'Blackberry Candy' (Patrick Stamile 1992). Dormant. Scape 25 in. (63.5 cm); flower 4 in. (10.2 cm). Midseason. A wide-petaled, round, gold self with a strong near-black eye. Tetraploid. 'Raging Tiger' × 'Tet. Siloam Virginia Henson'. PATRICK STAMILE

'Blood Spot' (Bryant Millikan 1983). Semi-evergreen. Scape 25 in. (63.5 cm); flower 4.5 in. (11.4 cm). Midseason late. A dark, rich, deep red with a small darker halo, and a lime-green heart. Tetraploid. 'James Marsh' × ('Gentle Dragon' × 'Annie Golightly'). PATRICK STAMILE

'Breed Apart' (Elizabeth H. Salter 1996). Semi-evergreen. Scape 26 in. (66.0 cm); flower 4.25 in. (10.8 cm). Midseason. An orange-coral blend with a green throat. Tetraploid. Parents unknown. TED L. PETIT & JOHN P. PEAT

'Bridget' (Clara Pittard 1974). Semi-evergreen. Scape 20 in. (50.8 cm); flower 3 in. (7.6 cm). Midseason. A dark red self of a triangular, tailored form with a green-yellow throat. Diploid. Parents unknown. GAIL KORN

'Broadway Angel' (Grace Stamile 1996). Dormant. Scape 22 in. (55.9 cm); flower 3.25 in. (8.3 cm). Midseason. A ruffled lavender-pink blend with a burgundy-purple eyezone and a strong green center. Tetraploid. 'Broadway Baby' × 'Angel's Smile'. PATRICK STAMILE

'Broadway Baby' (Grace Stamile 1991). Dormant. Scape 23 in. (58.4 cm); flower 2.75 in. (7.0 cm). Midseason. A round ivory-cream with a deep red eyezone above a green heart. Tetraploid. 'Tet. Siloam Virginia Hensen' × 'Tet. Siloam Red Toy'. PATRICK STAMILE

'Broadway Gal' (Grace Stamile 1991). Dormant. Scape 26 in. (66.0 cm); flower 3 in. (7.6 cm). Midseason. A ruffled, gold-edged, cream-pink-peach blend with a red eyezone above a green throat. Tetraploid. 'Tet. Siloam Virginia Henson' × 'Tet. Siloam Red Toy'. PATRICK STAMILE

'Broadway Gnome' (Grace Stamile 1997). Dormant. Scape 18 in. (45.7 cm); flower 3.5 in. (8.9 cm). Late. Pale yellow with a mauve eyezone and pale yellow throat. Tetraploid. ('Touch of Wonder' × seedling) × 'Tet. Priscilla's Rainbow'. PATRICK STAMILE

'Broadway Imp' (Grace Stamile 1996). Dormant. Scape 16 in. (40.6 cm); 2.75 in. (7.0 cm) flower. Midseason late. A wide-petaled, creped raspberry-rose with raspberry-red eyezone and a green heart. Tetraploid. 'Broadway Ingenue' × (seedling × 'Chorus Line Kid'). PATRICK STAMILE

'Broadway Ingenue' (Grace Stamile 1991). Dormant. Scape 26 in. (66.0 cm); flower 3.25 in. (8.3 cm). Midseason. A bright rose-red with a red eyezone above a green heart. Tetraploid. 'Tet. Siloam Virginia Henson' × 'Tet. Siloam Red Toy'. PATRICK STAMILE

'Broadway Pink Slippers' (Grace Stamile 1995). Dormant. Scape 16 in. (40.6 cm); flower 3 in. (7.6 cm). Midseason late. A round, loosely ruffled, deep pink self with rose halo and a green throat. Tetraploid. 'Broadway Ingenue' × (seedling × 'Chorus Line Kid'). PATRICK STAMILE

'Butterpat' (Robert Kennedy 1970). Dormant. Scape 20 in. (50.8 cm); flower 2.5 in. (6.4 cm). Midseason. A recurved medium yellow self with a green center. Diploid. Parents unknown. Award of Merit 1977. Donald Fischer Memorial Cup 1977. TED L. PETIT & JOHN P. PEAT

'Cherry Berry' (Patrick Stamile 1989). Dormant. Scape 30 in. (76.2 cm); flower 4.25 in. (10.8 cm). Midseason. A pale cream-pink with a wine eyezone, slight picotee, and a green throat. Tetraploid. 'Tet. Siloam Virginia Henson' × 'Chicago Picotee Ballet'. PATRICK STAMILE

'Cherry Candy' (Patrick Stamile 1989). Dormant. Scape 30 in. (76.2 cm); flower 4.25 in. (10.8 cm). Midseason. A ruffled, wide-petaled cream-peach with a bold cherry-red eye above a green throat. Tetraploid. 'Raging Tiger' × 'Siloam Virginia Henson'. PATRICK STAMILE

'Camden Gold Dollar' (Clarke Yancey 1982). Semi-evergreen. Scape 19 in. (48.3 cm); flower 3 in. (7.6 cm). Early midseason. A lightly ruffled, deep yellow self with a green throat. Diploid. Seedling × 'Squeaky'. Award of Merit 1989. TED L. PETIT & JOHN P. PEAT

'Chorus Line Kid' (Grace Stamile 1991). Dormant. Scape 26 in. (66.0 cm); flower 3.5 in. (8.9 cm). Early midseason. A round, recurved peach-pink with a chevron, rose eye above a large green center. Tetraploid. 'Tet. Siloam Virginia Henson' × 'Tet. Chorus Line Kid'.
PATRICK STAMILE

'Cinnamon Circle' (Harrold Harris and John Benz 1988). Dormant. Scape 24 in. (61.0 cm); flower 4.5 in. (11.4 cm). Midseason. A yellow self brushed with a cinnamon blend and a green throat. Tetraploid. 'Gentleman Lou' × 'Matt'. MELANIE MASON

'Ciao' (Ra Hansen 1986). Semi-evergreen. Scape 16 in. (40.6 cm); flower 4 in. (10.2 cm). Early. A rose-red with a chartreuse halo and large, deep olive-green throat. Diploid. ('Jumbo Red' × 'Luke Senior') × 'Christmas'. RA HANSEN

'Clairvoyant Lady' (Ra Hansen 1992). Semi-evergreen. Scape 22 in. (55.9 cm); flower 4 in. (10.2 cm). Late. A recurved, purple-veined, light violet self with a very large purple eye-zone above a large green throat. Very dramatic eye. Diploid. ('Futuristic Art' × 'Charlie Pierce Memorial') × ('Janice Brown' × 'Night Beacon').
RA HANSEN

'Custard Candy' (Patrick Stamile 1989). Dormant. Scape 24 in. (61.0 cm); flower 4.25 in. (10.8 cm). Early midseason. A round, recurved cream-yellow with a bold maroon eye above a green throat. Tetraploid. (('Chicago Picotee Queen' × 'Byzantine Emperor') × 'Frandean') × 'Tet. Siloam Virginia Henson'. Award of Merit 1996. Annie T. Giles Award 1996.
PATRICK STAMILE

'Daggy' (Enman R. Joiner 1993). Evergreen. Scape 20 in. (50.8 cm); flower 3.5 in. (8.9 cm). Early. A yellow-ochre with a dark burgundy-red eyezone above a green throat. Diploid. 'Enchanter's Spell' × 'Baby Fresh'. TED L. PETIT & JOHN P. PEAT

'Dark Avenger' (Elizabeth H. Salter 1988). Semi-evergreen. Scape 18 in. (45.7 cm); flower 2.5 in. (6.4 cm). Midseason. A dark, saturated red self with a yellow-green throat. Diploid. Parents unknown. Award of Merit 1997. Donald Fischer Memorial Cup 1997. JAY TOMPKINS

'Dead Ringer' (Elizabeth H. Salter 1991). Semi-evergreen. Scape 20 in. (50.8 cm); flower 2.75 in. (7.0 cm). Midseason late. A rose-lavender-pink with a deep, dark purple eye above a green throat. Diploid. 'Enchanter's Spell' × 'Siloam Bertie Ferris'. TED L. PETIT & JOHN P. PEAT

'Dee Dee's Baby' (Mac Carter 1996). Dormant. Scape 22 in. (55.9 cm); flower 3.75 in. (9.5 cm). Midseason. A peach-pink base with a large, dramatic purple eyezone and a green throat. Tetraploid. 'Paper Butterfly' × 'Daring Dilemma'. MAC CARTER

'Dewberry Candy' (Patrick Stamile 1990). Dormant. Scape 22 in. (55.9 cm); flower 3.75 in. (9.5 cm). Midseason. A round and recurved cream-pink with a purple eyezone and slight picotee above a deep green throat. Tetraploid. (seedling × 'Chicago Picotee Ballet') × 'Tet. Siloam Virginia Henson'. PATRICK STAMILE

'Dragon Heart' (Elizabeth H. Salter 1996). Evergreen. Scape 28 in. (71.1 cm); flower 4 in. (10.2 cm). Midseason. A rose-pink with a bright red eye and a green throat. Diploid. 'Eye of Newt' × seedling. TED L. PETIT & JOHN P. PEAT

'Dragons Eye' (Elizabeth H. Salter 1992). Semi-evergreen. Scape 24 in. (61.0 cm); flower 4 in. (10.2 cm). Midseason late. A famous rose-red eyezone on a clear, pastel pink self, and a green throat. Diploid. 'Enchanter's Spell' × 'Janice Brown'. Annie T. Giles Award 1997. TED L. PETIT & JOHN P. PEAT

'Dream Legacy' (Patrick Stamile 1995). Dormant. Scape 26 in. (66.0 cm); flower 4.5 in. (11.4 cm). Midseason. An ivory-cream-white with a deep wine-red eyezone and picotee above a green throat. Tetraploid. 'Cherry Drop' × 'Royal Braid'. PATRICK STAMILE

'Dragon's Orb' (Elizabeth H. Salter 1986). Evergreen. Scape 20 in. (50.8 cm); flower 2.75 in. (7.0 cm). Midseason. A pale ivory-white self with a black eyezone and a chartreuse-lemon throat. Diploid. 'Corsican Bandit' × 'Dragons Eye'. Donald Fischer Memorial Cup 1994. CURTIS & LINDA SUE BARNES

'Earth Angel' (Patrick Stamile 1987). Dormant. Scape 25 in. (63.5 cm); flower 4.5 in. (11.4 cm). Early midseason. A wide-petaled, very ruffled apricot self with a green throat. Very famous. Tetraploid. 'Touch Me' × 'Ever So Ruffled'. PATRICK STAMILE

'El Desperado' (Patrick Stamile 1991). Dormant. Scape 28 in. (71.1 cm); flower 4.25 in. (10.8 cm). Late. A mustard-yellow self with a striking wine-purple eye above a deep green throat. Tetraploid. 'El Bandito' × 'Blackberry Candy'. PATRICK STAMILE

'Elegant Candy' (Patrick Stamile 1995). Dormant. Scape 25 in. (63.5 cm); flower 4.25 in. (10.8 cm). Early midseason. A wide-petaled, ruffled, clear pink with a deep red band above a green heart. Tetraploid. 'Lady of Fortune' × 'Tet. Janice Brown'. PATRICK STAMILE

'Eye of Newt' (Elizabeth H. Salter 1988). Semi-evergreen. Scape 18 in. (45.7 cm); flower 3 in. (7.6 cm). Midseason late. A cream-yellow-gold with a bold near-black eye and a green throat. Diploid. Parents unknown. PATRICK STAMILE

'Faberge' (Ida Munson 1986). Evergreen. Scape 20 in. (50.8 cm); flower 4.5 in. (11.4 cm). Midseason. An orchid-pink-lavender with gold-edged, crimped ruffling, a chalk-pink eyezone, and a yellow-green throat. Tetraploid. 'Sir Oliver' × 'Ruffles Elegante'. TED L. PETIT & JOHN P. PEAT

'Fairy Filigree' (Elizabeth H. Salter 1990). Semi-evergreen. Scape 32 in. (81.3 cm); flower 3.5 in. (8.9 cm). Midseason late. A classic, triangular, cream-yellow to pink self with a gold edge and a green throat. Tetraploid. Parents unknown. TED L. PETIT & JOHN P. PEAT

'Fan Club' (John Shooter 1992). Semi-evergreen. Scape 27 in. (68.6 cm); flower 4 in. (10.2 cm). Midseason. A veined light lavender with a purple band above a chartreuse throat. Diploid. Parents unknown. TED L. PETIT & JOHN P. PEAT

'Forsyth Hot Lips' (Wyatt LeFever 1988). Dormant. Scape 23 in. (58.4 cm); flower 4.5 in. (11.4 cm). Early midseason. A wide-petaled peach-pink with a red band surrounding a green throat. Diploid. 'Ambivalent Angel' × seedling. JOHN EISEMAN

'Guiniver's Gift' (Elizabeth H. Salter 1989). Evergreen. Scape 18 in. (45.7 cm); flower 3.25 in. (8.3 cm). Early midseason. A cream-yellow-peach blend with a green throat. Lightly ruffled. Tetraploid. (('Adah' × ('Sabie' × ('Knave' × 'Chicago Royal'))) × ((('Grand Prize' × seedling) × 'Teahouse Geisha') × 'Stolen Base')) × 'Tet. Moonlight Mist'. TED L. PETIT & JOHN P. PEAT

'Her Majesty's Wizard' (Elizabeth H. Salter 1996). Semi-evergreen. Scape 24 in. (61.0 cm); flower 4.5 in. (11.4 cm). Early midseason. A gold-edged purple blend with a lighter watermark above a green throat. Tetraploid. ('Elizabeth's Magic' × 'Tomorrow's Dream') × ('Elizabeth's Magic' × 'Tomorrow's Dream').
TED L. PETIT & JOHN P. PEAT

'In the Navy' (Elizabeth H. Salter 1993). Semi-evergreen. Scape 18 in. (45.7 cm); flower 3 in. (7.6 cm). Midseason. A lavender to pink self with a dark navy-blue eye above a green throat. Very special. Diploid. Parents unknown.
TED L. PETIT & JOHN P. PEAT

'Indian Giver' (Elizabeth Ferguson 1991). Semi-evergreen. Scape 20 in. (50.8 cm); flower 4.5 in. (11.4 cm). Early midseason. A burgundy to purple with lighter edge and a medium purple watermark above a green throat. Diploid. Parents unknown. JOHN EISEMAN

'Jackie's Choice' (Mort Morss 1990). Dormant. Scape 24 in. (61.0 cm); flower 4.5 in. (11.4 cm). Early midseason. A rich burgundy-purple with a bluish lavender watermark and a green throat. Tetraploid. ('Mort's Magic' × ('Inner View' × 'Thais')) × ('Zinfandel' × (('Charles Hamil' × 'Tet. Oliver Monette') × 'Rings of Glory')). JOHN EISEMAN

'Little Angel Eyes' (Grace Stamile 1997). Dormant. Scape 18 in. (45.7 cm); flower 2.5 in. (6.4 cm). Midseason. A cream-lavender with a striking plum-purple eyezone and a green throat. Diploid. Seedling × (('Arcadian Sprite' × 'Alpine Mist') × 'Siloam Art Work'). PATRICK STAMILE

'Little Baby Mine' (Elizabeth H. Salter 1994). Semi-evergreen. Scape 18 in. (45.7 cm); flower 3 in. (7.6 cm). Midseason. A pale cream-pink with a deep rose-pink eye above a green throat. Diploid. Parents unknown. TED L. PETIT & JOHN P. PEAT

'Little Cadet' (Dalton Durio 1979). Dormant. Scape 18 in. (45.7 cm); flower 3 in. (7.6 cm). Early midseason. A tailored, loosely ruffled, clear yellow with a burgundy-red eyezone above a green throat. Diploid. 'Buffys Doll' × 'Little Suzie'. TED L. PETIT & JOHN P. PEAT

'Little Clown' (Grace Stamile 1997). Dormant. Scape 12 in. (30.5 cm); flower 2.5 in. (6.4 cm). Midseason. A soft cream-pink with a large rose eye, lighter petal edges, and a green throat. Diploid. 'Little Romance' × ('Siloam Tiny Tim' × 'Siloam Grace Stamile'). PATRICK STAMILE

'Little Deeke' (Lucille Guidry 1980). Evergreen. Scape 20 in. (50.8 cm); flower 4.5 in. (11.4 cm). Extra early. A ruffled orange-gold blend with a green throat. Diploid. Parents unknown. Award of Merit 1986. Annie T. Giles Award 1993. JOHN EISEMAN

'Little Fantastic' (E. L. Cunningham 1977). Semi-evergreen. Scape 20 in. (50.8 cm); flower 3 in. (7.6 cm). Early midseason. A warm, medium pink self with a green throat. Diploid. 'Little Dumplin' × 'Ella Thomas Riggins'. TED L. PETIT & JOHN P. PEAT

'Little Maggie' (W. Williamson 1981). Evergreen. Scape 12 in. (30.5 cm); flower 3 in. (7.6 cm). Early. A rose-pink with a burgundy eyezone and a green throat. Diploid. Parents unknown. JOHN EISEMAN

'Little Red Warbler' (Clarence Crochet 1985). Dormant. Scape 18 in. (45.7 cm); flower 3.5 in. (8.9 cm). A rose-red self with white midribs, a large dark maroon eye, and a yellow-green throat. Diploid. Parents unknown. PATRICIA LOVELAND

'Love Those Eyes' (George Rasmussen 1987). Dormant. Scape 24 in. (61.0 cm); flower 4.5 in. (11.4 cm). Midseason. A triangular, classically formed golden-yellow with a red eyezone and a gold throat. Tetraploid. 'Bandit Man' × seedling. TED L. PETIT & JOHN P. PEAT

'Little Zinger' (Edna Lankart 1979). Semi-evergreen. Scape 16 in. (40.6 cm); flower 2.75 in. (7.0 cm). Early midseason. A deep, clear red self with a green throat. Diploid. Parents unknown. Award of Merit 1989. Donald Fischer Memorial Cup 1986. JOHN EISEMAN

'Lullaby Baby' (Elsie Spalding 1975). Semi-evergreen. Scape 19 in. (48.3 cm); flower 3.5 in. (8.9 cm). Midseason. A very pale cream to light pink self with a strong green heart. Diploid. Parents unknown. Award of Merit 1983. Annie T. Giles Award 1982. Lenington All-American Award 1988. TED L. PETIT & JOHN P. PEAT

'Malmaison Plum' (R. W. Munson Jr. 1994). Semi-evergreen. Scape 24 in. (61.0 cm); flower 4.5 in. (11.4 cm). Midseason. A deep, rich purple with a distinct, chalky plum watermark above a green throat. Tetraploid. 'Nivia Guest' × 'Cameroons'. R. W. MUNSON JR

'Moonlight Mist' (Elizabeth H. Hudson 1981). Evergreen. Scape 18 in. (45.7 cm); flower 3 in. (7.6 cm). Midseason. A frost-pink-peach blend with a chartreuse throat. Diploid. 'Lullaby Baby' × ('Tropical Sherbert' × 'Munchkin Moon'). JOHN EISEMAN

'My Special Angel' (Elizabeth H. Salter 1996). Semi-evergreen. Scape 26 in. (66.0 cm); flower 3.5 in. (8.9 cm). Midseason. A bright cream flower with a heavily ruffled, fringed edge and a green throat. Tetraploid. 'Regency Summer' × 'Angel's Smile'. TED L. PETIT & JOHN P. PEAT

'Nacogdoches Bing Cherry' (Jean Barnhart 1987). Semi-evergreen. Scape 14 in. (35.6 cm); flower 2.5 in. (6.4 cm). Early. A cream-dusty-rose to cream-lavender with a dark, dramatic purple eyezone and a green throat. Diploid. Seedling × 'Siloam French Doll'. TED L. PETIT & JOHN P. PEAT

'Navajo Princess' (Ra Hansen 1992). Semi-evergreen. Scape 24 in. (61.0 cm); flower 4.5 in. (11.4 cm). Midseason late. A pale pink self with a large, bold, triangular, rose eyezone above a deep, triangular, dark green throat. Very distinctive. Diploid. 'Futuristic Art' × 'Janice Brown'. RA HANSEN

'Night Beacon' (Ra Hansen 1988). Evergreen. Scape 27 in. (68.6 cm); flower 4 in. (10.2 cm). Early midseason. A very dark black-purple with a large, striking lime-green center. Diploid. ('Motor Mouth' × 'Ciao') × 'Unique Purple'. RA HANSEN

'Oliver Dragon Tooth' (Mort Morss 1991). Semi-evergreen. Scape 20 in. (50.8 cm); flower 4.25 in. (10.8 cm). Midseason. A pale lavender-pink with a purple eyezone above a green throat. Tetraploid. 'Shadow Dance' × 'Tet. Siloam Virginia Henson'. TED L. PETIT & JOHN P. PEAT

'Oriental Mystery' (Elizabeth H. Salter 1992). Semi-evergreen. Scape 28 in. (71.1 cm); flower 4.5 in. (11.4 cm). Midseason late. A round pale lavender with a plum-purple eyezone above a yellow-green throat. Tetraploid. (('Fred Ham' × 'Pasha's Passport') × ('Fred Ham' × 'Pasha's Passport')) × 'Tet. Siloam Virginia Henson'. TED L. PETIT & JOHN P. PEAT

'Pandora's Box' (Dave Talbott 1980). Evergreen. Scape 19 in. (48.3 cm); flower 4 in. (10.2 cm). Early midseason. A triangular, pale cream with a purple eyezone and a green throat. Diploid. ('Prairie Blue Eyes' × 'Moment of Truth') × ('Apparition' × 'Moment of Truth'). Award of Merit 1987. Annie T. Giles Award 1987. JOHN EISEMAN

'Pardon Me' (Darrel Apps 1982). Dormant. Scape 18 in. (45.7 cm); flower 2.75 in. (7.0 cm). Midseason. A triangular, tailored, bright burgundy-red self with a yellow-green throat. Diploid. Seedling × 'Little Grapette'. Award of Merit 1987. Donald Fischer Memorial Cup 1985. TED L. PETIT & JOHN P. PEAT

'Pink Puff' (Walter Jablonski and Leo Sharp 1987). Dormant. Scape 21 in. (53.3 cm); flower 3.5 in. (8.9 cm). Early midseason. A very wide-petaled pink with a yellow halo and a green throat. Diploid. Parents unknown.
PATRICK STAMILE

'Plum Candy' (Patrick Stamile 1989). Evergreen. Scape 24 in. (61.0 cm); flower 4 in. (10.2 cm). Early midseason. A pale cream-peach with plum-purple eyezone and a gold throat. Tetraploid. 'Panache' × 'Tet. Siloam Virginia Henson'. PATRICK STAMILE

'Regency Summer' (Elizabeth H. Salter 1993). Semi-evergreen. Scape 26 in. (66.0 cm); flower 3.5 in. (8.9 cm). Early midseason. A gold-peach self with a ruffled, crunchy gold edge and a green throat. Tetraploid. 'Fairy Filigree' × 'Guinevere's Gift'. JOHN EISEMAN

'Renegade Lady' (Elizabeth H. Salter 1990). Evergreen. Scape 28 in. (71.1 cm); flower 4 in. (10.2 cm). Midseason late. A triangular, lightly ruffled yellow-gold with deep red eyezone and a green throat. Diploid. Parents unknown.
JOHN EISEMAN

'Robbie Salter' (David Kirchhoff 1982). Evergreen. Scape 24 in. (61.0 cm); flower 3.25 in. (8.3 cm). Midseason. A clear, medium coral-pink edged in buff with a deeper coral band above a green throat. Diploid. 'Fern Johnson' × 'Lullaby Baby'. DAVID KIRCHHOFF

'Roses with Peaches' (David Kirchhoff 1993). Semi-evergreen. Scape 22 in. (55.9 cm); flower 3.75 in. (9.5 cm). Extra early. A cream-peach with wire gold edge and a deep rose band above a yellow throat. Tetraploid. ('Ming Porcelain' × ('Dunedrift' × 'Dance Ballerina Dance')) × 'Tet. Siloam Virginia Henson'. TED L. PETIT & JOHN P. PEAT

'Ruffled Carousel' (Edwin C. Brown 1985). Semi-evergreen. Scape 23 in. (58.4 cm); flower 3.75 in. (9.5 cm). Early. A round cream self with an apricot-penciled eye and a yellow-green throat. Diploid. 'Siloam French Doll' × 'Ruffled Ivory'. TED L. PETIT & JOHN P. PEAT

'Selma Timmons' (R. W. Munson Jr. 1987). Semi-evergreen. Scape 18 in. (45.7 cm); flower 4.5 in. (11.4 cm). Early midseason. An apricot-pink self with a ruffled, crimped edge and a green heart. Tetraploid. ('Fugue' × 'Silk Brocade') × 'Dance Ballerina Dance'. PATRICK STAMILE

'Siloam Baby Doll' (Pauline Henry 1981). Dormant. Scape 18 in. (45.7 cm); flower 2.8 in. (7.1 cm). Midseason. A pale apricot self with a rose band and a green throat. Diploid. Parents unknown. PATRICK STAMILE

'Siloam Bo Peep' (Pauline Henry 1978). Dormant. Scape 18 in. (45.7 cm); flower 4.5 in. (11.4 cm). Early midseason. A striking orchid-pink blend with deep purple eyezone and a green throat. Diploid. Parents unknown. Award of Merit 1984. Annie T. Giles Award 1983. TED L. PETIT & JOHN P. PEAT

'Siloam Button Box' (Pauline Henry 1976). Dormant. Scape 20 in. (50.8 cm); flower 4.5 in. (11.4 cm). Early midseason. A pale cream self with maroon eyezone and a green throat. Diploid. Parents unknown. Award of Merit 1983. TED L. PETIT & JOHN P. PEAT

'Siloam Bye Lo' (Pauline Henry 1980). Dormant. Scape 16 in. (40.6 cm); flower 3.25 in. (8.3 cm). Midseason. A soft rose-pink with a red-banded eyezone and a green heart. Diploid. Parents unknown. JOHN EISEMAN

'Siloam Ethel Smith' (Pauline Henry 1981). Dormant. Scape 20 in. (50.8 cm); flower 3.25 in. (8.3 cm). Midseason. A very refined cream-pink-beige with a deep rose band and a dark green center. Diploid. Parents unknown. TED L. PETIT & JOHN P. PEAT

'Siloam Eye Shocker' (Pauline Henry 1987). Dormant. Scape 17 in. (43.2 cm); flower 3.5 in. (8.9 cm). Midseason. A striking, very dark, saturated red eye on a light rose self with green heart. Diploid. Parents unknown. PATRICK STAMILE

'Siloam Fairy Tale' (Pauline Henry 1978). Dormant. Scape 18 in. (45.7 cm); flower 2.5 in. (6.4 cm). Midseason. A pale ivory to pink with a deep orchid eyezone and a green throat. Diploid. Parents unknown. TOM ROOD

'Siloam Jim Cooper' (Pauline Henry 1981). Dormant. Scape 16 in. (40.6 cm); flower 3.5 in. (8.9 cm). Early midseason. A bright rose-red self with darker red eyezone and a green throat. Diploid. Parents unknown. Award of Merit 1989. Annie T. Giles Award 1988. JOHN EISEMAN

'Siloam Royal Prince' (Pauline Henry 1983).
Dormant. Scape 19 in. (48.3 cm); flower 4 in.
(10.2 cm). Midseason. A rich red-purple self
with a green throat and white midribs. Diploid. Parents unknown. JOHN EISEMAN

'Siloam Shocker' (Pauline Henry 1981). Dormant. Scape 28 in. (71.1 cm); flower 3.75 in. (9.5 cm).
Midseason. A pale ivory-pink with a bold red eyezone and a green throat. Diploid. Parents unknown. TED L. PETIT & JOHN P. PEAT

'Siloam Show Girl' (Pauline Henry 1981). Dormant. Scape 18 in. (45.7 cm); flower 4.25 in. (10.8 cm). Midseason. A triangular, lightly ruffled burgundy-red with a darker red eyezone and a green throat. Diploid. Parents unknown. TED L. PETIT & JOHN P. PEAT

'Siloam Sugar Time' (Pauline Henry 1981). Dormant. Scape 20 in. (50.8 cm); flower 2.75 in. (7.0 cm). Midseason. A loosely ruffled light apricot to peach-cream with a burgundy eyezone and a green throat. Diploid. Parents unknown. TED L. PETIT & JOHN P. PEAT

'Siloam Ury Winniford' (Pauline Henry 1980). Dormant. Scape 23 in. (58.4 cm); flower 3.25 in. (8.3 cm). Early midseason. A triangular deep cream with large, distinctive, purple chevron eyezone, and a green throat. Diploid. Parents unknown. TED L. PETIT & JOHN P. PEAT

'Siloam Virginia Henson' (Pauline Henry 1979). Dormant. Scape 18 in. (45.7 cm); flower 4 in. (10.2 cm). Early midseason. A pale ivory to pink with a precise ruby-red eyezone above a green throat. Very famous and popular for breeding. Diploid. Parents unknown. Award of Merit 1986. Annie T. Giles Award 1985. Don C. Stevens Award 1989. TED L. PETIT & JOHN P. PEAT

'Song of Singapore' (Mort Morss 1991). Evergreen. Scape 25 in. (63.5 cm); flower 4 in. (10.2 cm). Midseason. A rose-amethyst with slight bluish lavender halo above a yellow-green throat. Tetraploid. Parents unknown. JOHN EISEMAN

'Strawberry Candy' (Patrick Stamile 1989). Semi-evergreen. Scape 26 in. (66.0 cm); flower 4.25 in. (10.8 cm). Early midseason. A round, recurved, ruffled strawberry-pink blend with a rose-red eyezone and golden-green throat. Extremely popular. Tetraploid. 'Panache' × 'Tet. Siloam Virginia Henson'. Award of Merit 1996. Annie T. Giles Award 1994. Don C. Stevens Award 1995. PATRICK STAMILE

'Strawberry Fields Forever' (Patrick Stamile 1997). Evergreen. Scape 26 in. (66.0 cm); flower 4.5 in. (11.4 cm). Early midseason. A soft medium pink with a strawberry-rose eye and matching wide picotee on a braided edge above a green throat. Tetraploid. 'Blueberry Candy' × 'Creative Edge'. BETH CREVELING

'Sugar Cookie' (Darrel Apps 1983). Evergreen. Scape 21 in. (53.3 cm); flower 3.25 in. (8.3 cm). Early midseason. A very famous wide-petaled, ruffled cream self with a green throat. Diploid. 'Buffys Dolls' × 'Little Infant'. Award of Merit 1989. Annie T. Giles Award 1989. JAY TOMPKINS

'Sweet Sugar Candy' (Patrick Stamile 1991). Dormant. Scape 25 in. (63.5 cm); flower 4 in. (10.2 cm). Late. A circular, cream, clear pink with rose-red eyezone above a green throat. Tetraploid. 'Papillon' × 'Tet. Siloam Virginia Henson'. PATRICK STAMILE

'Taste of Paradise' (Matthew Kaskel 1996). Evergreen. Scape 20 in. (50.8 cm); 4.5 in. (11.4 cm) flower. Midseason. A very ruffled, wide-petaled, clear apricot-cream self. Tetraploid. Seedling × 'Senegal'. MATTHEW KASKEL

'Texas Sunlight' (Joyce Lewis 1986). Dormant. Scape 28 in. (71.1 cm); flower 2.75 in. (7.0 cm). Midseason. A round, recurved, bright gold self with a deep green center. Diploid. Parents unknown. JOHN EISEMAN

'Tigerling' (Patrick Stamile 1989). Dormant. Scape 25 in. (63.5 cm); flower 3.75 in. (9.5 cm). Midseason. A round, brilliant, light orange self with striking, bright red eyezone and picotee above a green throat. Tetraploid. 'Raging Tiger' × 'Tet. Siloam Virginia Henson'. Award of Merit 1997. PATRICK STAMILE

'Tigger' (Patrick Stamile 1989). Dormant. Scape 24 in. (61.0 cm); 4.25 in. (10.8 cm) flower. Midseason. A burnt orange-red self with a deeper red eyezone above a green heart. Tetraploid. Seedling × 'Tet. Siloam Virginia Henson'. PATRICK STAMILE

'Todd Monroe' (Edith Sholar 1974). Dormant. Scape 20 in. (50.8 cm); flower 3.25 in. (8.3 cm). Early midseason. A triangular, classic, light buff self with a bold fuchsia eyezone above a green throat. Diploid. 'Prairie Maid' × 'Joyful Heart'. JOHN EISEMAN

'Tropical Tangerine' (Elizabeth H. Salter 1986). Evergreen. Scape 20 in. (50.8 cm); flower 3.25 in. (8.3 cm). Midseason. A wide-petaled, round, slightly ruffled, orange, yellow, and salmon blend with a green heart. Tetraploid. (('Tet. Sabie' × seedling) × ('Dalai Lama' × 'Teahouse Geisha')) × 'Adah'. PATRICK STAMILE

'Tuscawilla Dave Talbott' (Ra Hansen 1991). Evergreen. Scape 26 in. (66.0 cm); flower 4 in. (10.2 cm). Early midseason. A pale almond self with a bold raisin eyezone above a deep emerald-green throat. Diploid. ('Summer Echoes' × seedling) × ('Summer Echoes' × seedling). RA HANSEN

'Unique Style' (Kate Carpenter 1985). Dormant. Scape 21 in. (53.3 cm); flower 3.75 in. (9.5 cm). Early midseason. A diamond-dusted cream-yellow with a dark rose-burgundy edge and a green throat. Diploid. 'Schoolmate' × seedling. JOHN EISEMAN

'Vanilla Candy' (Patrick Stamile 1990). Dormant. Scape 23 in. (58.4 cm); flower 4.25 in. (10.8 cm). Midseason. A cream-white with a burgundy-red eyezone and a green throat. Tetraploid. 'Tet. Siloam Virginia Henson' × 'Designer Gown'. PATRICK STAMILE

'Winter Mint Candy' (Patrick Stamile 1989). Dormant. Scape 30 in. (76.2 cm); flower 4.25 in. (10.8 cm). Midseason. A cream self with a wine-red eyezone and a green throat. Tetraploid. 'Tet. Siloam Virginia Henson' × 'Chicago Picotee Ballet'. PATRICK STAMILE

'Witch's Thimble' (Elizabeth H. Hudson 1981). Semi-evergreen. Scape 14 in. (35.6 cm); flower 2.25 in. (5.7 cm). Midseason. A cream to white-ivory with a striking black-purple eyezone and a green throat. Diploid. 'Elf Witch' × 'Dragons Eye'. PATRICK STAMILE

'Witches Wink' (Elizabeth H. Salter 1993). Semi-evergreen. Scape 26 in. (66.0 cm); flower 3 in. (7.6 cm). Early midseason. A very popular, clear, light yellow with a distinct plum eyezone above a green throat. Tetraploid. Seedling × 'Tet. Witch's Thimble'. TED L. PETIT & JOHN P. PEAT

'Wondrous' (R. W. Munson Jr. 1986). Semi-evergreen. Scape 22 in. (55.9 cm); flower 4.5 in. (11.4 cm). Early midseason. A very pale lavender-pink with a large, lighter watermark and a green throat. Tetraploid. ('Sir Oliver' × 'Doge of Venice') × 'Royal Saracen'. R. W. MUNSON JR

'Wynnson' (Olin Criswell 1977). Dormant. Scape 24 in. (61.0 cm); flower 4.5 in. (11.4 cm). Early midseason. A creped, light yellow self with a green throat. Diploid. 'Wynn' × seedling. PATRICK STAMILE

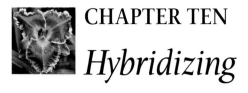 **CHAPTER TEN**
Hybridizing

Techniques

One great joy of daylilies is that it is so easy to create your own hybrids. Hybridizing allows for a wonderful expression of personal taste and a creative outlet for the spirit. Usually a person loves particular flowers more than others because of favorite colors or favorite forms, such as miniatures, spiders, or doubles. By breeding plants, you can create new plants that have enhanced or even new features just to your own personal liking. If you love miniatures but would like them even smaller, or would like some double miniatures, hybridizing is your chance to express those desires and create new, beautiful plants.

The actual technique of hybridizing daylilies is quite simple—anyone can do it. Creating new hybrids that express your specific interests is easy with daylilies and one reason so many people have become addicted to this plant. Simply take the pollen from one flower, paint it onto the pistil of another, harvest and plant the seeds, and within nine months to two years your newly created hybrids can bloom. Compare this to hybridizing orchids, for example, where the seeds must go to a laboratory to grow in test tubes, or camellias, which can take five to seven years to reach blooming size.

Hybridizing daylilies does have its pitfalls, but it also has tricks that can make it even easier. The steps of the hybridizing process are outlined below. They are also beautifully demonstrated in a 50-minute color video now available from We're In the Hayfield Now Daylily Gardens in Orono, Ontario (see Appendix A).

The easiest way to hybridize daylilies is to remove a stamen from one flower and brush its pollen onto the pistil of another flower. If the parents of a particular desired cross do not bloom at the same time, collect pollen from the pollen parent when it is in bloom and store it for use when the pod parent blooms. Many hybridizers pick the flower they wish to use as a pollen parent and place the entire flower in the refrigerator, where it will remain relatively fresh for two or more days, and use one or more stamens each day. The flowers should be collected early in the day since exposure to midday heat causes a progressive loss in pollen viability. If you have a limited amount of special pollen and would like to use it over a longer period of time, gently pull the anther with its attached pollen away from the stamen with a pair of tweezers. Alternatively, brush the pollen off the anther with a small artist's brush, which should be carefully cleaned of pollen between uses. In either case, the pollen (with or without the anther) can then be stored in the refrigerator for several months, or in the freezer for several years. We have used a number of different storage containers for pollen, from simple packets made by folding aluminum foil, to inexpensive plastic contact lens cases. Be sure to label the pollen, either directly on the container or on a piece of tape stuck to the container. Take care to keep the pollen dry, which may mean leaving the packet of pollen on the kitchen counter for a few minutes after removing it from the refrigerator or freezer to allow the condensation to evaporate. Pollen can be taken from the refrigerator many times and returned with little loss of viability as long as it is kept dry and away from the midday heat. Pollen can stay fresh for long periods of time and be used to make many, many crosses. When it is time to use the pollen, simply open the container and apply the pollen with an artist's brush or touch the stored anther to the pod parent's pistil with a pair of tweezers (reverse tweezers are very helpful here, since they are normally clamped shut rather than open). Instead of the normal fluffy texture with a yellow to orange color, the pollen of a very few flowers (such as 'Exotic Echo') is hard and white, a sign that it is not viable. In such cases, the plant can be used only as a pod parent.

Unlike breeding the flowers of other genera, daylily breeders rarely bother to remove the stamens from flowers chosen to be the pod parent since the pistil of a daylily is such a long distance from the stamens and pollen. Early morning is the best time for pollinating daylilies; successful crosses become less and less likely as the day progresses. In general, diploids are more fertile than tetraploids and therefore can have a higher percentage of takes later in the day. Successful seed set is temperature dependent. Hot days are not good for pollination since few pods will set; any crossing should be made as early in the morning as possible, and preferably on plants in the shade. Cool, overcast days generally result in excellent seed set, even on crosses made late in the day. It is not necessary to cover the pollinated pistil to ensure that no unintended pollen reaches it, since the stigma is only receptive for a short period of time and the flower is open for only a single day.

Label the crosses as you make them, including the names of both parents. Many hybridizers use small white paper tags on strings, like those generally used for marking prices, which are readily available in most office supply stores. Be sure to use permanent markers so the label will withstand the eight weeks of weather until harvest. You may wish to use a record book as well, where more detailed information about the cross may be included. Methods of labeling, numbering, or otherwise recording crosses vary from person to person, and each breeder must find a system that works best for him or her.

A few days after pollination, the daylily flower will drop off. If pollination has been successful a very small, green seed pod will be at the former flower base. If the cross did not take, no seed pod will form, which happens about half the time even under the best conditions. The seed pod, once formed, will slowly enlarge and reach maturity within six to ten weeks, in midsummer to fall depending on the climate. When mature, the seed pod will turn brown and split open to reveal glossy black seeds. Keep a close watch on the seed pods as they mature, for once the pods crack open the seeds will easily scatter by wind and rain. Because of an untimely vacation or early frost, you can ripen seed pods indoors if they are already very near maturity. Simply break off the entire flower scape and place it in a vase of water.

Collect the seeds and store them in envelopes or zip-lock bags labeled with the parentage. Refrigerate the seeds for a minimum of three weeks if they are to be planted without outdoor overwintering. Pure evergreen varieties will sprout without any chilling, but daylily seeds with dormancy in their background require refrigeration in order to sprout. Some research suggests that completely dried out seeds do not benefit from refrigeration; therefore, most hybridizers attempt to keep the seeds in a moist environment by placing a moist paper towel in the zip-lock bag with the seeds. Ideally, the paper towel should not be soggy, as the seeds can rot if they get too wet. We have found it most convenient to squirt a solution of mild fungicide and water into the zip-lock bags (using an old shampoo bottle) to keep the seeds moist and prevent rot during refrigeration.

Daylily seeds may be planted outside in the fall or spring or started inside. Treat them no differently from any other seeds. Sowing daylily seeds outdoors in the fall in cold climates runs the risk of killing some plants, they also lose the benefit of the winter growing time. Most gardeners in cold climates start the seeds inside and overwinter seedlings in a greenhouse, sunny window, or under grow lights. In warmer climates, the seeds can be started outdoors in late summer to early fall, and they will grow all winter. Indoors or out, germination usually takes place within two weeks, although some seeds can be slow to germinate. Since daylily seeds do not sprout well and even can be killed in extreme heat, such as 90°F (32°C), germination rates may be reduced by planting in full sun in the late summer in hot climates, or by overheating the seeds during indoor sprouting. Ideal sprouting rates generally occur between 70 and 80°F (21–27°C). When planting seedlings outdoors, they should be set about 4 in. (15 cm) apart in rows 1–1.5 ft. (30.5–45.7 cm) apart. Be sure to transfer the parentage information to the garden with the plants.

Once planted out, plants will flower in one to three years. In warm climates or in a greenhouse, if the seeds are planted in the early fall and the plants are fertilized heavily, they can bloom the following spring, within nine months.

Goals

One critical question in any attempt to hybridize daylilies is ploidy—are the plants you want to cross diploids or tetraploids? This question is critical since diploids, those with the normal set of 22 chromosomes, will only cross with diploids, and tetraploids, those with 44 chromosomes, will only set seed with tetraploids. A diploid will not cross successfully with a tetraploid, no matter how hard you try to make seed.

Hybridizers have discussed the possibility that some diploid daylilies may contain unreduced gametes which would make them capable of crossing with both diploids and tetraploids. Under normal circumstances, the cells that form pollen are produced by cell division, during which the amount of chromosome material is divided in half, resulting in two cells that each have half the full number of chromosomes. The male half-set of chromosomes in each pollen cell is destined to combine with the female half-set to form a whole set of chromosomes for the offspring. Unreduced gametes result when the cell division leading to the formation of pollen does not occur. The pollen thus formed has twice the normal amount of chromosomes. Such pollen from a diploid plant has twice the normal genetic complement, theoretically making it capable of successfully pollinating a tetraploid plant. According to Robert Griesbach (personal communication), although unreduced gametes are not uncommon in other plants, a case of their occurrence in daylilies has never been confirmed. There have been some reports of tetraploid seed set from the pollen of diploid plants such as 'Ed Murray'. However, it is possible that hybridizers unknowingly purchased plants of 'Tet. Ed Murray,' or the pistil was pollinated by other means, such as insects or wind.

How do you know whether your plants are diploid or tetraploid? Most nursery catalogs list plants' ploidy levels, so look up the plant in the garden catalog from which you purchased. If the plant is from a friend or some other source, look it up in a catalog from a major daylily garden (see Appendix B). The ultimate source is the *American Hemerocallis Society Checklist*. This series of books lists all registered daylilies as well as their characteristics. An additional source of information is the yearly *Eureka Daylily Reference Guide* (see Appendix A). It lists most daylilies in commerce and where to buy them and compares prices between the different sources. Further, we have produced a CD-ROM titled *A Pictorial History of the Daylily* that contains information on registered cultivars and thousands of images (see Appendix A). The more time-consuming but least expensive way to check for ploidy is to cross the unknown plant with a plant that you know is a diploid or tetraploid. Plants of opposite ploidy may initially develop seed pods, but within a few weeks the pods will dry up and abort since no viable seeds are inside.

Once establishing whether a plant is diploid or tetraploid, you can cross it with any other daylily of the same ploidy. Then you must decide where you want to take the plant. You can cross almost any two flowers, but most crosses are designed to make improvements in the different key categories. Daylilies are generally categorized based on the factors of flower size (large, small, or miniature), single or double, polytepal, spider, and so on. In order to officially fit into the categories, flowers have to meet the American Hemerocallis Society's designated criteria for that category, such as the petal length-to-width ratios for spiders. However, the flowers themselves often fall between official groups. For example, a flower may be very spidery looking, with long, narrow petals, but not actually reach the criterion for a spider as set forth by the American Hemerocallis Society. This same plant would be very important for breeding, though.

When a flower falls within one group, do not hesitate to cross it with flowers from another group if it offers characteristics in the direction of your hybridizing goal. For example, the prominent and showy gold edge found on the newer tetraploid daylily hybrids originally appeared only on large-flowered, wide-petaled, single daylilies. Therefore, hybridizers interested in getting this petal edge on miniatures, spiders, or doubles had to breed them across categories. This route does, however, mean losing many desirable characteristics, such as size, narrowness, or doubling, in the first generation in order to ultimately achieve the goal of the gold edge. Though the categories listed above delineate most breeding—doubles to doubles and spiders to spiders—enthusiasts should not be afraid to cross flowers of different groups on the path toward a specific goal.

Pollinating a daylily. TED L. PETIT & JOHN P. PEAT

Newly forming seed pod. TED L. PETIT & JOHN P. PEAT

Maturing seed pods. TED L. PETIT & JOHN P. PEAT

Mature pod with seeds. TED L. PETIT & JOHN P. PEAT

CHAPTER ELEVEN
Cultivation

Daylilies are among the most carefree plants in modern gardens. Compared to many other garden plants, their horticultural requirements are minimal, and they are highly disease resistant. This carefree nature has been a major factor contributing to the popularity of the daylily.

Climate

Daylilies will thrive in virtually any climate. While most daylilies do well across a large climatic range, certain varieties perform better in extreme climatic zones. For example, in very cold climates such as Canada dormant daylilies generally perform better, although many cold-hardy evergreen daylilies also thrive in these conditions. In very hot climates such as the deep southern United States and northern Australia, evergreen varieties generally tend to perform better. Even in locations that receive only mild frosts, many dormant daylilies perform very well. Although most daylilies require some degree of winter chilling in order to survive or bloom, some varieties perform well even in frost-free climates.

Planting

Consider sunlight, soil, and water when planting daylilies. Daylilies prefer full sun, although they will grow happily in partial shade. The flowers benefit from midday to late-afternoon shade when the sun is at its hottest, particularly in hot, sunny climates and for dark-colored flowers, such as reds, purples, and blacks. These richly colored flowers often will scorch in full, hot sun. If grown in full shade, daylilies will usually survive but will produce fewer flowers or none at all, the scapes will be tall and lean toward the sun, and the foliage will be lanky.

Daylilies are not overly particular about soil conditions, although they do perform best in moist but well-drained soil. Prior to planting daylilies, loosen the soil as you would for any plant. Adding organic matter, such as manure, rotted leaves, compost, and so on, to your soil is always a benefit. Daylilies particularly like pine bark mulch, because it helps aerate the soil and improve drainage. Remember that any decaying organic matter requires nitrogen and will take it from the soil. Therefore, if you use uncomposted organic matter, be sure to compensate by increasing the amount of nitrogen fertilizer. Prepare a hole large enough to accommodate the plant and form a mound at the bottom of the hole on which to set the plant. Place the plant and fill in the soil to the same height as before. The difference in the color of the leaves will indicate the level of the soil: the leaves will be white where they were below the soil. Although daylilies are tolerant of a wide range in soil pH, they prefer a neutral to slightly acidic soil. It is rare for daylilies not to flourish in the average garden because of an imbalance in soil pH; however, if plants fail to thrive, consider having the soil tested for pH by a local agricultural agent.

Daylilies need a lot of water but do not like to be in standing water. Although daylilies will survive in standing water far better than most other plants, do not plant them in areas where standing water is expected after heavy rains. Standing water strains the plant and decreases its disease resistance. During bloom season, daylilies especially need plenty of water to produce large, voluptuous blooms. Therefore, locate the plants where they can receive an adequate supply of water when needed. Although not required, mulch, including some organic matter, helps to retain water and keep the soil moist and cool.

While not absolutely necessary, some fertilizer is beneficial in order to get the maximum enjoyment from your daylilies, particularly the newer hybrids. Any balanced fertilizer is adequate, such as 6-6-6 or 20-20-20 (nitrogen-phosphorus-potassium), and can usually be purchased in any local garden center. Generally, applications of fertilizer in the spring and prior to bloom time are sufficient to ensure good growth and healthy bloom.

Diseases and Pests

One of the few and rare disease problems found in daylilies is fungal infection. It generally takes two forms: spring sickness or crown rot. Spring sickness most commonly occurs in colder climates in the spring when the plants are just beginning to come out of winter dormancy. The emerging center leaves are often notched and ragged. Often only several fans in a clump are afflicted, and these fans may bend over at a 45-degree angle to the soil surface. The fan or clump afflicted by spring sickness does not die, but an individual fan may fail to flower.

Crown rot develops almost exclusively during extremely hot and humid conditions. Therefore, this problem is most prevalent in climates closest to the equator during mid- to late summer. The plants begin to turn yellow, and an entire clump may die. If the leaves are pulled the entire plant typically will pull from the ground, accompanied by a strong smell of rot. Certain hybrids seem more susceptible to crown rot than others. Some daylily growers suggest using fungicides to treat rotting plants, but once the rot has appeared it is often too late to save the plant. Many daylily enthusiasts insist that any cultivar that appears to be susceptible to rot should not be treated but should be destroyed and culled from the garden, thus ensuring that this genetic weakness is not passed on to any progeny through hybridization.

A number of insects can attack the daylily, although none cause serious problems for the average gardener. We have approximately 120,000 daylily plants. Such a large-scale monoculture generally leads to increased disease and insect vulnerability, but daylilies are so disease and pest resistant that we do not use any pesticides or other chemicals in the garden to combat these problems. However, under certain conditions some insects will attack the daylily.

Thrips typically thrive in cooler weather, making them mainly a problem in early spring. Thrips are very tiny insects, just barely visible to the naked eye, that resemble the top of an exclamation point (!). They do not kill the daylily, but they attack the developing scape and flower buds. The most common and irritating symptoms of thrip damage are flower buds that fail to develop, turn yellow, and fall off. Most gardeners simply ignore this problem and wait for the weather to warm. Other gardeners use pesticides or organic means, such as introduced predators, to control thrips.

Spider mites and aphids are other insect pests that affect daylilies. Spider mites generally attack daylilies that are drought stressed or grown in greenhouse conditions. They live on the underside of the leaf and create small webs similar to spider webs. Spider mites can be treated with insecticides, but often they can be easily controlled by frequent watering that includes spraying the leaves with water. Aphids, which are small white insects, are also sometimes found on daylily leaves, particularly in the spring. They do little harm and can generally be washed off with water through a garden hose.

Slugs and snails can also attack the daylily, most frequently in cooler wet climates. They chew on the sides of leaves, giving them a ragged edge. They tend to proliferate in wet garden areas, such as in mulch and dead leaves. Slug pellets can be used to control them if necessary. In most regions, simply removing the mulch or dead plant material is usually sufficient for their control.

Growers in Europe have reported instances of the hemerocallis gall fly (or gall midge) affecting their daylilies. The tiny white fly deposits its eggs in the newly forming flower buds. The growing larvae feed on the developing flower bud, which becomes wider, distorted, and discolored and typically drops off before a flower is formed. The recommended treatment is to remove any distorted blooms and destroy them.

Most daylily growers insist that the few insect and disease problems that affect daylilies are so minimal that no spraying or other treatment should be used. In fact, many are adamant that chemicals not be used on daylilies, insisting that the plants should be able to resist such maladies with little help other than routine care. They believe that any daylily not able to withstand insects and diseases without chemical intervention has no place in the garden.

Thrip damage to flower buds. TED L. PETIT & JOHN P. PEAT

Thrip damage to flower blossom. TED L. PETIT & JOHN P. PEAT

Propagation

Daylilies typically increase from one plant, or fan, into several during the average season, soon forming a clump. Early fall is the ideal time to divide daylily clumps, since it gives the newly planted fans a long time to become fully adjusted prior to the next spring's bloom time. Though the plants can be divided into single fans, the flowers often look better if left in small clumps of two to three fans. Large clumps left undivided for years generally produce blooms of inferior quality. Therefore for optimal enjoyment of the plants, though it is not necessary, it is best to divide daylily clumps periodically. It is difficult to suggest exactly how often to divide daylilies, since it depends on how quickly they increase, which in turn is dependent on the particular variety and growing region. Some daylilies, particularly diploids, will increase rapidly, while others, particularly tetraploids, may take many years to form large clumps. Daylilies generally multiply more rapidly in warmer climates, which also means more frequent dividing.

To divide a clump, first dig it up and remove as much soil as possible from the root mass. The dirt can be removed by spraying the roots with a garden hose. Removing the dirt allows a clearer view of the individual plants and their root mass. Often, plants in a clump will have separated their root systems naturally, allowing you to simply pry the plants apart. If the plants do not pull apart, use a knife to divide them. If the clump is cut into separate plants, make sure that each plant has some roots attached to it. Cutting the plant, however, makes it more susceptible to fungus infection on the open wounds, leading to rot. It is best not to cut plants during the hot summer months. If forced to divide daylilies in the heat of summer, use a mild fungicide-and-water solution to soak the daylily roots for a few minutes prior to planting.

Digging clump for division. TED L. PETIT & JOHN P. PEAT

Trim the leaves of newly divided plants back to approximately one-half to one-third their original length. Since the roots have been disturbed, the plants are less capable of supplying the leaves with water. Trimming the leaves allows the plant to survive while it reestablishes its root system. Dead or rotten roots can be removed, but it is best to leave all live roots on the plant and not to trim the roots, since the plant needs as much root system as possible to quickly reestablish.

Cutting a double division. TED L. PETIT & JOHN P. PEAT

Dividing a double division. TED L. PETIT & JOHN P. PEAT

Some daylilies develop proliferations, or small plants on the flower scapes. Although they typically do not form roots, they can and often do so during prolonged rainy weather. Proliferations can be removed from the scape and treated like any other small plant or cutting. Induce the new plant to form new roots by placing it in a glass of water or treating it as you would a cutting.

Replanting a single division. TED L. PETIT & JOHN P. PEAT

Freshly planted and labeled cultivar.
TED L. PETIT & JOHN P. PEAT

CHAPTER TWELVE

Daylilies of the Future

How can we predict the future, especially for something as complex and diverse as the daylily? A number of years usually elapse for each new hybrid daylily between its virgin bloom and its introduction into commerce. But by looking into the seedling fields of daylily hybridizers, we can catch a glimpse of what the future will hold, at least the near future. Though these plants may not be available for a few years, it is exciting to see the breaks and new features they exhibit. To show some of the newest hybridizing achievements, this book must picture flowers that are "still under number," those that have not yet been named; therefore, the plants in this chapter are grouped by hybridizer. Those who contributed photos to this chapter are listed in Appendix B and can be contacted directly about their flowers.

Before exciting new seedlings can be introduced into commerce they are selected and removed from the seedling field for further evaluation, which can span three to six years depending on the climate and cultivar. This evaluation generally involves assessing overall plant characteristics, including dormancy, plant measurements, bud count, and so on, as well as the beauty and distinction of the flower. If the hybridizer is satisfied with both the plant and its flowering habits and feels that the daylily is worth introducing he or she will name the plant and register that name with the American Hemerocallis Society. Most daylilies pictured in this chapter are newly discovered seedlings, or those still under evaluation by the hybridizers. Since these plants have not yet been named or fully evaluated, much of the information pertaining to them is currently not available. A few cultivars pictured are further along in their evaluation process; therefore, they may already have names or more complete information.

In addition to those hybridizers mentioned previously in this book, a number of hybridizers have contributed photographs of their work for this chapter. These individuals include Jean Duncan and Henry Ruhling, who have been working on increasing refinement in the large-flowered tetraploids. In addition, John Kinnebrew, Karol Emmerich, George Doorakian, McNeil Carter, Dan Hansen, and Betty Harwood have been concentrating on producing extremely ruffled, heavily substanced, large and medium-sized tetraploids. Pat Sayers has worked with flowers containing interesting color patterns. Ludlow Lambertson and Bob Schwarz have worked on spiders and unusual forms, Bobby Baxter has concentrated on producing polytepal daylilies, and Bill Reinke has worked with both spiders and polytepal forms. Lee Pickles has hybridized bold-eyed and -edged daylilies, whereas Frances Harding has worked on ornate filigree edges. Douglas Lycett and Henry Lorrain took many lines of R. W. Munson and bred a very hardy northern line that flourishes in Canada.

These latest seedlings show many future trends in the daylily. Crosses between plants of differing hardiness are producing daylily plants much more tolerant of a wide climatic range. Flowers are becoming larger, with sturdier scapes, and flower substance is heavier and thicker, resulting in more weather-resistant blooms. Efforts to extend the bloom season continue to increase branching, bud count, and recurrent bloom. The beginning of carved and sculpted textures within the petal are adding a whole new dimension to the look of the flower. And the original push to widen the petals and make the daylily a round flower continues—many future cultivars are close to achieving this goal.

Flower colors are becoming clearer and more intense. The whites are whiter, and the reds and purples are more saturated and sunfast. The elusive blue daylily appears to be on the horizon, developing out of the blue eyes. Eye patterns are larger, more dramatic and complicated, and available in a diverse range of colors. The latest styles mimic rainbows, butterfly wings, spider webs, and concentric circles. Stippled patterns are more pronounced and refined. Patterned daylilies generally are becoming more exotic and complex.

Picotee edges are becoming wider and more pronounced, including multiple colors or shades, often mimicking the pattern within the eye. These picotee edges are often surrounded by gold or lighter ornate edges. With the widening of the picotees and the expanding of the eyes, the petal self is progressively shrinking. The light edges are more complex, often involving gold, silver, yellow, orange, white, and more. These edges are often diamond dusted, creating a sparkling and glittering effect in the sun. The ornate edges are becoming wider, too, and vary in texture from shark's teeth to hooks and horns, often combined with intense ruffling and crimping.

Spiders are growing narrower and larger, with ornate toothed and gold edges. Unusual forms are more diverse and consistent, often combining twisted and curled segments within one flower. Doubles are more fully double, with ornate gold and picotee edges and increased size and bud count. The relatively new midrib doubling is becoming very popular. Miniatures are even smaller, and double and tetraploid miniatures are starting to appear.

The daylily is changing and evolving at an accelerating pace. Clearly, in the years to come the daylily's beauty and popularity as a garden plant will be increasing around the world. As this occurs, hybridizers must also consider the overall plant habit, ensuring good branching and bud count, vigor, insect and disease resistance, and wide climatic adaptability.

Looking at the latest innovations makes the future possibilities seem endless. Some flower forms, such as the tetraploid doubles, spiders, and miniatures are in their infancy, as are polytepals and unusual form daylilies. It is exciting to think what the future might bring to these flower types as well as others. If the latest trends continue, the singles will be round, ruffled, heavily substanced, and in every possible color, with ornate contrasting eyes, watermarks, and edges. The doubles will share many of these features, and the spiders will probably become enormous and ornately decorated. The five-petaled polytepal will likely become a reality. The future of daylilies appears to be limited only by the imagination of hybridizers everywhere, and the flower will surely continue to change as long as gardeners can dream.

'Beyond the Rim' (Bobby Baxter). A dark burgundy-red, spidery flower with curling segments and a large green center. BOBBY BAXTER

'DA-BG-1' (John Benz). A very rich, dark purple double with white picotee on the petals and petaloids. JOHN BENZ

'Shirley Farmer' (John Benz). A wide-petaled rose-red flower with a heavily ruffled gold edge. JOHN BENZ

'Z-BG-b1-1' (John Benz). A dark burgundy-purple, double flower with a wire white edge on the petaloids. JOHN BENZ

'RLBM-RLas-1' (John Benz). A wide-petaled, ruffled, dark red with a deep green throat. JOHN BENZ

'White Fang' (John Benz). A very toothy-edged, dark burgundy-red flower with a green center. JOHN BENZ

'EM-C1-1' (John Benz). A very round, intensely colored, blood-red flower with a large green center. JOHN BENZ

'LS-GM-2' (John Benz). A richly colored, wide-petaled, ruffled, dark purple flower with a green throat. JOHN BENZ

'THBM-JDP-ro' (John Benz). A very round, wide-petaled, ruffled, silvery pink flower with a green throat. JOHN BENZ

'Janet Benz' (John Benz). A very wide-petaled, ruffled rose-pink flower with a darker band above a deep green throat. JOHN BENZ

'Shirley Supreme' (John Benz). A dark burgundy-red flower with a green center and ornate, ruffled gold edge. JOHN BENZ

'Belle Cook' (Malcolm Brooker). A very wide-petaled, round flower of medium pink with heavily ruffled gold edges and a green throat. 'Seminole Wind' × 'Ed Brown'. MALCOLM BROOKER

'Boo Hoo' (Mac Carter). Semi-evergreen. Scape 21 in. (53.3 cm); flower 3.75 in. (9.5 cm). Midseason. An apricot-peach flower with a dark burgundy eye and very ruffled matching picotee. Tetraploid. Seedling × 'Daring Dilemma'. MAC CARTER

'Zing' (Mac Carter). Semi-evergreen. Scape 22 in. (55.9 cm); flower 6 in. (15.2 cm). Midseason. A cream-apricot-peach flower with complex washed and patterned eye and darker picotee. Tetraploid. 'Zareba' × 'Creative Edge'. MAC CARTER

'5D-3331' (George Doorakian). A medium pink flower with a large rose chevron eye and striking, large green chevron throat. GEORGE DOORAKIAN

'6D-577-2G' (George Doorakian). An ivory-cream flower with a huge, dramatic green throat surrounded by a wire rose halo. GEORGE DOORAKIAN

'Queen Kathleen' (George Doorakian). A cream-yellow spidery flower with a very large dramatic green throat. GEORGE DOORAKIAN

'Nancy Britz' (George Doorakian). A triangular cream-peach flower with very strong dark green throat. GEORGE DOORAKIAN

'Malachite Prism' (George Doorakian). A rose-pink flower with a large rose-purple chevron eye and an extremely pronounced green chevron throat. GEORGE DOORAKIAN

'7D-303-J' (George Doorakian). A rose flower with a large dramatic green chevron throat. GEORGE DOORAKIAN

'Stargate' (George Doorakian). A triangular, patterned flower of rose-lavender with a darker eye and extremely large, green chevron throat. GEORGE DOORAKIAN

'7T-1069-C' (George Doorakian). An apricot-melon polytepal flower with darker gold crimped edges on the petals. GEORGE DOORAKIAN

'Laura Girl' (Jean Duncan 1998). A wide-petaled, recurved flower of clear medium pink with a deep green throat. JEAN DUNCAN

'Perfect Poise' (Jean Duncan). A wide-petaled, round, ruffled melon-peach-pink flower with a darker banded eye. JEAN DUNCAN

'126-POLI-99' (Jean Duncan). A very ruffled, wide-petaled apricot-cream flower. JEAN DUNCAN

'Wesley Hayes Hamiter' (Jean Duncan). A richly colored burgundy-purple flower with a large green throat. JEAN DUNCAN

'3399' (Karol Emmerich). A rose-lavender self with a large, bold, dark purple eye and very wide matching picotee. KAROL EMMERICH

'7999' (Karol Emmerich). A very dark, rich burgundy flower with a lighter watermark, ruffled silver edge, and a green throat. KAROL EMMERICH

'16399' (Karol Emmerich). A dark, richly colored purple with a lighter watermark, wide petals, and very ornate edge. KAROL EMMERICH

'1899' (Karol Emmerich). A clear yellow-gold of recurved form with large looping ruffles. KAROL EMMERICH

'18999' (Karol Emmerich). A wide-petaled purple with heavily crimped edges, a large lighter watermark, and a green throat. KAROL EMMERICH

'3699' (Karol Emmerich). A lavender-rose flower with a very heavy gold edge, lighter watermark, and green throat. KAROL EMMERICH

'6199' (Karol Emmerich). A richly colored burgundy flower with a lighter watermark and green throat. KAROL EMMERICH

'2999' (Karol Emmerich). A tailored cream flower with a patterned eye of dark purple and matching wire picotee. KAROL EMMERICH

'3999' (Karol Emmerich). A large and unusually patterned rose-red eye and matching wire picotee on a pink flower with a green throat. KAROL EMMERICH

'J. T. Davis' (Larry Grace). A wide-petaled, round, heavily ruffled cream-pink flower with a green center. LARRY GRACE

'55699' (Larry Grace). A very round, ruffled, heavily substanced flower of peach to salmon-pink with a green throat. LARRY GRACE

'21598' (Larry Grace). A wide-petaled, ruffled pink flower with a striking red eye and very wide matching picotee. LARRY GRACE

'698' (Larry Grace). A wide-petaled, heavily substanced, lavender-rose flower with a green center and gold edges. LARRY GRACE

'55599' (Larry Grace). A clear ivory flower with a patterned dark purple eye and matching ruffled picotee. LARRY GRACE

'6095' (Larry Grace). A very wide-petaled, round, ruffled, warm pink flower with a green throat and lighter edge. LARRY GRACE

'18198' (Larry Grace). An ornately ruffled clear, light purple self, picotee-edged and eyed in dark purple. LARRY GRACE

'58499' (Larry Grace). A textured, clear baby-ribbon-pink, recurved flower with a heavily ruffled gold edge and a green throat. LARRY GRACE

'57799' (Larry Grace). A clear shell-pink, wide-petaled, heavily ruffled flower with a green throat. LARRY GRACE

'53399' (Larry Grace). A very round, wide-petaled, rich burgundy-purple with a large watermark and ruffled gold edge. LARRY GRACE

'5298' (Larry Grace). A dark, richly colored burgundy flower with a precise watermark and gold edging. LARRY GRACE

'See His Glory' (Larry Grace). A wide-petaled, heavily ruffled, gold-edged, soft cream-ivory-pink flower with a green throat. LARRY GRACE

'49897' (Larry Grace). A pale ivory-pink flower with a pale rose eye and matching narrow picotee on very ruffled petals. LARRY GRACE

'42997' (Larry Grace). An ornately ruffled, very wide-petaled, gold-edged lavender with a green throat. LARRY GRACE

'57899' (Larry Grace). A heavy substanced cream-pink flower with a green throat and large, looping ruffles. LARRY GRACE

'Bill Robinson' (Larry Grace). A very ornately ruffled heavy gold-edged pink flower with a green throat. LARRY GRACE

'Felecia Grace' (Larry Grace). An extremely heavily ruffled apricot-gold flower with a green throat. LARRY GRACE

'99-013' (Betty Hudson). An orange-rose double flower with a darker eye and lighter petal edges. BETTY HUDSON

'99-014' (Betty Hudson). A cream-yellow, spidery, double flower with a green throat. BETTY HUDSON

'99-015' (Betty Hudson). An apricot-cream, lightly ruffled, double flower with a large rose-purple banded eye. BETTY HUDSON

'99-017' (Betty Hudson). A cream-peach double flower with a very large darker rose eye extending onto the petals and petaloids. BETTY HUDSON

'Lori Goldston' (John Kinnebrew). A heavily ruffled, gold-edged, lavender-pink with a lighter watermark and a green throat.
JOHN KINNEBREW

'Royal Heron' (Marc King-Lamone). A lightly ruffled, lavender, spidery flower with a lighter watermark and a large green throat.
MARC KING-LAMONE

'Moonlit Pirouette' (Marc King-Lamone). An ivory-cream spidery flower with a green throat.
MARC KING-LAMONE

'DKCRP:1-99R' (David Kirchhoff). A heavily textured cream-pink flower with a ruffled gold edge and a green throat. DAVID KIRCHHOFF

'R59' (David Kirchhoff). A bright red, lightly ruffled, double flower with deep green center.
DAVID KIRCHHOFF

'SS-SS' (John Kinnebrew). A very heavily ruffled, wide-petaled, round flower of apricot-melon. JOHN KINNEBREW

'Virginia Little Henson' (David Kirchhoff). A bright rose-peach-pink flower with a darker eye and heavy ruffled gold edge.
DAVID KIRCHHOFF

'RWE-7-8' (David Kirchhoff). A deep red flower with precise white edges and a green throat.
DAVID KIRCHHOFF

'R69' (David Kirchhoff). A very wide-petaled tomato-red flower with ruffled, crimped edges.
DAVID KIRCHHOFF

'BSH-198' (David Kirchhoff). A heavy-substanced beautifully ruffled rose-red with a dark green heart. DAVID KIRCHHOFF

'KF&D-1-9' (David Kirchhoff). A lavender-pink double flower with a very large, dramatic, complex eye. DAVID KIRCHHOFF

'Jerry Pate Williams' (David Kirchhoff). A bright orange-apricot-melon-pink double with heavy ruffling on petals and petaloids. DAVID KIRCHHOFF

'JOWE-1-98' (David Kirchhoff). A very full, ruffled, clear medium pink double. DAVID KIRCHHOFF

'Sdlg.-IE' (Ludlow Lambertson). A cream-lavender flower with a charcoal, purple, and bluish complex eye and a dark purple picotee. LUDLOW LAMBERTSON

'JB-AL' (Ludlow Lambertson). A triangular, lavender flower with a large, complex, purple chevron eye and matching picotee. LUDLOW LAMBERTSON

'Art Gallery Explosion' (Ludlow Lambertson). A very large, dramatic purple eye and matching wide picotee on lavender-rose petals. LUDLOW LAMBERTSON

'On Silken Thread' (Ludlow Lambertson). An unusual-formed, rusty orange flower with a darker eye and curling segments. LUDLOW LAMBERTSON

'CS-FD' (Ludlow Lambertson). A dark purple, spidery flower with a darker eye and pronounced shark's tooth edge. LUDLOW LAMBERTSON

'CS-WC' (Ludlow Lambertson). A rose-pink spidery flower with a darker rose eye, white midribs, and distinct shark's tooth edge.
LUDLOW LAMBERTSON

'Doug's Memento' (Henry Lorrain and Douglas Lycett). A richly colored, dark purple flower with a lighter watermark above a green throat.
HENRY LORRAIN & DOUGLAS LYCETT

'James Douglas Lycett' (Henry Lorrain and Douglas Lycett). A lightly ruffled, gold-edged cream-pink flower with a green throat.
HENRY LORRAIN & DOUGLAS LYCETT

'DF-BWW-Sdlg.98' (Henry Lorrain and Douglas Lycett). A wide-petaled, ruffled, orange-gold flower with a green throat. 'Divine Magic' × ('Femme Osage' × 'Betty Warren Woods').
HENRY LORRAIN & DOUGLAS LYCETT

'TLP-TEE-1' (Mort Morss). A lightly ruffled cream-pink flower with a large, complex, patterned eye of purple and charcoal. MORT MORSS

'FD-1-99' (Mort Morss). A lavender-rose flower with a white shark's tooth edge and a green throat. MORT MORSS

'MtRP-19' (Mort Morss). A lavender-peach flower with a large, complex, banded eye of purple and charcoal. MORT MORSS

'UME-WOW' (Mort Morss). A cream-peach flower with a darker eye and matching picotee surrounded by a wide, ruffled, gold edge. MORT MORSS

'MSE-197' (Mort Morss). A lavender flower with a dark purple eye and striking, iridescent throat pattern extending out the midribs. MORT MORSS

'Scott-2-99' (Mort Morss). A cream-apricot flower with a lavender eye and matching wide picotee below a gold edge. MORT MORSS

'TEE-GB-198' (Mort Morss). A lightly ruffled ivory-cream flower with a complex, patterned eye of purple, lavender, and charcoal. MORT MORSS

'FD-HD-WS-1-98' (Mort Morss). A wide-petaled rose-lavender flower with a crunchy hooked edge and a green throat. MORT MORSS

'99-007' (R. W. Munson Jr.). A very dark, rich blood-red with a lighter red watermark above a green throat. R. W. MUNSON JR

'99-011' (R. W. Munson Jr.). A dark claret-purple flower with a large lavender watermark surrounding a green center. R. W. MUNSON JR

'99-005' (R. W. Munson Jr.). A clear lavender-purple with a very large, dramatic, lighter lavender, patterned watermark above a green throat. R. W. MUNSON JR

'99-003' (R. W. Munson Jr.). A dark, rich burgundy-purple with a rose-pink watermark and a wire gold edge. R. W. MUNSON JR

'99-004' (R. W. Munson Jr.). A slate-lavender with large watermark above a green throat and a heavily ruffled gold edge. R. W. MUNSON JR

'55-PR' (John P. Peat). A pink flower with a burgundy-red eye and wide matching picotee surrounded by a wide, ruffled gold edge. JOHN P. PEAT

'Ted Gardian' (John P. Peat). A clear lavender flower with a heavy, braided gold edge and a green throat. JOHN P. PEAT

'AWR' (John P. Peat). A pink-peach flower with dark rose eye and matching wide picotee surrounded by an ornate gold edge. JOHN P. PEAT

'EE-LYA-300-55' (John P. Peat). A dramatic lavender flower with a darker lavender chevron eye and matching picotee surrounded by a heavy gold edge. JOHN P. PEAT

'VP-LYA' (John P. Peat). A cream-pink flower with darker rose petal edges surrounded by a heavy gold ruffle. JOHN P. PEAT

'55-300' (John P. Peat). A lavender flower with a purple eye and wide edges of purple surrounded by gold. JOHN P. PEAT

'ES-300' (John P. Peat). A lavender-rose flower with a darker rose eye, matching picotee, and heavy, white popcorn edge. JOHN P. PEAT

'CC' (John P. Peat). A rose self with red patterned midribs and a precisely etched deep red eye. JOHN P. PEAT

'EU-1' (John P. Peat). A apricot-melon flower with heavy cinnamon stippling and a darker stippled eye. JOHN P. PEAT

'LSAS' (John P. Peat). A complex, patterned rose flower with a wide, pink, ruffled edge and a rose eye above a green throat. JOHN P. PEAT

'QRAS' (John P. Peat). A very dark lavender-purple with a broad lighter edge that fades to near white. JOHN P. PEAT

'55-TSVH' (John P. Peat). A recurved, voluptuously formed, peach-pink flower with a rose eye and very ornately ruffled, matching picotee. JOHN P. PEAT

'Complicated Lifestyles' (John P. Peat). A very ornately gold-edged lavender flower with a darker eye and matching picotee. JOHN P. PEAT

'RTSdlg.' (John P. Peat). A very large wide-petaled flower of deep velvet-red and a green throat. JOHN P. PEAT

'EU-2' (John P. Peat). A wide-petaled, ruffled cream-yellow with rose stippling that darkens at the eye and midribs. JOHN P. PEAT

'AGAS-1' (John P. Peat). A rose-pink flower with a very large, red chevron eye and pattern surrounding a green throat. JOHN P. PEAT

'SC' (John P. Peat). A ruffled apricot-melon flower with heavy sculpting from the midribs. JOHN P. PEAT

'SFF-55' (John P. Peat). A pale cream-peach flower with precise, dark red eye and matching picotee. JOHN P. PEAT

'SSMF2ES' (John P. Peat). A strong, wide, rubbery, tangerine-orange edge on a lavender-rose flower. JOHN P. PEAT

'AGAS-2' (John P. Peat). A triangular pink flower with patterned red splotching and white midribs. JOHN P. PEAT

'AGAS-3' (John P. Peat). A rose-pink flower with a precisely banded red eye and red patterned midribs. JOHN P. PEAT

'ASAG-1' (John P. Peat). An orange-apricot flower with two layers of precisely edged eyes, red on rose. JOHN P. PEAT

'TFC' (John P. Peat). A very large, burnt orange-red, hose and hose double. JOHN P. PEAT

'Just One Look' (John P. Peat). A very large, striking red eye and matching picotee on a cream-ivory flower. JOHN P. PEAT

'Susan Pritchard-Petit' (Ted L. Petit). A dramatic rose-lavender double with a lighter watermark and heavy gold edging. TED L. PETIT

'20-SWW' (Ted L. Petit). A large peach-pink flower with a lavender-rose eye and an edge of rose picotee surrounded by gold. TED L. PETIT

'EBG' (Ted L. Petit). A lightly ruffled cream flower with a large, extremely complex, banded, purple-cream and charcoal eye. TED L. PETIT

'RBF2KV' (Ted L. Petit). A pink flower with a ruffled gold edge and heavily sculpted, raised tissue extending from the midribs. TED L. PETIT

'RBSD77' (Ted L. Petit). An intense blood-red, velvety heavily ruffled flower with a wire gold edge. TED L. PETIT

'STSCIM' (Ted L. Petit). A very dark blood-red flower with a rose watermark above a striking green throat. TED L. PETIT

'Berenice Pappas' (Ted L. Petit). A heavily ruffled gold flower with a green throat. TED L. PETIT

'300-FD' (Ted L. Petit). A dark purple flower with a large popcorn edge, lighter watermark and green throat. TED L. PETIT

'Bill Munson' (Ted L. Petit). An ornate, heavily ruffled rose-pink flower where the petal color darkens toward the edge surrounded by a lighter edge. TED L. PETIT

'77' (Ted L. Petit). An intensely color-saturated red flower with heavily ruffled petals and a green throat and a wire gold edge. TED L. PETIT

'SCAWGF' (Ted L. Petit). A very heavy-substanced, bright orange-gold flower with crimped ruffled edges. TED L. PETIT

'SCAWPS' (Ted L. Petit). A wide-petaled tangerine-orange flower with heavily crimped ruffled edges. TED L. PETIT

'FG-SW' (Ted L. Petit). A wide-petaled, round, soft pink with ruffled gold edges and green throat. TED L. PETIT

'SSRB77' (Ted L. Petit). A very wide-petaled black-red flower with a gold ruffled crimped edge. TED L. PETIT

'55-2' (Ted L. Petit). A very ruffled, gold-edged flower with a rose eye surrounded by a darker band and a matching rose picotee. TED L. PETIT

'55-SG' (Ted L. Petit). A very ornate pink flower with a muted rose eye and matching picotee with an extremely pronounced gold edge. TED L. PETIT

'WP-TPR-WB' (Ted L. Petit). A very wide-petaled, heavy-substanced pink flower with rose halo and ruffled gold edge. TED L. PETIT

'Baby Jane Hudson' (Ted L. Petit). A very dark red, dramatic flower with a heavy, crunchy gold edge and a green center. TED L. PETIT

'20-512' (Ted L. Petit). A dramatic rose-pink flower with a large, dark rose-red eye and wide matching picotee surrounded by a gold edge. TED L. PETIT

'55-1' (Ted L. Petit). An ivory cream flower with a rose-pink eye and matching picotee surrounded by a wide gold edge. TED L. PETIT

'EBSdlg.' (Ted L. Petit). A very formal baby-ribbon-pink flower with precise gold edges and a green throat. TED L. PETIT

'AH' (Ted L. Petit). An apricot-peach flower with a patterned eye containing dramatic arrowhead forms. TED L. PETIT

'KA3' (Ted L. Petit). A heavily ruffled, gold-edged, lavender-rose flower with a large lighter watermark and a green throat. TED L. PETIT

'KA3B' (Ted L. Petit). A rose-purple flower with a very pronounced gold edge and lighter rose-pink watermark above a green throat. TED L. PETIT

'KBF2' (Ted L. Petit). A cream-yellow double with a darker eye and a dark red picotee on petals and petaloids. TED L. PETIT

'KBPR' (Ted L. Petit). A very ornately edged yellow double with a darker eye and matching picotee. TED L. PETIT

'KPF2ST' (Ted L. Petit). A very heavy-substanced, wide-petaled medium pink with heavily ruffled edges and a green throat. TED L. PETIT

'LSKV' (Ted L. Petit). A very large rose-red flower with looping white edges and a green center. TED L. PETIT

'LIS' (Ted L. Petit). A clear yellow flower with complex, banded, burgundy-purple eye above a green throat. TED L. PETIT

'A-DB' (Lee Pickles). A very ruffled, wide-petaled, cream to peach-pink flower with a green throat. LEE PICKLES

'Doc Branch' (Lee Pickles). A very round, ruffled apricot-gold with a green throat. LEE PICKLES

'Dream Queen' (Bill and Joyce Reinke 1998). Dormant. Scape 39 in. (99.1 cm); flower 11.5 in. (29.2 cm). Late. A golden yellow blend spider variant with a green throat. Diploid. BILL & JOYCE REINKE

'Tomorrow's Song' (Bill and Joyce Reinke 1999). Dormant. Scape 32 in. (81.3 cm); flower 9 in. (22.9 cm). Midseason. A rose-lavender bitone classic spider with a chartreuse throat. Diploid. BILL & JOYCE REINKE

'El Nino' (Bill and Joyce Reinke). Scape 26 in. (66.0 cm); flower 9 in. (22.9 cm). Late. An apricot spider-looking double. Diploid. BILL & JOYCE REINKE

'99-120' (Henry Ruhling). An ivory-cream flower with a complex, banded, purple eye surrounding a green throat. HENRY RUHLING

'99-FD-Sdlg.' (Jeff Salter). A very large dark purple with a lighter watermark, green throat, and extremely pronounced gold, shark's tooth edge. 'Fortune's Dearest' × Salter seedling. JEFF SALTER

'Macho Macho Man' (Jeff Salter). A very large heavy-substanced yellow-cream with a green throat and heavily ruffled, wide petals. JEFF SALTER

'Edge of Heaven' (Jeff Salter 1996). Semi-evergreen. Scape 28 in. (71.1 cm); flower 6.5 in. (16.5 cm). Midseason. A cream-pink self with a heavy gold edge and green throat. Tetraploid. Parents unknown. JEFF SALTER

'99-VB-EB' (Jeff Salter). Red with a gold hooked edge above a green throat. 'Ed Brown' × 'Velvet Beads'. JEFF SALTER

'Passion's Promise' (Pat Sayers). A patterned flower with petals red along the middle, surrounded by lighter edges and a green throat. PAT SAYERS

'West of the Moon' (Bob Schwarz). A creampink unusual-formed flower with a darker eye and twisted, spatulate sepals. BOB SCHWARZ

'Bimini Twist' (Bob Schwarz). An unusual-formed deep red flower with spatulate sepals. BOB SCHWARZ

'Laughing Giraffe' (Bob Schwarz). A spidery bitone with orange-red, toothy petals and lighter sepals. BOB SCHWARZ

'Hurricane Bob' (Bob Schwarz). A orange-red spidery flower with twisted and curling segments. BOB SCHWARZ

'Strike Up the Band' (Bob Schwarz). An unusual-formed dark red flower with pinched petals and large green center. BOB SCHWARZ

'Rose Corsage' (Patrick Stamile). A clear rose-pink double flower with ruffled edges and a green throat. PATRICK STAMILE

'Web Browser' (Patrick Stamile). A very narrow-petaled spidery flower of rich red color with a cream to green center. PATRICK STAMILE

'Daniel Webster' (Patrick Stamile). A red spidery flower with pinched and twisted segments and large green center. PATRICK STAMILE

'730A' (Patrick Stamile). A cream-yellow double flower with a large, dramatic purple eye on the petals and petaloids. PATRICK STAMILE

'933A' (Patrick Stamile). A rose-red spidery flower with curled segments and a dark green center. PATRICK STAMILE

'Bas Relief' (Patrick Stamile). An apricot-melon flower with deeply carved grooves at the midribs and heavy, looping ruffles. PATRICK STAMILE

'Victorian Lace' (Patrick Stamile). An extremely ruffled, wide-petaled ivory flower with a green throat. PATRICK STAMILE

'868A' (Patrick Stamile). A lavender spidery flower with twisted segments and a very large green center. PATRICK STAMILE

'9132A' (Patrick Stamile). A rose-red double flower with a wire gold edge on petals and petaloids. PATRICK STAMILE

'Treasure of Love' (Patrick Stamile). A very clear rose-pink flower with wide ruffled petals and a green throat. PATRICK STAMILE

'863B' (Patrick Stamile). A rose spidery flower with a darker rose eye and large green throat. PATRICK STAMILE

'Sungold Candy' (Patrick Stamile). A cream-yellow flower with a dramatic red eye and matching wire picotee above a dark green throat. PATRICK STAMILE

'Ain't She Nice' (Patrick Stamile). A heavy-substanced, recurved, deep rose-pink flower with ruffled edges and a green throat. PATRICK STAMILE

'Awesome Candy' (Patrick Stamile). A large burgundy-red eye on a cream-yellow flower with a green center. PATRICK STAMILE

'8516C' (Patrick Stamile). A very large dramatic eye of dark black-purple on a cream flower with a narrow picotee edge. PATRICK STAMILE

'8324A' (Patrick Stamile). A wide-petaled, heavily ruffled, gold-edged flower of medium pink with a green throat. PATRICK STAMILE

'Sedona' (Patrick Stamile). An apricot-peach flower with a rose-lavender eye, wide matching picotee, and heavily ruffled gold edge. PATRICK STAMILE

'8286A' (Patrick Stamile). A rich royal purple flower with a braided gold edge and lighter purple watermark above a green throat. PATRICK STAMILE

'Dan Mahony' (Dan Trimmer). A cream-pink with a large, dramatic deep-red eye and matching picotee. DAN TRIMMER

'Gillian' (Dan Trimmer). A rose-lavender flower with a large, dark burgundy eye and matching picotee. DAN TRIMMER

'Mohican Summer' (Dan Trimmer). A burnt orange flower with heavily crimped ruffled edges and a green throat. DAN TRIMMER

'Penny Pinsley' (Dan Trimmer). A cream-peach double flower with a dark purple eye and matching picotee. DAN TRIMMER

'Raspberry Beret' (Dan Trimmer). A cream flower with a raspberry chevron eye and matching braided picotee. DAN TRIMMER

'Ruby Moon' (Dan Trimmer). A bright orange-gold flower with a striking, feathered ruby eye above a green throat. DAN TRIMMER

APPENDIX A
Additional Resources

A great way to begin enjoying daylilies is to join a daylily society. The American Hemerocallis Society (A.H.S.) is the largest. It is also the international society responsible for registering daylilies. It costs U.S.$18 per year, which includes a subscription to *The Daylily Journal*, a thick quarterly on glossy paper with many full-color pictures of daylilies and articles about daylily gardening. To join, send a check payable to the American Hemerocallis Society to:

American Hemerocallis Society
Pat Mercer
P.O. Box 10
Dexter, Georgia 31019 U.S.A.
tel 912-875-4110
gmercer@nlamerica.com

The official A.H.S. home page may be viewed at www.daylilies.org/html. In addition to the A.H.S., other societies are active in countries around the world.

British Hosta and Hemerocallis
    Society
Lynda Hinton
Hon. Membership Secretary
Toft Monks, the Hythe
Rodborough, Stroud Common
Gloucestershire GL5 5BN
United Kingdom

Hemerocallis Society of Australia
Helen Reid
16 Farnsworth Street
Sunshine, Victoria 3020
Australia

Hemerocallis Europa
Elke Brettschneider
General Secretary and Treasurer
Schlomerweg 22
41352 Korschenbroich
Germany

Fachgruppe Hemerocallis
Gellschaft der Staudenfreunde
Norbert Graue
Stockflethweg 208
22417 Hamburg
Germany

The techniques of hybridizing daylilies are expertly illustrated in a very helpful and informative, step-by-step, beautiful color video available for U.S.$25 from

Henry Lorrain
We're In the Hayfield Now Daylily Gardens
4704 Pollard Road, R.R. 1
Orono, Ontario L0B 1M0
Canada
tel 905-983-5097
fax 905-983-6271
withndg@osha.igs.net

A problem for many gardeners new to daylilies is the overwhelming number of named varieties. We produce a CD-ROM entitled *A Pictorial History of the Daylily* that offers a quick and easy identifying reference for thousands of cultivars. It is updated every year or two to keep pace with new introductions. For more information contact

John P. Peat
Cross Border Daylilies
16 Douville Court
Toronto, Ontario M5A 4E7
Canada
tel 416-362-1682
fax 416-861-9300
www.distinctly.on.ca

The Eureka Daylily Reference Guide, published annually, is an excellent source of information about where to find daylilies. It prices thousands of daylily cultivars, pictures some, and gives the addresses of nurseries that offer the cultivars. The guide is available from

Eureka Daylily Reference Guide
Ken Gregory
P.O. Box 7611
Asheville, North Carolina 28802
tel 828-236-2222
www.gardeneureka.com

Hundreds of display gardens officially recognized by the A.H.S. are located across North America. A complete list appears in the spring issue of *The Daylily Journal*. Also, most gardens listed in Appendix B welcome visitors during the bloom season.

APPENDIX B
Sources for Daylilies

Most daylilies found in large gardening centers are very old hybrids or unnamed varieties. The sources below offer the latest named varieties. Prices for daylilies newly introduced by top hybridizers usually fall between U.S.$100 and $200. Prices quickly drop, however, as the plants multiply and become more readily available. Excellent daylilies can be had for as little as $10. The lists from these sources range from expensive new introductions to inexpensive tried-and-true daylilies. Many offer color catalogs.

United States

Bobby Baxter
Happy Moose Daylily Gardens
4109 Lodge Allen Court
Raleigh, North Carolina 27616-9519
tel 919-217-1961

Bell's Daylily Garden
1305 Griffin Road
Sycamore, Georgia 31790
tel 912-567-2633

John Benz
12195 6th Avenue
Cincinnati, Ohio 45249-1143
tel 513-489-1281

Brookwood Gardens
303 Fir Street
Michigan City, Indiana 46360-4812

Browns Ferry Gardens
13515 Browns Ferry Road
Georgetown, South Carolina 29440
tel 888-329-5459
fax 803-546-0318

Carolina Daylilies
209 Secret Cove Drive
Lexington, South Carolina 29072

Robert Carr
9900 N.W. 115th Avenue
Ocala, Florida 34482-8636
tel 352-629-3081

McNeil Carter
219 Tomotla Drive
Marble, North Carolina 28905-8709

Coburg Planting Fields
573 E. 600 North
Valparaiso, Indiana 46383
tel 219-462-4288

Covered Bridge Gardens
1821 Honey Run Road
Chico, California 95928-8850
tel 530-342-6661

Crochet Daylily Garden
P.O. Box 425
Prairieville, Louisiana 70769

Daylily Heaven
24 Beaman Lane
North Falmouth, Massachusetts
    02556
tel 508-564-9923
Fax 508-564-9912

George Doorakian
4 Bandera Drive
Bedford, Massachusetts 01730-1242
tel 617-275-2343

Jean Duncan
Garden Path Daylilies
P.O. Box 8524
Clearwater, Florida 33758

Karol Emmerich
7302 Claredon Drive
Edina, Minnesota 55439-1722
tel 612-941-9280

Larry Grace
Graceland Gardens
12860 West U.S. 84
Newton, Alabama 36352
tel 334-692-5903

Grey Wood Farm
85 River Road
Topsfield, Massachusetts 01983
fax 978-887-8625

Dan Hansen
Ladybug Daylilies
1852 S.R. 46
Geneva, Florida 32732
tel 407-349-0271

Curt Hanson
Crintonic Daylily Gardens
County Line Road
Gates Mills, Ohio 44040
tel 440-423-3349

Frances Harding
Forestlake Gardens
HC 72 Box 535
Locust Grove, Virginia 22508

Betty Harwood
Box 28
Farmingdale, New Jersey 07727-0028
tel 908-938-9001

Betty Hudson
Wimberlyway Gardens
7024 N.W. 18th Avenue
Gainesville, Florida 32605-3237

Jeff and Jackie's Daylilies
179 Smith Road
Clinton, Tennessee 37716-5005
tel 423-435-4989

E. R. Joiner
Joiner Gardens
9630 Whitfield Avenue
Savannah, Georgia 31406

Matthew Kaskel
Kaskel Farms
10295 S.W. 248th Street
Homestead, Florida 33032
tel 305-258-5300
fax 305-258-2150

John Kinnebrew
Box 224
Scottsmoor, Florida 32775-0224
tel 407-267-7985

David Kirchhoff and Mort Morss
Daylily World
P.O. Box 1612
260 N. White Cedar Road
Sanford, Florida 32772-1612
tel 407-322-4034
fax 407-322-4026

Ludlow Lambertson
Art Gallery Gardens
203 Oak Apple Trail
Lake Helen, Florida 32744
tel 904-228-3010

Lily Farm
Route 4, Box 1465
Center, Texas 75935

Majestic Gardens
2100 N. Preble County Line Road
West Alexandria, Ohio 45381
tel 937-833-5100

Marietta Gardens
P.O. Box 70
Marietta, North Carolina 28362
tel 910-628-9466
fax 910-628-9993

Steve Moldovan
Moldovan's Gardens
38830 Detroit Road
Avon, Ohio 44011-2148
tel 440-934-4993

Oakes Daylilies
8204 Monday Road
Corryton, Tennessee 37721
tel 800-532-9545
fax 423-688-8186
paradisegarden@oakes.html
www.oakesdaylilies.com

Ted L. Petit
Le Petit Jardin
P.O. Box 55
7185 N.W. County Road 320
McIntosh, Florida 32664-0055
tel 352-591-3227
fax 352-591-1859
www.distinctly.on.ca

Lee Pickles
Chattanooga Daylily Gardens
1736 Eagle Drive
Hixson, Tennessee 37343-2533
tel 423-842-4630
fax 423-842-1411

Pinecliffe Daylily Gardens
6604 Scottsville Road
Floyds Knob, Indiana 47119-9202
tel 812-923-8113 or 9618
dcs923@aol.com

Bill Reinke
Stephen's Lane Gardens
Route 1, Box 136 H
Bells, Tennessee 38006

Ridaught Daylily Farm
12309 N.W. 112 Avenue
Alachau, Florida 32615
tel 800-256-9362

Roycroft Daylily Nursery
942 White Hall Avenue
Georgetown, South Carolina 29440-
2553
tel 800-950-5459
fax 803-546-2281
roycroft@worldnet.att.net
www.roycroftdaylilies.com

Henry Ruhling
6129 Johnson Road N.W.
Hahira, Georgia 31632-3315
tel 912-794-2151

Jeff and Elizabeth Salter
Rollingwood Gardens
21234 Rollingwood Trail
Eustis, Florida 32726

Pat Sayers
16 Green Meadow Lane
Huntington, New York 11743-5123
tel 516-367-8630

Bob and Mimi Schwarz
Rainbow Daylily Garden
8 Lilla Lane
East Hampton, New York 11937
tel 516-324-0787

Singing Oaks Garden
1019 Abell Road
Blythewood, South Carolina 29016
tel 803-786-1351

Patrick and Grace Stamile
Floyd Cove Nursery
1050 Enterprise-Osteen Road
Enterprise, Florida 32725-9355
tel 407-860-1230
fax 407-860-0086

Thoroughbred Daylilies
6615 Briar Hill Road
Paris, Kentucky 40361
tel 606-988-9253
fax 606-988-9021

Tranquil Lake Nursery, Inc.
45 River Street
Rehoboth, Massachusetts 02769-
1395
tel 800-353-4344
fax 508-252-4740

Dan Trimmer
Water Mill Daylily Garden
1280 Enterprise-Osteen Road
Enterprise, Florida 32725-9401
tel 407-574-2789

Woodside Nursery
327 Beebe Run Road
Bridgeton, New Jersey 08302

Canada

Pam Erikson
Erikson's Daylily Gardens
24642 51st Avenue
Langley, British Columbia V2Z 1H9
tel 604-856-0716

Henry Lorrain
We're In the Hayfield Now Daylily
Gardens
4704 Pollard Road, R.R. 1
Orono, Ontario L0B 1M0
tel 905-983-5097
fax 905-983-6271
withndg@osha.igs.net

Joan Messer
Box 28
Macoun, Saskatchewan S0C 1P0
tel 306-634-4364

John P. Peat
Cross Border Daylilies
16 Douville Court
Toronto, Ontario M5A 4E7
tel 416-362-1682
www.distinctly.on.ca
jpeat@distinctly.on.ca

The Potting Shed
81 Talbot Street East
Cayuga, Ontario N0A 1E0
tel 905-772-7255

Australia

Daylily Display Centre
Gin Gin Road
Bundaberg, Queensland 4671
tel 071-574353

Mead's Daylily Gardens
203 Watson Road Acacia Ridge
Brisbane, Queensland 4110
tel 07-3273-8559

Mountain View Gardens
Policeman's Spur Road
Maleny, Queensland 4552
tel 07-5494-2346

Europe

Apple Court
Hordle Lane
Hordle, Lymington
Hampshire SO41 0HU
United Kingdom

Cor Govaerts
Broechemsesteenweg 330
B-2560 Nijlen
Belgium
tel 32-34-8178

Marc King-Lamone
Via Santa Caterina 6
14030 Rocca d'Arazzo
Italy

Francois Verhaert
Fatimalaan 14
B-2243 Zandhoven
Belgium
tel 03-484-5086

 *Bibliography*

Dahlgren, H., T. Clifford, and P. F. Yeo. 1985. *The Families of the Monocotyledons.* Berlin/New York: Springer Verlag.

Eddison, S. 1992. *A Passion for Daylilies: The Flowers and the People.* New York: Henry Holt and Co.

Erhardt, W. l992. *Hemerocallis: Daylilies.* Portland, Oregon: Timber Press.

Gatlin, F. 1995. *Daylilies—A Fifty Year Affair: A Story of a Society and Its Flower.* Edgerton, Missouri: American Hemerocallis Society.

Grenfell, D. 1998. *The Gardener's Guide to Growing Daylilies.* Portland, Oregon: Timber Press.

Hemerocallis Check List: 1893 to July 1, 1957. 1957. Compiled by M. Frederick Stuntz, Paul D. Voth, Earl A. Holl, Wilmer B. Flory, Harry I. Tuggle, Jr., William E. Monroe. Edgerton, Missouri: American Hemerocallis Society.

Hemerocallis Check List: July 1, 1957 to July 1, 1973. Compiled by W. E. Monroe. Reprint Edgerton, Missouri: American Hemerocallis Society, 1990.

Hemerocallis Check List: July 1, 1973 to December 31, 1983. Compiled by W. E. Monroe. Edgerton, Missouri: American Hemerocallis Society.

Hemerocallis Check List: January 1, 1984 to December 31, 1988. Compiled by W. E. Monroe and W. C. Monroe. Edgerton, Missouri: American Hemerocallis Society.

Hemerocallis Check List: 1989 to 1993. 1994. Compiled by W. C. Monroe. Edgerton, Missouri: American Hemerocallis Society.

Hemerocallis Cultivar Registrations. Vols. 50–53. 1994–1997. Compiled by W. C. Monroe. Supplement to *The Daylily Journal.* Kansas City, Missouri: American Hemerocallis Society.

Hu, S.-Y. 1968. "An Early History of Daylily" in "Daylily Handbook." *American Horticulture Magazine* 47, no. 2: 51–85.

Munson, R. W., Jr. 1989. *Hemerocallis: The Daylily.* Portland, Oregon: Timber Press.

Stout, A. B. 1934. *Daylilies: The Wild Species and Garden Clones Both Old and New of the Genus.* Reprint Millwood, New York: Sagapress, 1986.

Stout, A. B. 1947. "The Character and Genetics of Doubleness in the Flowers of Daylilies: The Para Double Class." *Herbertia* 12:113–123.

Index of Pictured Cultivars